Talking Music

Talking Music

Conversations with New Zealand Musicians

Sarah Shieff

Foreword by Witi Ihimaera
Photographs by Robert Cross

AUCKLAND UNIVERSITY PRESS

This book is dedicated to the memory of my father,
Bernard Shieff (1916–2001),
whose love and support never faltered.

Auckland University Press
University of Auckland
Private Bag 92019
Auckland
New Zealand
http://www.auckland.ac.nz/aup

ISBN 1 86940 228 6

The publishers gratefully acknowledge the assistance of the Lilburn Trust.

National Library of New Zealand Cataloguing-in-Publication Data
Shieff, Sarah.
Talking music : conversations with New Zealand musicians / by Sarah Shieff ; photographs by Robert Cross.
ISBN 1-86940-228-6
1. Musicians—New Zealand—Interviews. 2. Composers—New Zealand—Interviews. 3. Singers—New Zealand—Interviews. I. Cross, Robert, Photographer. II. Title.
780.92293—DC 21

Printed by Astra Print Ltd, Wellington

Contents

ACKNOWLEDGEMENTS

I would like to thank the subjects of this book, who so generously gave of their time, and of themselves. I would also like to thank Robert Cross, Witi Ihimaera, and Elizabeth Caffin of Auckland University Press. For their unstinting practical help, support and encouragement, I would also like to thank Scilla Askew, the Auckland Philharmonia, Tracy Bowell, Paul Bushnell, Max Cryer, Wystan Curnow, Ron Dellow, Tim Dodd, Norman Franke, Annie Goldson, Karen Grylls, Tim Gummer, Miguel Harth-Bedoya, Marilyn Hayr, Ross Hendy, Roger Horrocks, Mark Houlahan, Michael Houstoun, Kai Jensen, Elizabeth Kerr, Wayne Laird, Lu Jihong, Martin Lodge, Rachel Lord, Judith Macdonald, Honor McKellar, Lisa McLean, Andrew Mason, Kate Mead, Brett Morris, the New Zealand Symphony Orchestra, Margaret Nielsen, Richard Nunns, Mary O'Brien, Terence O'Neill-Joyce, Jill Palmer, Pascale Parenteau, John Ritchie, Iain Sharp, Jenny Shieff, June Shieff, Rob Shieff, Geoffrey Smith, Roger Smith, Sophie Tomlinson, Murray Vincent, John Ure, Anya Welle, Ken Wilson, Ivan Zagni, the late John M. Thomson and the Estate of Mervyn Thompson. Most of all I wish to thank Alex Calder – my companion in this undertaking, as in all others.

This book was produced with the assistance of the Department of English at the University of Waikato, the Humanities Research Committee of the University of Waikato, the Lilburn Trust, and the New Zealand Lottery Grants Board.

FOREWORD

The Working Musician: a Writer's Perspective

Witi Ihimaera

'Sometimes I've found myself standing in the wings with a cold or a headache, thinking, "What am I doing here?" People have no idea what you go through.'– Malvina Major

Of all the arts practitioners, I have always had the greatest admiration for the working musician. Take composers, for instance: not only do they write the music (often without commission), they also write the various orchestral and vocal parts for woodwind, brass, strings and percussion, soloists and chorus – and, when that's done, negotiate the business of obtaining a performance of the work. The equivalent for a writer like myself would be to write the same novel about thirty times for the various components in the strings, woodwind and percussion sections and hope to hell people will still understand it.

Think of performers, too: they must learn the score, their role within the orchestral or operatic performance, rehearse (often within a limited time-frame) with stage director or conductor, and then deliver performances which are true to the composer's intentions, the conductor's interpretation and the stage director's vision. They have to be all things to all people while facing the most important critic of all – you and me sitting in the audience with our own expectations of the music and the performance. And sometimes they will perform the piece only once or twice. All that work! Again, the equivalent for the writer would be to have his or her work turned into a dramatic production. I can tell you that, if the collaboration is cordial, it's a terrific experience. If it isn't, misericordia.

Then there's the music critic: they don't just appear fully formed, you know. Most have had a life-long engagement with music and require concert-going experience sufficient to be able to critique solo, chamber, orchestral and operatic performances for radio, television or print media. Their reviews can make or break a performance or production. As a past reviewer myself, I take my hat off to the music critic. Next time you're at a performance, look for the man standing all by himself in the foyer, alone and friendless. That's the music critic. And if he's William Dart, go and shake his hand: this man is a tireless champion and eloquent advocate of artistic excellence in the music arts.

Unlike the composer, as a writer I don't have to think of what the piccolo is doing while the violin is playing. Unlike the soloist, I don't have to worry about making the right entry at the right point of an orchestral score teeming with demi-semiquavers. Unlike the music critic, I can keep my friends, including the soprano who has been just trashed in a review.

Thank God I'm just a writer.

> 'If I was just composing – and not doing a drag show here or a gig with Strike there – there'd be no way I'd be able to pay the rent.' – Gareth Farr

I think it was the author Anthony Burgess who, during a lecture at Victoria University of Wellington in the 1960s to starry-eyed students including myself, put me onto the notion that all art aspires to the condition of music.

Whether or not you agree, I have certainly tried to apply the verities of music to the structure, form and development – counterpoint, if you like – of the books I have written. My first collection of short stories (unpublished) was titled *Exercises for the Left Hand*, and I had in mind pianoforte pieces. I like to think of *Pounamu, Pounamu* as my 'Songs of the Auvergne'. Both *The Matriarch* and *The Dream Swimmer* are operatic in conception and are structured into acts. *Tangi* is based on the model of the symphony.

However, would I really want to be a working musician? I don't think so. And why not? In my opinion, literature (including theatre) has better working conditions and better pay. If you're a musician, you work in a totally exposed arena with high risk and low pay. If you're lucky as a composer, you get a stipend working for some tertiary institution. There are not many grants available and only one university, Otago, has a fellowship for New Zealand musicians. As for performance opportunities, if you're lucky here you can be employed by one of our two main orchestras and two opera companies. The odds just aren't worth it.

Yet the working musician has just as much to add to the nation's narratives – the stories we tell about ourselves – as do our writers, poets, playwrights, painters and other artists. Indeed, we are fortunate that there have been passionate men and women in all our arts – Katherine Mansfield, Colin McCahon, Te Rangi Hiroa, Frances Hodgkins, Ramai and Rudall Hayward, Bruce Mason, Inia Te Wiata, Robin Hyde, Allen Curnow and many others – who have enabled us to gain access to international excellence. Just as important, through the creation of New Zealand-specific works, they have enabled us to see ourselves and the country we live in. They have 'created' us as well as the country we live in. Without their skills of 'seeing', New Zealand wouldn't exist. You and I would not exist.

Of all these creative people, the one whose talents are not recognised is the working musician. If you don't believe me, at your next dinner party ask your guests to name at least five New Zealand composers. If they get past that question, ask them to name two of each composer's works. If you have even one successful participant, please let me know and I will send ten dollars to the lucky person.

My point is that, except for the occasional biography – usually of a 'star' opera performer like Dame Kiri Te Kanawa, Inia Te Wiata or Malvina Major – New Zealanders know very little about who has been and who is contributing to the culture of New Zealand music.

> 'I chose [poems which showed how women faced up to colonial life] because I felt I was a pioneer myself, in a sense.' – Dorothea Franchi

I therefore welcome Sarah Shieff's collection of fourteen interviews, *Talking Music: Conversations with New Zealand Musicians*. Indeed, I've been lucky enough to know personally eleven of the fourteen musicians who appear here. I knew Frank and Sylvia Gurr as marvellous hosts when I was living in Wellington. Edwin Carr and I have been friends of long standing – we still have a piece which we wrote together, *Ariki Nui*, unperformed. Donald McIntyre I first met in New York, after he had sung Wotan in *Die Walküre* at the Met in 1988; he was a brilliant Hans Sachs in *Die Meistersinger* at the Wellington International Festival of the Arts in 1990. I saw the young and ravishing Malvina Major (if I remember correctly, she was wearing a stunning red dress) in Wellington in 1969 in one of her homecoming performances after she had performed in *The Barber of Seville* for Claudio Abbado at Salzburg. Jenny McLeod and I have been colleagues and good friends; unable to work on a piece I had written called

The Clio Legacy, she recommended fellow composer Dorothy Buchanan. Jack Body and I have always planned on doing an opera together but the right project hasn't come along yet. Then of course there's Hirini Melbourne (we met at an education conference in Melbourne way back in the 1970s), who together with Richard Nunns has added so much to our knowledge of traditional Maori instruments and music-making. Helen Medlyn and I always have the time for a hug, the last time at *Der Rosenkavalier* in Wellington in 2002, and Peter Scholes and I worked together on *Symphonic Legends*, premiered in 1996. I met the fabulous Gareth Farr when he was percussionist for *Tanz Der Schwane* (the second opera I wrote for Ross Harris); Gareth did the splendid music for my play, *Woman Far Walking*. As for William Dart, when he discovered my love of the music of Bernard Herrmann, he took time out from his busy duties to send me a tape of Herrmann's score of *Obsession*. Wilma Smith and Diedre Irons I have known from the concert platform. I think I met Dorothea Franchi at a music party in Wellington and, if I'm right, I hope she will forgive the rash and untutored youth who spoke in arrogant terms about what was wrong with New Zealand music, not what was right with it. Miss Franchi was one of the things that were right about New Zealand music culture – and, indeed, we have much to be thankful to our working musicians for. Their love of music, joy in collaboration and belief in their artistry has helped create a music culture in New Zealand.

Sarah Shieff's interviews affirm this history. They are acts of reclamation, affirming the lives of working musicians. Fourteen musicians tell their fascinating stories about how they became who they are, the commitment required, the struggles, failures and successes, and the fierce ambition which has driven them. What is just as fascinating is how the interviews criss-cross with one another. They may be national stories but they are also international stories, hooking us into world music. They may be about musicians but they are also about artists, writers, sculptors, theatre practitioners and the intersections our art-forms have with one another. In the telling of their stories, through Sarah Shieff's interviews, all these working musicians invoke the much greater hinterland of culture-making and history-making in our country.

I believe that New Zealand has actually inhibited the growth of New Zealand music and forced it into shapes that a more generous society might not have required of our musicians. Their triumph has been to surmount the limitations and to create the splendid and – dare I say it? – accidental history that has been New Zealand music.

INTRODUCTION

In the summer of 1946 Douglas Lilburn rose to address the first Cambridge Music School. 'Music has been written here and is being written here,' he said, 'but I feel that all of it is only the most tentative of beginnings towards solving that problem – the discovery of our own identity.' It was easy enough then to see classical music in New Zealand as a barren field: in that historic talk, Lilburn called for the establishment of a New Zealand musical tradition, one which would 'satisfy the parts of our being that cannot be satisfied by the music of other nations'.[1] Almost sixty years later, the abundance and diversity of professional music-making in New Zealand is at least a partial realisation of Lilburn's vision for music in this country.

Although the intervening years have complicated our notions of identity and belonging, the phrase 'New Zealand music' still has about it an aura, if not of wholeness, then of an obviousness one need not enquire into. But, while the effort to quantify the 'New Zealandness' of New Zealand culture has long been a dead horse critically, the challenge of thinking outside that square remains. We might well raise an eyebrow at those earlier (and futile) efforts to isolate 'New Zealand music' in some static, transcendental essence that was presumed to derive from the landscape, the sea coast or 'the national character', and that might in turn set it apart from the music of other places. We are now more likely to say that there are many New Zealand musics, popular and high, drawing on all manner of imported and indigenous traditions – and that all, in their own ways, are valuable and important to their audiences. But such a story about New Zealand music, dwelling on its great multi-faceted variety, would be in danger of falling victim to the obvious, or to grand rhetorical gestures. That is why I make no apologies for this book's very particular scope: I am interested in what might broadly be termed 'classical' music in New Zealand since the 1940s – a period that can still be described as within living memory. The memories of New Zealand musicians, spanning six decades of professional music-making in New Zealand, form the substance of this biographical history. Some may suggest that such a focus is a form of élitism. This charge is no source of embarrassment: the days when classical music was a monument, keeping all else in its shade, are long gone. Besides, professional classical musicians form an élite much as our top sportspeople do. Only a few may perform at the highest levels, but when an élite is open to newcomers – as sport and music both are – we should celebrate achievement wherever we find it.

So, rather than trying to sum up or even adequately represent a totality of 'New Zealand music', *Talking Music* proceeds on the assumption that classical music in New Zealand has evolved as – and continues to evolve through – a series of conversations. The term is not as vague as it might at first appear: it means music in dialogue with other music, and musicians in dialogue with each other and with an audience. Since earliest colonial times, conversations have been going on between the music of the present and the past, between this geographical space and variously remote ones, among the musics of Maori and other peoples indigenous to the Pacific and the musics of the colonisers. Conversations between 'high' and 'popular' musical idioms are part of the everyday experience of many of the people in this book; I have found that, instead of disparaging popular music in order to value what they do, most of these musicians readily include popular music among their most formative musical experiences.

The vitality of New Zealand music culture depends partly on the vitality of these conversations. It also depends on sustained conversations between composers and performers, and on the quality of the critical intervention in these conversations. (It goes without saying that orchestras, broadcasters, record companies, and public and private sponsors also participate in these conversations: it is impossible to imagine a lively professional music culture without an equally lively music infrastructure.)

While an audience is obviously essential to these conversations too, a healthy music culture requires spaces in which musicians can talk in private – musicians talking to musicians. Without these spaces, dialogue between musicians and audiences would be impoverished, at best. These private conversations take place in music lessons, in composition classes, in rehearsals and in recording studios. Audiences hear the results of these conversations in live or recorded performances. *Talking Music* lends an ear to what happens behind the studio door. But books about music – without music – can be arid things indeed. The CD which accompanies this book gives an example of each musician's work: track numbers appear in the text in square brackets.

Talking Music is not, however, just an expanded programme note. It aims to give an insight into the kinds of conversation that may have taken place in the years leading up to, and following, a particular composition or performance. Whose music was this composer listening to as a student? What facet of technique did this pianist acquire during lessons with that teacher? What might this singer have learned from that director, or conductor, or colleague? Sometimes these conversations are in an unfamiliar language: for example, what might unaccustomed Pakeha listeners need to learn about traditional Maori music before they can actively engage in Hirini Melbourne's musical conversation? *Talking Music* also introduces readers to the individuals participating in these conversations. How was their love of music fostered? What led them to music as a profession? What challenges have they had to overcome? What do they regard as their greatest triumphs?

These conversations go some way towards describing the shape of classical music in New Zealand over the last sixty-odd years. This story could well have been told differently, in different voices, but my selection is neither haphazard nor star-struck. I have tried most of all to present a musician's sense of the *range* of participants in the larger conversation that is classical music in New Zealand. Readers will find conversations with composers, performers, conductors and critics, men and women, Maori and Pakeha. They live and work in many areas. Some are household names, others are less well-known. At the time of writing, they range in age from their early thirties to their early eighties; the chapters are in chronological order of each musician's year of birth. My selection was based in part on the availability of the participants themselves. In no way did I decide to exclude people: some preferred not to participate, for reasons of their own. I hope those who feel they should have been asked and were not will excuse me – all could have been here. A book that did justice to all the individuals who have made an important contribution to New Zealand music would have been many times this size. So *Talking Music* is necessarily a partial picture, but I hope a representative, engaging and suggestive one.

1 Douglas Lilburn, *A Search for Tradition* (Wellington: Alexander Turnbull Library Endowment Trust, 1984), pp.9-10.

Dorothea Franchi : Pioneering Spirit

When I wrote the *Four Pioneer Portraits* I wanted to find a group of poems which showed how women faced up to colonial life, and what a lot they had to put up with. The poems I chose are all about settlers. I think I chose them because I felt I was a pioneer myself, in a sense.

Dorothea Franchi (born 1920) lives quietly in Warkworth, north of Auckland. Although she doesn't play much any more, New Zealand's most senior woman composer depended for her livelihood on her work as a pianist, harpist, teacher, accompanist and arranger; she was also an occasional percussionist, and the first woman to conduct the New Zealand Broadcasting Corporation (NZBC) Symphony Orchestra. In the course of her working life, Franchi saw professional music in New Zealand become highly centralised and increasingly specialised, but when she started work in the early 1940s, her versatility enabled her to survive in a musical environment that was remarkable for its vitality, and for its proliferation of generally small, community-based, semi-professional music organisations. Between her return from study in England in 1952 and her retirement from active performance in the late 1980s, there was hardly a professional music group in New Zealand with which Dorothea Franchi had not been actively involved.

Dorothea was born in Auckland. As a four-year-old she began piano lessons with her mother, but she attributes her life-long love of jazz to her father: Peter Franchi, a furniture designer by trade, loved to sing the songs of Irving Berlin and ragtime ballads. 'We had fabulous musical evenings at our place. We would never have dreamed of turning on the gramophone – we made our own music.' From the age of nine, Dorothea continued her piano lessons at St Joseph's Convent School in Balmoral, Auckland. The musical education she received there laid the foundation for the rest of her life. 'I was with Sister Olga for eight years. She was a wonderful pianist and a splendid teacher. I also got my theory training there, which took me on to university.' However, apart from piano, the music that made the biggest impression on her at school was Gregorian chant. 'We really did learn to sing it properly, and we sang the Mass every Sunday at school. It was a great love of mine.'

Even though Dorothea excelled at her music studies, her father fiercely opposed her taking up music as a career, feeling that a trade would offer her more security. 'He pushed my brothers into trades – one into building and one into upholstery – and the only thing he would allow me to do was to go into a factory and learn dressmaking. I'd never sewn a stitch in my life!' For the first time in her life Dorothea stood up to him. 'I told him I was going to university. He said he couldn't afford it, but I'd been teaching the piano since I was fifteen – my first pupil was the girl next door – and I was earning enough to pay my way and even pay my mother some board, so he had to give in.' Franchi was sixteen when she started her music degree in Auckland in 1936, and had completed a Bachelor of Music degree before her nineteenth birthday. 'I was one of Professor Hollinrake's first fully trained Bachelors of Music. There was no performance then – that didn't start until after Charles Nalden arrived – so I did my degree in composition.'[1]

War put paid to Franchi's immediate plans for further study overseas. 'I graduated in 1939, but I didn't go away until 1948. All those years I kept in touch with Holly: I was really still his pupil. He'd give me counterpoint exercises in seven and eight parts, more or less like a doctorate, and I'd take him work for comment.' Hollinrake's advice also saved Franchi from arduous war work: 'it was a case of farm work, factory work or working in a market garden'. She could see gardening ruining her hands, so at Hollinrake's suggestion she enrolled at Auckland Teachers' College. 'I didn't particularly like the idea, but he persuaded me that it wouldn't do me any harm.' Franchi graduated from training college as a music specialist, and in the years before she left New Zealand she was in charge of music at Epsom Girls' Grammar School, taking four choirs and the school orchestra as well as teaching class music: 'I had to arrange most of the music for the orchestra because there were always some instruments missing.' Franchi also composed for her students: her largest composition was a *Magnificat* for women's voices, contralto soloist and organ. In it she revisited her early memories of Gregorian chant, finding in it a freedom that profoundly influenced her own subsequent writing. 'I realised it could be used in a melodic way, and it made me more aware of modes in music.'

In January 1946, Franchi attended the first summer school for music held at St Peter's School, Cambridge.[2] 'I was there as a pianist and sort of musical dog's-body. I was in everything that was going.' She found herself in demand as a jazz pianist. 'Every night after the serious stuff was over another chap and I would sit down at the two grand pianos. We never knew what we were going to play, but hey presto, they had dancing for the next two hours.' In 1947 Franchi joined Douglas Lilburn's first Cambridge composers' workshop. She remembers Lilburn as a quiet presence: 'Douglas was not what you would call communicative. There used to be great silences: he'd sit there and say nothing unless someone came up with a question, which he answered very briefly. Although he was encouraging, I don't think he was as much of a musical influence on me as he was on his own students.'

Franchi found her first harp at the 1946 Cambridge school. She had been enchanted by the instrument as a child – Harpo Marx had set her dreaming of becoming a harpist – and when she was twelve she tried to persuade her father to buy her one. 'By then I'd been learning the piano for eight years, but I wanted to play in an orchestra because I loved playing with people.' It seemed an obvious choice for a pianist to take up the harp, but it was the Depression, and times were hard. 'He told me I'd have to wait until I grew up.' She did wait: at the summer school, at the age of twenty-six, she heard of a disused instrument in the possession of a Cambridge family. 'It was an old double-action Erard – fully chromatic – built around 1860. It was what we'd call a lady's boudoir harp, about the size of Mozart's time.'[3] Although the instrument had been in the family for three generations and had been lovingly maintained, it was no longer played. 'I went over and talked sweetly to the lady who owned it and persuaded her to part with it.'

The next problem was finding someone to teach her. New Zealand-born harpist Winifred Carter had recently returned home from the United States, and had been appointed to the newly formed National Orchestra of the New Zealand Broadcasting Service (NZBS).

> Winifred was a fabulous harpist, technically – she'd been in the Detroit Symphony Orchestra for years. The only woman amongst all those men. Since she'd been back in New Zealand I'd done some arranging for her, and I knew she was teaching, so I rang her up and asked if she could give me a few lessons. I only wanted her to get me started and show me how to hold my hands. She was completely uninterested:

> she offered to send to America for a book so I could teach myself. That's why I had to go to England – her refusing to teach me made me all the more determined. I'd take composition as a first study, and harp as my second.

In 1948 Franchi left New Zealand for London. Her first choice of composition teacher had been William Walton – she had been impressed by his Viola Concerto as a student in Auckland – but when she arrived in London she found he didn't take students. Instead she enrolled at the Royal College of Music, studying composition with Herbert Howells. 'Although I had already found my own direction in my writing by the time I came to study with Howells, he guided me. He was a very, very discerning teacher, and a marvellous stylist.' Franchi studied orchestration with Gordon Jacob, and keyboard and continuo with Dr Thornton Lofthouse. She also found herself in demand as an accompanist. 'Frederick Thurston roped me in to accompany all his pupils, including Jack McCaw and Frank Gurr. They'd arrived from New Zealand shortly after me, to study clarinet.'

Franchi also wanted to study conducting, but was dissuaded by the college advisors. 'They told me I'd be wasted. I'd be put in with the opera students as a *répétiteur*, and I'd be lucky to get the college orchestra once in the year. They were more or less saying it was no job for a woman. I *wish* I hadn't listened to them, but at the time I was very much put off.' Franchi had few illusions about the chauvinism of the musical establishment. 'A friend who played in the Philharmonia used to sneak me into rehearsals, and I would watch. I've been at the Philharmonia in the EMI studios with Furtwängler conducting, and not another woman in the place, because there were no women in the orchestra.'

Before she left New Zealand, Franchi's single harp lesson had been with the newly arrived Charles Nalden. 'When I got to [the Royal] College I told them I wanted to start on the bottom rung, but they made me sit an examination anyway, so I muddled my way through Bach's C major Prelude from Book I of *The Well-Tempered Clavier*. And of course I got in on the bottom rung.' Franchi started lessons with Welsh harpist Gwendolen Mason. 'She was fantastic. At the age of sixteen she'd been playing in the Covent Garden orchestra under Hans Richter. There wasn't much of her – she was even shorter than I was – but she was playing into her nineties.' Franchi studied with Mason for five years, first at the Royal College of Music and then privately.

Within fifteen months of beginning lessons at the college, Franchi had made her début as a harpist.

> I'd been working solidly at my technique – exercises and studies – and suddenly dear Gwen announced that I was going to perform Britten's *A Ceremony of Carols* with the Westminster Cathedral Boys' Choir under George Malcolm. My knees were knocking like castanets on the soundboard. I kept saying to myself, 'You stupid git. What are you doing sitting here when you could quite easily be a pianist? What did you take this instrument up for?' I got through it all right, but it took me about ten years to overcome nerves, which I'd never experienced with the piano.

While in London, Franchi threw herself into as many music activities as she could. She joined the University of London Choir as an alto; the conductor – her keyboard tutor Thornton Lofthouse – suggested she should write something for them. The result was a setting for unaccompanied choir of Eileen Duggan's poem 'The Oxen'.[4] The work was first performed in St Paul's Cathedral in December 1949, in a Christmas programme which included works by Purcell, Bach, Peter Warlock and Benjamin Britten. 'I remember the poor vergers moaning about having to open the great west doors, because Princess Margaret had decided to come. Those doors were only used for royalty. The place was packed: there must have been three or four thousand people there. It was a great occasion.' The lights were lowered after the performance. 'A very romantic figure appeared out of the gloom. He was wearing a cloak, and carrying one of those flat sombrero-type hats. Dr Lofthouse said to me, "Come over here, Dorothea. There's someone I want you to meet." It was Zoltán Kodály, and he was very complimentary about my carol.' A year later Franchi received a commendation from Roger Quilter, this time for *Eventide*, a song-cycle for tenor, string quartet and harp, written for New Zealand tenor Andrew Gold.

Franchi's next triumph was winning the 1951 Lionel Tertis Prize with her *Rhapsody for Viola and Orchestra*. The prize had been established by the Royal College of Music at the instigation of Tertis, a renowned violist, who felt that the viola had been neglected as a concerto instrument. The conditions of the prize were fairly broad: the competition was open to any British composer under the age of thirty-five; the work had to be about twenty minutes long and scored for an orchestra without brass. The three works chosen as finalists would be performed by the London Symphony Orchestra in front of the judge, Sir Arthur Bliss. Concerti by Ronald Tremain – another New Zealander studying at the Royal College of Music – and Franchi were selected as two of the three finalists. 'Of course it was vital to find a good performer. I immediately got hold of Frederick Riddle, who was teaching at the college. He liked the look of my piece, but couldn't take it on because he was due to play the Walton concerto in Berlin.' Riddle instead introduced Franchi to Herbert Downes, principal violist in the Philharmonia Orchestra. 'He was a wonderful player. It was through him I won the Tertis Prize.' Tremain was awarded second place, and Bridget Fry (an English composer studying with Gordon Jacob) came third. 'It was worth £75, which was a fair amount in those days.' Downes refused to take a fee, but Franchi gave him £20. 'The only reason I ended up with any money at all was because I'd copied all the parts myself – and given myself conjunctivitis in the process.' Writing in *The Times* in 1951, English reviewer Frank Howes noted 'several glimpses of poetry in the viola's cleverly disposed brooding'; after hearing the work performed in New Zealand in 1953, critic Owen Jensen commented that 'if Dorothea Franchi ever wore a felt hat, either figuratively or actually, I am sure she must have sent it flying in the air as she wrote her *Rhapsody*, for the music is as fresh as the morning breeze'.[5]

In London, Franchi also completed her *Four Pioneer Portraits* (1949) for mezzo-soprano and piano [CD Track 1].[6] She regards these as her greatest achievement, feeling that they express her identity as a New Zealander and make a feminist statement. The songs also grew out of a sense of identification with isolated pioneering women. 'The poems all show what a grim life it was for the women. I set Robin Hyde's "The Farmer's Wife", and Eileen Duggan's "The Bushfeller" and "The Blacksmith". I had to go to Australia for the last one – "The Shearer's Wife" by Louis Esson.' Franchi began the songs during her first Christmas in England. 'My family had always spent Christmas together, but some family friends up in Preston had invited me and my friend Ted Carr to spend Christmas with them.' It was snowing as the two returned to London by bus. 'I'd been chewing over words of the Hyde poem, and I remember telling Ted to shush: I was thinking out the opening chords. As soon as I got home, I shot in and started to write. I think the songs were caught up with a form of homesickness.' The cycle was first performed in 1953 by mezzo-soprano Honor McKellar in an NZBS radio broadcast.

Despite her homesickness, Franchi soon realised that she needed to stay in England longer than she had originally planned. She had left New Zealand with enough saved from her schoolteacher's salary, and from playing for dance bands and ballet classes, to keep herself for two years.[7] Once in England she applied for a New Zealand government bursary (instituted after she left New Zealand) which gave her a further £5 a week. 'Things were not easy. My harp lessons alone cost a pound a week, and I was paying 30 shillings a week for my room.' On top of that there was travel, tickets for concerts, and food. 'I had about half a dozen music pupils, which helped me get to the Continent during the holidays, but I lived on next to nothing.' The largest single expense of her years in London was buying a harp. She had travelled to England with the harp bought in Cambridge, but this proved too small for orchestral work. 'Gwendolen Mason found me a harp through John Morley, who did all the harp repairs in those days. It was an Erard and about sixth-hand when I got it, but it was a marvellous instrument.'

Franchi graduated Bachelor of Music in 1950 and returned to New Zealand in 1952, abandoning her plans to complete a doctorate. 'I keep saying I don't know why I came back. If it hadn't been for the fact that my mother wasn't well I wouldn't have. At least you could push for things when you were overseas: there were more opportunities. We were not well done by as composers, especially in Auckland.' The National Film Unit had begun to produce documentaries, but commissions for scores were falling to Wellington composers David Farquhar, Ashley Heenan, Larry Pruden and Douglas Lilburn:

> Ron Tremain and I wrote to the Film Unit and told them there were composers in Auckland too. They replied that they couldn't afford to send film up to Auckland and if we wanted the work we should move to Wellington. So that was completely lost to us because of our region. There were occasional commissions for incidental music from Broadcasting, which had a strong drama section in those days, but other than that it was an absolute desert.

If public commissions were scarce, Franchi made the most of private opportunities. Not long after her return she was approached by a neighbour whose son was studying singing with the charismatic tenor Hubert Milverton-Carta.

> Mrs McIntyre was a violin teacher, and she rang me up and asked for some help. Donald was going in for the competitions – he would have been seventeen or eighteen, just out of school – and he needed a New Zealand composition. They couldn't find anything suitable for his voice, so I told her I'd write him something. I shot off a setting of Thomas Campion's 'Man of Life Upright'. He sang it, and he won, and I got a terrific commendation from the judge. Years later, when Donald was here to sing the Verdi *Requiem*, I went backstage to see him. I hadn't seen him since, and he had his wife with him, whom I'd never met. He scooped me up in his great big bear-hug and said to her, 'This is the lady who wrote me a song once.' And he started singing it. He remembered it all those years.

Income from commissions and performing was at best unreliable, so Franchi returned to teaching piano and theory. However, life as a private music teacher didn't remain quiet for long. 'Winifred Carter was still playing in the National Orchestra when I got back, but her mother was increasingly ill and she was finding it difficult to get to Wellington for rehearsals. Broadcasting – who ran the orchestra in those days – heard I was home and one day I got a call to go down to the Town Hall to play for Warwick Braithwaite.[8] That was the only audition I had, and I was in.' From 1953 until the mid-1970s, Franchi was on call as the NZBC Symphony Orchestra's second harp and deputy principal harpist.

Her involvement with what would become the Royal New Zealand Ballet began around the same time. 'Not long after I got back, a former pupil of mine from Epsom Grammar asked me if I'd like a job playing for a ballet teacher. I told her no thanks: ballet teachers are too unscrupulous with music. They cut the parts they don't like and make a travesty of the rest. But she said, "This is someone quite different".' Danish dancer Poul Gnatt had toured New Zealand in 1952 with the Borovansky Ballet and had returned the following year with the intention of establishing a professional ballet company, for which he required the services of a rehearsal pianist. 'I'd always loved ballet, and his name rang a bell – he'd trained with the Royal Danish Ballet in Copenhagen and had been dancing with the Ballet Russe when I was in London – so I trotted down to the hall where he was working.' Gnatt asked Franchi if she could start that afternoon. 'I said yes, and from then on we were a team. He'd just give me a tempo, whistle a bar or two, and I'd catch it up and carry it on.'

She travelled with the embryonic company on its first tour to Northland in 1953, under the auspices of the Community Arts Service (CAS).[9] There were only four dancers on the tour – Gloria Young, Marion Newman, Pamela Bishop Williams and Gnatt. 'We did our first performance in Kaikohe, followed by a six-week tour of the provincial centres. The thing just gradually blossomed. Wellington got to hear of us – they had an organisation similar to the CAS – and we were taken under their wing.' By the time Franchi stopped touring with the company in 1958, they had grown from a group of four dancers to twelve, working virtually fulltime for nine months of the year, and touring the whole country. 'There were very few places in New Zealand we didn't visit – only places we didn't think we could get an audience, like the Bluff, or Cape Reinga. We were billeted everywhere we went, and we really got to know people. It was a great era in my life.' Financially, however, it was less rewarding. 'I was absolutely stony broke at the end of every year. I couldn't keep my piano pupils going, of course – I'd be away for six weeks at a time – but I carried on teaching theory by correspondence. The New Zealand Post Office used to track me down wherever I was with bundles of work from theory pupils.'

Franchi was the young company's arranger as well as pianist and musical director. 'In those days there were very few piano reductions available, and one of the first things we ever did were some excerpts from *Giselle*. Poul seemed to think he was still living in Europe. He asked me if I had a piano arrangement, but there was no score in the country, let alone a piano reduction, so I took down half a dozen of the dances from a recording.' In the same programme Gnatt wanted to include the long *pas de deux* from Tchaikovsky's *Romeo and Juliet*. 'There was no piano score for that either, so I transcribed the whole thing. I've still got the pencil-written copies. I never had time to write them out.' Other feats included playing the whole of Stravinsky's *Petrouchka* on the piano, and a huge programme of Chopin for a ballet choreographed by young Australian dancer, designer and choreographer Arthur Turnbull, who had been with the company almost since its inception. 'I think I landed up playing about three études, the *Barcarolle*, a couple of nocturnes, a scherzo, a polonaise and the *Tarantelle*, one after the other, in one fell swoop, every night.'

The ballet *Do-Wack-a-Do*, written for the New Zealand Ballet Company and first performed in 1961, is perhaps Franchi's best-known and most frequently performed work. Arthur Turnbull conceived the idea of a ballet based on 1920s jazz dances, and asked Franchi to write the music for it. By then she had stopped touring with the ballet, so she could write a score that didn't rely solely on her own piano-playing. 'I wrote the original for a small combo of piano, percussion, clarinet doubling sax, trumpet and double bass. We put it on tape, because they couldn't afford to travel with a band.' *Do-Wack-a-Do* tells the story of a society hostess besotted by her daughter, who unfortunately can't dance to save herself. 'Mama plans to launch the daughter at a private party and invites all her friends. But she doesn't invite the terrible vamp who lives down the road. Somehow the vamp and her dancing partner – Nadine Walker and Jon Trimmer – gatecrash the party, and create mayhem.'

The work, which critic Bruce Mason later described as 'music of an Ibertian exuberance'[10], parodies popular dances of the 1920s.

> It took me ages to find an example of a 'black bottom'. Eventually I ran to earth a very early recording in Beggs. Then there was the 'soft shoe shuffle', the tango, and

> a very twee piece I wrote for the daughter. It took off like a bomb and had a lot of performances, which was good for me as I got ten bob a time royalties. It was one of the few works that's ever earned me anything.

Orchestras were available in the main centres, so Franchi expanded her original score for jazz combo into an arrangement for small concert orchestra. 'I didn't use strings – I used brass and woodwind – but still couldn't get the four saxophones I would have liked.' Unfortunately, the score and all the parts were lost in 1967, in a disastrous fire which destroyed the Adelaide Road premises where the New Zealand Opera and the New Zealand Ballet stored their props and costumes.

The fire didn't mean the end of *Do-Wack-a-Do*. 'The NZBC wanted something for the orchestra's Proms programme for the summer of 1965, so I arranged *Do-Wack-a-Do* as a suite for full orchestra. They asked me if I'd be interested in conducting it myself, and I thought, "Why not?" I was the first woman conductor they'd had, and I ended up conducting it everywhere we went. It was a great joy to hear it blossom like that.' Franchi conducted the work again in 1975 in a concert commemorating the fiftieth anniversary of commercial radio broadcasting in New Zealand, and in 1988, after a twenty-four-year absence from the group she had helped found, she conducted the Royal New Zealand Ballet's revival of *Do-Wack-a-Do*.

Franchi's stint as pianist with the ballet came to an end when she decided not to move to Wellington when the company relocated there in 1958. 'Nothing would induce me to live there. I just cannot stand the weather. You come out of the hairdresser's, go around a corner, and you need another hair-do.' Her years as a pianist had, in any case, been due largely to circumstance. 'The harp I'd bought in England didn't last long: New Zealand Railways smashed it beyond repair. I'd only paid £100 for it, so you can imagine how much I got back, and I couldn't afford to replace it. That was partly why it was easy for me to go back to the piano: I didn't have a big harp suitable for orchestral work.' Her association with the NZBC Concert Orchestra[11] began once she had replaced the damaged harp with another second-hand Erard. She thereafter played both harp and piano when the Concert Orchestra visited Auckland.

> When I wasn't needed as a pianist or harpist, I offered to ting a triangle or shake a tambourine, so I quickly became a sort of second percussionist. I got jobs as a percussionist with the Symphonia of Auckland, and the Auckland Choral Society

> made quite frequent use of me as a timpanist. I played most of the other percussion instruments as well: once I even played the anvil in *Il Trovatore*. But I never played the side drum. That really is a specialised instrument.

Franchi played that second-hand Erard until the mid-60s, but by 1967 she felt she needed a new harp – her first. On the advice of John Morley, Franchi ordered an Obermayer harp from the factory of Max Horngacher in Munich. 'They were only making twelve harps a year, so I had to order it in advance. It cost about $5000, but I dodged import duty on it by keeping it out of the country for a year. It's rosewood and gold – a magnificent instrument.' While waiting for the harp to be completed, and for the year to elapse, Franchi spent five months in Vienna studying with Hubert Jelinek, harpist with the Vienna Philharmonic Orchestra. She also returned to London for further lessons with Gwendolen Mason.

While in Europe, Franchi represented New Zealand at the UNESCO Rostrum for Broadcasters in Paris in May 1967: 'Ashley Heenan heard I was going away, and asked me to do some work for Broadcasting.[12] They couldn't afford to send someone from New Zealand, so they paid my fare from London.' Franchi found herself sitting alongside twenty-nine other delegates – all men – vetting new works on tape, advising their respective broadcasting companies. On the same trip Franchi attended the Prague meeting of the International Society for Contemporary Music (ISCM): she had been secretary of the society's Auckland chapter and had frequently performed in its Auckland concerts. In Prague she detected what she describes as a certain musical decadence:

> I remember sitting at a concert listening to an orchestral work by a Scandinavian composer. The orchestra had been given brown paper bags which they blew up and burst, and bottles filled with water which they tapped with their bows. It was laughable. And that's just what the audience did. They laughed, because they thought it was a comic turn. The composer got up and walked out.

At another concert she encountered a French harpist playing with gloves on. 'I couldn't work out why. I think the composer had run out of ideas.'

Franchi characterises her own musical language as neo-romantic. 'I'm not inhibited by key; I think if anything has influenced me, it's atonalism, but without Schoenberg's strict rules.' Her style has become more chromatic over the years, but she has never been interested in electro-acoustic music:

> I don't consider it music. I've never quite forgiven Douglas Lilburn for having gone into the electronic field – I felt that was a great talent gone to waste. Electronic music is music robbed of its spirituality. My friend Michael Wieck – who'd played violin in contemporary music concerts with me in Auckland – once said to me, 'Dorothea, it has no art. *Keine Kunst*.' I said, 'Michael, it has *kein Herz*.' No heart. And I will stick to that. It lacks rhythmic interest, for a start. And to me rhythm is the be-all and end-all of music.

Franchi's patience for the extreme reaches of the avant-garde has worn rather thin:

> If there's been a new music festival somewhere I'll turn the radio on to hear what they've been doing, but I usually end up turning it off because it bores me stiff. I can't find a connection with anything I call music. When someone like Xenakis has to write a whole volume of programme notes to tell you what his music is about, why did he bother writing the music in the first place? Music is supposed to communicate, and if it doesn't communicate, it's lost its purpose. All right, I may not be able to take it all in at once, but I'll give it a go, and if I can see some form or rhythm or colour in it, then I'm willing to listen again. But I'm afraid too much new music lacks all three, and it's like a block of concrete. It leaves me unmoved.

Franchi still composes. She has recently completed a suite for a young friend in Warkworth, to whom she lent a small harp. 'She was taking music at school, and had to be able to play with someone. There was a fabulous young flautist at Mahurangi College with her, so I wrote a suite for them.' This practical, occasional approach to composition places Franchi in the same musical family as other great pragmatists – Vaughan Williams, Walton, Britten – who also wrote for particular occasions and performers, and for friends.

Franchi is an indefatigable organiser of house concerts, in which she still occasionally plays herself when her health permits. She also keeps in close contact with friends made during a lifetime of music. If, in pursuing the life about which she was passionate, Franchi made some unusual choices for a woman of her generation, those choices also took her to places inaccessible to many of her contemporaries. This may have necessitated some sacrifices, but she has few regrets. 'I've had a great joy, and a great reward from it, and I wouldn't have changed it for quids.'

1 English musician Horace Hollinrake (1902–55) arrived in New Zealand in 1926, appointed initially as a lecturer in music at Auckland Teachers' College. He became Professor of Music at the University of Auckland in 1935. In 1948 Hollinrake appointed English harpist, cellist and conductor Dr Charles Nalden to a lectureship in music; as Hollinrake's successor to the chair, Nalden instituted an executant diploma course in music, and 1956 saw the university's first intake of performance students.

2 Musician, music journalist and teacher Owen Jensen (1907–97) initiated the annual residential summer school for music at St Peter's School, Cambridge, in 1946. Administered through the Adult Education Centre of the University of Auckland, of which Jensen was music director, the Cambridge Music School ran until 1986, bringing together amateur and professional musicians of all ages. 'No other single organization has done as much to integrate and stimulate New Zealand musical life in so many fields.' – John M. Thomson, *The Oxford History of New Zealand Music* (Auckland: Oxford University Press, 1991), p.274.

3 Single action pedal harps emerged during the eighteenth century and were capable of playing in sharp keys up to E major and flat keys up to E flat major. Double-action harps were developed by Sebastian Erard in the early nineteenth century. An improved pedal system enabled pitches to be raised either a tone or a semitone, making it possible to play in all keys.

4 Dorothea Franchi, *The Oxen* (London: Novello, 1949).

5 Owen Jensen, 'Variations on a Felt Hat,' *NZ Listener*, 4 Dec. 1953, p.7.

6 Dorothea Franchi, *Four Pioneer Portraits* (Wellington: Waiteata Music Press, 1995); Dorothea Franchi, *Four Pioneer Portraits*, with Margaret Medlyn (soprano) and Bruce Greenfield (piano), on *Burning Bright: Four New Zealand Women Composers* (Kiwi-Pacific CD, SLD 110, 1999).

7 Franchi's savings were supplemented by the £25 attached to the Philip Neill Memorial Prize, awarded in 1947 for her song-cycle *The Desolate Star*, a setting of Robin Hyde poems. Franchi tied for the 1947 award with Dorothy Scott of Dunedin; previous winners had been Douglas Lilburn (1944), Harry Luscombe (1945) and Frank Callaway (1946).

8 Dunedin-born Warwick Braithwaite (1896–1971) became the first New Zealand conductor to reach international prominence. He first conducted the National Orchestra of the NZBS in 1947 and was its principal conductor for two years (1953–54), between positions at Sadler's Wells Opera (1950–53) and the Australian National Opera (1954–55). He was musical director of the Welsh National Opera 1956–60, then rejoined Sadler's Wells. He retired in 1968.

9 The Auckland-based Community Arts Service, established by Owen Jensen in 1946 and run through the Adult Education Centre of Auckland University, took music, theatre, ballet and art exhibitions to rural centres otherwise cut off from the visual and performing arts.

10 Bruce Mason, 'Dorothea Franchi', *Every Kind of Weather* (Auckland: Reed Methuen, 1986), pp.182-3.

11 The NZBC Concert Orchestra was formed in 1962, as an adjunct to the NZBC Symphony Orchestra. Conducted by James Robertson and led by Ruth Pearl, this small touring orchestra supported the activities of the New Zealand Ballet Company and the New Zealand Opera Company. It was disbanded at the end of 1964.

12 Conductor and composer Ashley Heenan (born 1925) also worked for many years as a music administrator in Broadcasting.

Frank Gurr : Forging a Heritage

It can be easy to lose sight of the fact that the National Orchestra was set up to give employment to New Zealand musicians. We should be giving opportunities to promising young New Zealanders rather than looking overseas for players. If we had unlimited finance, we could bring in the best players from all over the world – but would it be 'our' orchestra?

In 1946, just out of the Air Force, twenty-one-year-old clarinettist Frank Gurr (born 1924) joined the brand new National Orchestra of the New Zealand Broadcasting Service as a foundation player. Despite the national pride and musical optimism that surrounded the orchestra's first performances in March 1947, reviewers found its early efforts 'strident and unpleasing' and 'more notable for hearty goodwill than for refinement'.[1] However, by the time of his retirement in 1989, Gurr could look back not only over the National Orchestra's adolescence, but over the years in which it came of age as a 'world-class' performing ensemble.[2]

As one might expect of a boy growing up in the 1930s, Gurr was initially drawn to the jazz clarinet. 'I first heard the clarinet when I was fourteen years old, at Takapuna Grammar School. A friend lent me some Fats Waller recordings, and I immediately became an addict.' As his interest developed, he discovered jazz clarinettists Artie Shaw and Benny Goodman, but he was also attracted to the 'straight' clarinet: one of the first recordings he owned was Bartók's *Contrasts* (1938) for clarinet, violin and piano, played by Goodman, Szigeti and Bartók himself. 'Whenever I heard an orchestra I'd listen for the clarinet. I'd fallen in love with the instrument, and the wonderful sound it made.'

The resourceful young man set about saving to buy his first clarinet. A holiday scheme offered farm work to secondary school students, and he went to work on a dairy farm near Morrinsville. In two weeks he had saved £5, which was enough to buy the clarinet he had seen in Robinson's second-hand shop in Queen Street in Auckland. 'I didn't know anything about clarinets, so I asked a friend to look at it for me. He said it was all right, so I went in and bought it.' In fact it was far from all right. 'It was at the old high pitch – nearly a semi-tone sharper than the pitch we use now – and it had old-fashioned Albert system keywork.[3] But I started playing on that clarinet, and I loved it dearly.'

When he left school Gurr went to work as an office junior in the New Zealand Insurance Company (NZI). He hated it, and nurtured his passion for the clarinet outside working hours. Although there was a dearth of good clarinet teachers in Auckland, he managed a few lessons with Lionel Montgomery, 'the best clarinet player in Auckland at the time', and it wasn't long before he had to replace his beloved but obsolete instrument with a modern Boehm system clarinet. 'My eldest sister, Betty, who taught the piano and was a very competent pianist herself, helped me to buy a good instrument, which cost £30. That was a lot of money in 1941.'

Through Montgomery, Gurr met the talented young clarinettist Ken Wilson. The two became firm friends. 'Ken had had good tuition at school – he'd gone through high school in the United States – and I thought he was the most wonderful clarinet player I'd heard.' Wilson, a year older than Gurr, had been called up for military service in 1942, joining the Central Band of the Royal New Zealand Air Force. On a visit to Auckland, Wilson asked his friend what he planned to do when he turned eighteen and was himself conscripted. 'I said I didn't know. I'd only been playing for eighteen months or so, and really couldn't play very well.' Wilson told him the band was short of clarinettists and suggested he make enquiries. Gurr paid a visit to the band's conductor, H. Gladstone Hill, and when he was called up in 1943 he found himself in the RNZAF Band. 'It was the luckiest thing that could have happened to me under the circumstances.'

The RNZAF Band counted among its members some of the country's finest musicians, including Bob Girvan, who became principal bassoonist in the National Orchestra when it was formed in 1946, and clarinettist Jack McCaw, who formed its founding clarinet section with Gurr and Wilson. In his otherwise acerbic review of the National Orchestra's first concert, J. C. Beaglehole singled out the wind section for commendation: 'Thanks largely, it seems to the Air Force Band, the woodwind section is both adequate and potentially very good, and it gave us some very nice bits of playing, when left to itself.'[4] McCaw, who would later receive international acclaim as a soloist, acted as a mentor for the younger Gurr. 'Jack has been by far the biggest influence on my playing. I have always admired him tremendously. He was a wonderful role model.'

Since the demise of the short-lived Centennial Orchestra formed for the Treaty of Waitangi centennial celebrations of 1940, there had been no full-time professional orchestra in New Zealand. Gurr and his air force companions dreamed that the country would one day support such an orchestra again: 'there was ongoing talk in the band that a national orchestra would be formed when the war ended'. However, when he was demobilised in December 1945, the orchestra was still only a dream and Gurr returned to the insurance company. 'It was even worse than I remembered. I was desperately hoping that the talk of an orchestra would come to something, so I kept practising.' He was also playing part-time in the 1YA studio orchestra, in the days when most main cities had semi-professional radio orchestras. 'We did one programme a week, which went out live. Very few of the musicians I worked with were full-time. Most of them taught, and played in theatres or touring shows that came through New Zealand from Australia.'

Through the 1YA orchestra Gurr heard that auditions for the new National Orchestra were to be held early in 1946: English pianist and conductor Andersen Tyrer[5] had been engaged to conduct, and he travelled around the country auditioning applicants.

> The auditions were absolutely petrifying. I had never auditioned for anything before. Tyrer had a great collection of the orchestral repertoire you might give someone if you were trying to find out what they *couldn't* play. I didn't think I stood a chance, but, to my great delight, I received a letter offering me a job in the National Orchestra at twice the salary I was earning at NZI. I think I was getting £5 a week, and I was offered £10 to go and do the thing I most wanted to do. I thought I was in heaven.

The orchestra first met on 24 October 1946, in the 2YC broadcasting studio in Waring Taylor Street, Wellington. 'It was an old building with a very low ceiling, and with sixty-odd people jammed in there, plus the official party, it was pretty uncomfortable.' Despite the discomfort, excitement ran high. 'We all thought it was marvellous. We were doing what we all wanted to do.' Most of the first day of rehearsals was taken up with official speeches. 'The Prime Minister, Peter Fraser, came down, and Professor Shelley, who was the director of the Broadcasting Service.[6] The orchestra had been his passion, and he used to appear occasionally at rehearsals. It was like a visitation from on high when Professor Shelley appeared.'

Once the formalities were over, the players knuckled down to a gruelling rehearsal schedule. 'Our regular rehearsal routine sounded fine – we did three hours in the morning and two in the afternoon – but not many of us were used to intensive rehearsal, and we found it absolutely exhausting. People used to go home at lunchtime for an hour's rest.' On top of that was private practice and a great deal of new music to learn. 'The conditions in the studio didn't help much – the place was completely airless and poorly lit. Looking back, it was pretty ghastly, but we were just happy to be there.'

The orchestra had less than four months to prepare the enormous programmes Tyrer had designed for the inaugural concerts, due to begin in March 1947.

> The first programme seemed to last for ever. It began with 'God Save the King', followed by Dvořák's *Carnival Overture* and Brahms's Second Symphony. After the interval – and a cup of tea and a lie-down – came Butterworth's *A Shropshire Lad*, Enesco's *Romanian Rhapsody No. 1*, Johann Strauss's *Moto Perpetuo*, the 'Prelude' and 'Liebestod' from *Tristan und Isolde*, followed by *Till Eulenspiegel* by Richard Strauss. It must have been about a quarter to eleven before we'd even started playing encores – Percy Grainger's *Handel in the Strand* and the polka from Weinberger's *Schwanda the Bagpiper*. Not only were the musicians tired – the audience must have been just about asleep too. All Tyrer's programmes were like that. It took a long time before he realised that there was a limit to the attention span of an audience as well as the physical endurance of the performers.

Despite the demands the huge programmes placed on audiences, Gurr remembers the enthusiasm which greeted the orchestra in every centre they visited. In all the main centres people waited in long queues to book seats for concerts: in Auckland the bookings for the first concert opened at Lewis Eady's in Queen Street, and the queue went around the block and up onto Durham Street East. Public support continued to grow, despite the Broadcasting Service's apparent lack of interest in promoting concerts. 'Advertising was generally minimal. Sometimes Broadcasting displayed placards in shop windows, but there was never any radio advertising. Even as late as the 1950s we'd meet people after concerts and they'd tell us they hadn't known the orchestra was in town.'

Although the orchestra covered an astonishing repertoire in its first year, Gurr and McCaw realised that they would be unable to continue their musical development in New Zealand. In 1948 the friends left the orchestra, and travelled to London to study with Frederick Thurston at the Royal College of Music. 'College said they couldn't guarantee us a place until they heard us play, so we went under our own steam, without a government bursary.' The two were accepted as students and applied for New Zealand government bursaries, but found themselves being turned down time after time. They couldn't understand why. 'Jack had been ill and was in hospital. We were beginning to run short of money and things were getting a bit desperate.' Tony Curnow, the press officer at New Zealand House, suggested Frank approach Prime Minister Peter Fraser, then in London for a Commonwealth Prime Ministers' Conference. 'I went down to the Savoy Hotel, found the New Zealand delegation, and asked to see the Prime Minister. I was told he was very busy, but I said I'd wait.' Eventually Fraser appeared. 'He asked if I had problems, and I told him about the frustrations we'd been having with our bursary application. He promised to look into it, and sent in one of his secretaries to get the details.' Within six weeks the clarinettists had been granted bursaries and had their back fees refunded. It was only later that Frank discovered the cause of their problems. Hugo Anson, the Bursar of the Royal College of Music, was a New Zealander. 'He told us that Andersen Tyrer had been blocking our applications all along. Apparently he was upset about losing Jack – his principal clarinet and one of the stars of the orchestra.'

Towards the end of their first year in London, McCaw joined the London Philharmonic. Gurr stayed at the Royal College for a further year, and in 1950 joined the Yorkshire Symphony Orchestra (YSO) in Leeds: although he had been freelancing successfully in London, he found he needed the regular salary offered by the northern orchestra. Over the next three years, however, the YSO's funding became increasingly unstable, and in 1954 Gurr and his English fiancée, Sylvia, returned to New Zealand.

The newly-weds lived in Auckland for two years before another job came up in the National Orchestra. 'We found it very difficult to get any sort of work in Auckland. Sylvia was doing anything that came along – although she was a trained art teacher, she worked in shops as a salesperson.' Frank worked as an itinerant clarinet teacher. 'I used to trail out to Avondale College from Devonport, where we were living at the time, and on Saturday mornings I'd trek from Devonport out to Manukau Road to teach about three private clarinet students at my sister's piano studio.'

There was little orchestral work available in Auckland. 'I did some playing for Frank Poore and Gordon Cole, who had pit orchestras that played for the musicals which used to go on at His Majesty's.' Radio broadcasts with pianist David Galbraith proved more musically rewarding. 'David and I recorded most of the sonata repertoire for radio, although we didn't make much money out of it: radio held the national broadcasting rights, and could repeat the programme as many times as they liked, while we only got one fee.' Better still, Owen Jensen, then director of music for the Community Arts Service, arranged for Gurr to tour with pianist Janetta McStay and violinist Glynne Adams. Jensen also invited Gurr to tutor at the 1955 Cambridge summer school. 'While I was there my old friend Alex Lindsay[7] said, "Look, there's plenty of work in Wellington. You must come down."'

Frank and Sylvia moved down in late February 1956. At the beginning of April the principal clarinet chair became vacant. Gurr held the position until 1984, when he turned sixty, and Alan Gold took over as principal clarinet. 'I kept playing – mostly second and sometimes third clarinet. It was nice not to have the strain and responsibility of being principal. It doesn't get any easier as you get older.' Gurr left the orchestra in 1989, just before he turned sixty-five. 'It was time to go.' A little over a year after the death of his wife in 1998, he moved to Waikaura Bay, near Picton. For the first time in his life he no longer feels a daily urge to play the clarinet, preferring instead to listen to music, read and play golf. 'At last I'm free of the tyranny of daily practice. I don't feel guilty about it any more.'

In the course of over forty years with the orchestra, Gurr met some of the century's great musicians. Russian conductor Nicolai Malko visited New Zealand in 1957 and 1958. 'He'd conducted the first performance of Shostakovich's First Symphony. I'd worked with him in Yorkshire – he'd just been appointed there, more or less at the end of his career. He was an old-school Russian conductor. Very precise and very clear and wonderful to work with.' The distinguished Viennese conductor Josef Krips visited in 1959. 'He was another splendid conductor. At the big climaxes he used to shout, "*Vot you haf, vot you haf.*" What he meant was, "Give it all you've got!"' Italian conductor Alceo Galliera visited several times in the 1960s.

> He was outstanding. We liked working for him very much, but he was a hard task-master. He would curse the orchestra in Italian when things weren't to his liking. Although you don't have to like these people, it is important that they make you want to play. The really good ones do that, whatever your personal feelings may be.

An elderly Igor Stravinsky visited New Zealand in 1961, to conduct two concerts of his own work. Although the orchestra found the maestro's direction held few surprises, they learned that he expected performers to follow his printed instructions to the letter. Although he was becoming frail by that stage, and his assistant Robert Craft conducted the main part of the concerts, Stravinsky always did at least one or two of his own works. 'He was very meticulous. When he wasn't conducting he sat there with the score and carefully checked all the markings he'd put in the music. He found quite a lot of anomalies – mistakes and things. What we discovered was that he didn't want his music to be interpreted: he wanted it played literally. He annotated everything very carefully and you had to play exactly what was there.' Gurr still treasures his copy of the trio version of Stravinsky's *The Soldier's Tale*, autographed by the composer.

A few years later, English composer Sir William Walton arrived to conduct seven concerts of his own compositions. 'He was a charming man. He was not a great conductor and had no pretensions in that direction, but he was clear and efficient and easy to work with.' Walter Susskind was another great favourite. 'He knew the repertoire backwards, and his tempi were always playable. No matter what difficulties the music may have presented with other conductors, with Susskind you always seemed to have time.' Franz-Paul Decker began his regular visits to New Zealand in 1968. 'He's somewhat eccentric, but marvellous to work with, especially the big Mahler symphonies and Richard Strauss works.'

John Hopkins became another regular visitor to New Zealand.[8] Appointed as resident conductor in 1957 at the age of only twenty-nine, Hopkins was an energetic champion of contemporary music, and introduced difficult new repertoire to surprisingly receptive audiences. 'We covered a terrific amount of music with Hopkins. In 1960 and 1961 we did a series of programmes called 'Music of Our Time', which probably don't sound so new now, but were then.' The first programmes included Hindemith's *Nobilissima Visione*, Alban Berg's *Three Fragments from Wozzeck*, Vaughan Williams's *Sinfonia Antartica*, Bartók's First Violin Concerto and the first New Zealand performance of Shostakovich's

Eleventh Symphony. 'The following year we played more Stravinsky, Schoenberg, Vaughan Williams and Bartók, plus works by Martinu and Jolivet. The final two concerts were terrific: Stravinsky's *The Song of the Nightingale* and Bartók's *Duke Bluebeard's Castle*, which made our hair stand on end. The last concert in the series was Hindemith's *Symphonic Metamorphosis of Themes by Carl Maria von Weber* and Bartók's *Concerto for Orchestra*. They were all first New Zealand performances.' Also under Hopkins, the National Orchestra premiered Douglas Lilburn's Third Symphony in 1962. 'We were very proud of Douglas and tremendously impressed with his music. We'd had little exposure to New Zealand composers in the early years, and he was somebody who seemed to write with real authority.'

Deriving at least part of its founding impulse from the nationalist idealism of the 1930s and 40s, the orchestra was from its inception a touring body: if the whole country contributed to its maintenance, the whole country should reap the benefit. The orchestra's inaugural tour, which included schools concerts as well as evening performances, began in April 1947, less than a month after the first Wellington concert. 'As a national orchestra we were to play in as many places as possible, but touring took a huge amount of organisation. In the early days we had to split up into smaller groups because Broadcasting still needed studio orchestras in Auckland, Christchurch and Dunedin.' Players would travel back to their centres to keep the studio orchestras going, and a nucleus of musicians remained in Wellington. The whole orchestra would assemble for six months of the year, when it would tour and give concerts.

> I was in the Auckland sector, and we spent an enormous amount of time travelling, mostly by train. If you were heading back to Auckland from Invercargill, you got on the train at a quarter past eight in the morning and spent the whole day getting to Christchurch, where you changed to the overnight ferry to Wellington. You waited around in Wellington until half past three in the afternoon for the overnight express, which got to Auckland at about seven thirty the next morning. It was horrendous.

On tour, the musicians paid for their food and accommodation out of a travel allowance of a pound a day. 'You could stay at quite a reasonable hotel for a pound a day in 1947. Of course there were people who would stay at some pretty grotty places to save a bit of money – you could do that if you chose.'

Small-town hotels didn't always provide relief for tired travellers:

> The hotels gave the impression they really didn't like people coming to stay at all, and treated you accordingly. At about six in the morning the door would be flung open – they didn't have locks on the doors because you were up to no good behind locked doors – the light would be put on (usually a naked 40-watt bulb hanging over your head on a long piece of string) and you'd feel something being pushed into your hand or balanced on your chest. A voice would say, 'You take sugar?' You'd say, 'No, thank you.' Then just before the door slammed shut she'd turn around and say, 'Well, don't stir it then.' It was a sort of a ritual – all the hotels did it. You got a cup of tea – with milk and sugar – whether you wanted it not.

At one stage Frank thought he'd live it up, and moved into the St George Hotel in Wellington. 'You actually had a room with its own bathroom, which was quite rare in those days.'

Orchestral touring also took its toll on instruments. 'It's more streamlined these days, but there were always instruments being damaged and broken. For a long time you couldn't take violins onto aircraft. And there were some bitter arguments with taxi drivers, too. They'd say, "That thing has to go in the boot." "No, it's not going in the boot." When the driver objected, you'd have to explain that the fiddle was worth about ten times more than his taxi.'

Another constant problem was damage caused to instruments by the weather. 'I had a rather good new clarinet which I'd used for the Auckland Proms season, in sweltering temperatures. We then went down to New Plymouth and played in the Brooklands Bowl during a freak cold snap – it was in February, and there was snow right down on Mount Taranaki. The sudden change in temperature made the top joint of the clarinet split. The instrument was ruined.' The cold was also a problem in some of the smaller South Island centres, although Invercargill was the exception. 'The wonderful old Civic Theatre had a heating system that worked! But we froze in places like Timaru and Oamaru. The draughts were strong enough to blow the music off the stands. The players and the audience kept their overcoats on trying to keep warm.' In the end, players decided they could play only in halls heated to a minimum temperature of 19°c. 'We had no option. Instruments – particularly woodwind instruments – are designed to play in tune at about 21°c. Much colder than that and you run into terrible problems with intonation, and cracking instruments. And frozen fingers don't work too well either.'

The warm response from audiences in the small centres compensated for the hardships endured by the performers. 'They were just delighted to have us there. It always makes you feel good when you know the customers come out happy at the end of a concert.' Gurr, and some of his colleagues, lament that the smaller centres have been progressively eliminated from the orchestra's touring schedule. Budgetary constraints notwithstanding, many regard this as a betrayal of the orchestra's founding principles.

International touring began in 1974, with a two-week tour to Australia. English conductor Brian Priestman[9] had been appointed chief conductor, but he was still working in the United States and arrived only a few days before the orchestra was due to leave. 'Alex Lindsay had been rehearsing the orchestra because Priestman had so little time, and for that reason they were not what you'd call comfortable concerts.' In Sydney the orchestra performed six concerts in seven days. 'It was a very busy time. Each concert was a totally new programme, and each programme had a major work which wasn't necessarily part of the normal repertoire. We were doing big things like Vaughan Williams's Fourth Symphony, and Richard Strauss's *Don Quixote*.' The first five concerts were all in the new Sydney Opera House. 'We didn't find it a particularly congenial place in which to play, but the concert we did in the old Town Hall was splendid. That programme included the *Four Last Songs* of Richard Strauss, which Kiri Te Kanawa sang superbly.' The next overseas tour was to the Hong Kong Festival of 1980. 'That was pretty busy too, but not quite as concentrated as the Australian tour.'

Gurr's own career as a musical ambassador began several years earlier. In 1971 he was asked to join the World Symphony Orchestra, organised by the United Nations 'People to People Program' and the US State Department. Musicians from sixty countries were invited to participate, and New Zealand was asked to send a clarinettist. 'The offer came out of the blue. Peter Nisbet, who was the concert manager at the time, asked me if I'd like to go.' The rest of the clarinet section came from Ethiopia, Italy, Malta, the United States and Yugoslavia. Musical differences of opinion proved more challenging than language barriers: the most formidable problem proved to be establishing a common tuning pitch. 'At the first rehearsal, the oboist from Bonn gave such a high tuning A that we were all left wondering how on earth we were going to tune up to him.' The orchestra eventually settled down to make 'quite an impressive sound' under Boston Pops legend Arthur Fiedler. 'He was no spring chicken at that stage. It was amazing the way he kept going, full of energy.' The first concert – 'a great gala and chiefly a diplomatic affair' – was at New York's Lincoln Center. 'Each member of the orchestra – the whole 140 of us – was introduced individually: your name and country were read out and you walked onto the stage and took your place.' The next concert was in Orlando, Florida, at the opening of Walt Disney World. 'We played in front of Cinderella's Magic Castle, and afterwards there were speeches. Then all these ghastly, weird Walt Disney characters came out in their thousands and lined up on either side of the castle area. It wasn't really my idea of a jolly evening, but it was an experience. The customers all seemed to like it.' The next day the orchestra flew to Washington for a reception at the White House. 'It all got rather boring so I sneaked away and went to the National Gallery.' There was a concert at the John F. Kennedy Center that night, and the following day the orchestra disbanded. 'The most valuable thing for me was meeting musicians from other countries and talking to them about their playing problems, how they studied, and conditions in their orchestras. There was a marvellous spirit of friendship and co-operation that lasted the whole time we were there.'

Although Gurr's first commitment has always been to orchestral playing, he has also specialised in chamber music, forming what became the New Zealand Wind Quintet almost as soon as he rejoined the orchestra in 1956. All the members of the quintet played in the National Orchestra, so the group had to fit their radio broadcasts and chamber music tours around the orchestra's touring schedule. 'If the orchestra was in Christchurch, for example, the others would go back to Wellington and have a day or two off, and we'd stay on in Christchurch and do our quintet concerts.' The New Zealand Wind Quintet inspired local composers to write especially for the group. 'We gave Douglas Lilburn's quintet its first performance in 1957, and David Farquhar wrote his *Concerto for Wind Quintet* for us in 1966. There were also works by Bob Burch and Ken Wilson.'

Other composers wrote pieces especially for Gurr. In 1957 Christchurch composer John Ritchie, himself a clarinettist, wrote his *Concertino for Clarinet and Strings* for the Alex Lindsay String Orchestra and the National Orchestra's new principal clarinettist.[10] 'John and I became great friends. We used to have a beer and play golf when the orchestra visited Christchurch. He came up with the idea that he'd like to write a work for Alex and me, and produced the *Concertino*. It's a very successful piece.' [CD Track 2] Edwin Carr also wrote for Gurr, dedicating his *Aubade* for clarinet and orchestra to him. Gurr gave the work its first performance, and later recorded it with the National Orchestra.

Although he enjoyed the variety of his musical life, orchestral playing remained Gurr's abiding love.

When I first started playing the clarinet, I felt that if I could ever perform the Mozart quintet I would have achieved something in my life. When the Czech Quartet was resident in Canterbury some years ago, I played both the Mozart and the Brahms quintets with them. It was an unforgettable experience, playing such wonderful music with such a good quartet. But being part of an orchestra, the thrill of the sound of the orchestra around you, is something that has never ceased to amaze me. It's the most exciting and wonderful thing to do. Most of the time you wish you'd played better, but very occasionally you'd come off stage saying, 'Hey, that wasn't bad tonight.' That makes all the years of hard work feel worthwhile.

1 Frederick Page, 'A Music Chronicle', in *Third Year Book of the Arts* (Wellington: H. H. Tombs, 1947), pp.18-20; J. C. Beaglehole, 'Reflections on an Orchestral Performance', *NZ Listener*, 21 Mar. 1947, pp.8-9.

2 Peter Shaw, 'Lively Arts: A New Era for the NZSO', in *Metro*, Jan. 1990. pp.174-5. The National Orchestra of the New Zealand Broadcasting Service became the NZBC Symphony Orchestra in 1964, and the New Zealand Symphony Orchestra (NZSO) in 1975.

3 The modern clarinet exists in two main variants: the French Boehm system, now played almost everywhere except Germany, and the German Oehler system. Boehm clarinets offer greater ease of fingering, whereas so-called 'Simple System' instruments (including the Oehler clarinet and its obsolete relative, the Albert system clarinet) have advantages in terms of tone and intonation but require the mastery of awkward cross-fingering.

4 J. C. Beaglehole, op. cit.

5 Tyrer was music director of the 1940 Centennial celebrations, and resident conductor of the National Orchestra between 1946 and 1949.

6 Born in England in 1884, James Shelley arrived in New Zealand in 1920, appointed to a chair in education at Canterbury University College. Also an actor, art critic and designer, he became Director of Broadcasting in 1936 under the First Labour Government. He retired in 1949 and died in England in 1961.

7 Violinist Alex Lindsay (1919-74) had also been a foundation player of the National Orchestra. He left after a year, and from 1947 until 1956 pursued a freelance career. He rejoined the orchestra in 1956 as leader of the second violins. Between 1963 and 1967 he enlarged his professional experience in England, returning to New Zealand in 1967 as leader of the NZBC Symphony Orchestra. He held the position of Concertmaster until his death. Lindsay also founded and conducted the Alex Lindsay String Orchestra, which played a key role in the promotion and performance of New Zealand music in the late 1950s and 1960s.

8 John Hopkins (born 1927) had been the first apprentice conductor of the Yorkshire Symphony Orchestra at the age of twenty-one, and in 1949 became assistant conductor of the BBC Scottish Orchestra. In 1952 he succeeded Charles Groves at the BBC Northern Orchestra in Manchester, and was resident conductor of the NZBS Symphony Orchestra until 1963.

9 Appointed in 1972, Brian Priestman was contracted to conduct the orchestra for three months a year for three years, 1973–75.

10 John Ritchie, *Concertino for Clarinet and Strings* (London: Novello, 1963); Ritchie's *Concertino for Clarinet and Strings*, recorded by Gurr and the Alex Lindsay String Orchestra in 1962, has been re-released on *Alex Lindsay String Orchestra 50th Anniversary Commemorative Issue* (Kiwi-Pacific CD, SLD 107, 1998).

Edwin Carr : Strong Opinions

> Music must be magic – even if it's intellectual, it still must be magic. I may be reactionary, but I want to relate to my audiences. It takes a great deal of effort to relate, but there's nothing like the feeling you get when you've succeeded in communicating. It's the most wonderful thing in the world.

Edwin Carr (born 1926) has categorical views about music generally, and New Zealand music in particular. His credentials as a pundit are impressive: to date, four symphonies, four piano concertos, an opera, ballet scores, cantatas, sonatas, overtures, song cycles, chamber works, and more. He is one of the country's most prolific and successful composers, an achievement all the more remarkable given his early decision to work without the security of a permanent academic position. Yet Carr's name is comparatively unfamiliar in this country – his longing for a cosmopolitan musical environment led him to leave New Zealand in 1948 and, aside from infrequent extended visits home, most of his working life has been spent 'in voluntary exile'. Carr finally succumbed to the homeward pull in 1984, but he still describes himself as a displaced person: while he feels he belongs physically in New Zealand, he continues to regard Europe as his spiritual home.

Although he was 'a delicate child', Carr's early memories of life in Auckland's Bayswater are bathed in the same golden glow as those of his near-contemporary Bruce Mason. 'I learned to swim at Lansdowne Beach when I was four. There was a feeling of picnic living about the whole place.' The Bayswater Boating Club was the hub of local social life. 'They used to have regattas, and bazaars, and balls. Jazz bands would come over from Auckland, and my parents would take me along. I loved those balls.' His father, Harold Carr, worked as an accountant for the New Zealand Shipping Company and the family's neighbours and friends were predominantly English visitors. 'My father would bring home visiting officers, and we had the most marvellous parties. My mother was a wonderful hostess and used to entertain all these English people. I adored them. I think I was very influenced by English people.'

Huge excitement surrounded the arrival of the family's first radio, around the time of Carr's sixth birthday. 'My father had a very special wooden cabinet made, but he made us wait for the radio until this damned cabinet was built. Every day when I came home from school I'd ask my mother if the radio had arrived yet.' The family also had a majestic 'Apollo' cabinet gramophone and many recordings: Levitsky playing Liszt's First Piano Concerto, Delibes's ballet *Sylvia*, Beethoven's *Moonlight* sonata, Liszt's *Liebestraume* and Rachmaninov's popular Prelude in C sharp minor. 'The Rachmaninov terrified me. I'd seen a film where someone had been buried alive to the strains of the C sharp minor Prelude. It gave me nightmares for years.' The little boy especially hated the sound of the cello – 'we had a recording of Bruch's *Kol Nidrei* which struck the fear of death into me' – and was much happier listening to the popular pieces his mother played by ear on the piano at the kindergarten he attended. 'I loved all the popular tunes of the 30s. I think my love of music all came from that, really.'

Although Carr had longed for a piano since the age of four, the radio had been his father's first priority, so the youngster turned to neighbours when he wanted to make his own music. 'Our friends down the road had a piano, and the two young daughters used to look after me when my mother went off to town, or down to the boating club. They'd play me all the popular songs, and they'd let me play the piano.' He would occupy the neighbours' piano room for hours on end, producing torrents of music. 'One of their old aunts used to come and tell me to use two fingers, probably because I was making such an awful row.'

The seaside idyll came to an end in 1935, when the family was transferred to Wellington. Edwin's mother died at a tragically young age the following year, but his first formal music lessons provided a point of stability in a life without a maternal anchor. Notwithstanding some indifferent teaching, he made rapid progress. 'My teacher in Kelburn wasn't terribly encouraging. The one thing that impressed her was my ear: I could tackle ear tests many levels ahead of my keyboard skill.'

Edwin and his father moved to Dunedin early in 1939, and Carr once again found himself in his element. His new piano teacher, the 'vivacious and clever' Alice Wilson, saw the potential his Wellington teacher had missed. 'She inspired me in all directions.' When Wilson married and moved to Christchurch,

Carr continued piano lessons with University of Otago music lecturer Mary Martin. He also attended Martin's evening music appreciation classes, which she based on the record library donated to the university by the Carnegie Institute. 'It was a huge collection – the whole heritage of Western music, with all sorts of modern things as well – Stravinsky, Honegger, Bartók, Hindemith. The library had times you could go in and make requests. There'd be somebody operating the great big electric gramophone, and you'd all be sitting there – twenty people in that tiny room – and you'd just listen. It was wonderful.'

Although Carr remembers his years at Otago Boys' High School as some of the happiest of his life, he found the school did not take music particularly seriously. 'The best thing that happened was meeting John Matheson.[1] We played the marvellous piano duets we found in the Dunedin Public Library. It had the most extraordinary collection: all the modern French and Russian composers. We played at student festivals and recitals – quite outlandish things like Walton's overture *Portsmouth Point*, arranged for piano duet.' Carr's passion for the music of the twentieth century – and Stravinsky in particular – was confirmed at secondary school. 'I studied the enormous score of *The Rite of Spring* which was part of the Carnegie collection. It taught me a great deal about the development of musical language in the twentieth century.'

Despite his obvious talent, Carr's decision to pursue music as a career was not an active one. 'I let circumstances decide for me, because I really wasn't sure what to do for the best. I relied on my teachers, and on the judges of the piano competitions, who gave me a great boost. When I started to win things I realised I had it in me.'

Carr started a BA in music at the University of Otago and worked part-time at a local printing company. Not far into his studies, however, he sustained an injury that would eventually put paid to his hopes of becoming a concert pianist.

> One day I turned up for work, and didn't notice that a cleaner had moved an old iron heater so that it got in the way of the paper guillotine I operated. When I brought down the handle my right thumb was crushed between the wood and the metal. I fainted, and when I came to I found the upper joint of my thumb had swollen to twice its normal size. Someone put some ice on it, and I returned to work.

At the time, Carr and Matheson were preparing a two-piano recital, including Stravinsky's Suite No. 2 and Carr's own arrangement for two pianos of the 'Danse Russe' from *Petrouchka*. By the time of the concert the swelling had gone down enough for him to play. The concert went well, and he put the injury out of his mind until years later. 'It became very painful while I was preparing for a diploma examination in London, and required drastic treatment.' It was only then that he discovered the joint had been broken. 'It had set badly and was surrounded by scar tissue, so that was it, really. I learned ways around it, but it's always been a limitation on my technique.'

At the end of his second year at Otago, Carr transferred to the University of Auckland. 'The Dunedin climate didn't suit me, and I found Otago University very stifling, especially Professor Galway's classes – he was terribly boring.'[2] Auckland was altogether different. 'Professor Hollinrake was inspirational.' Hollinrake, however, was about to go on sabbatical leave. 'I was horrified. I was twenty-one, and I thought, "I can't do a year without this man at this point", so I was more or less catapulted overseas.'

The summer before his departure, Carr had attended Douglas Lilburn's composition class at the Cambridge Music School. 'Douglas was in as full a flight as he could have been, ever. It was hard to winkle anything out of him, because his personality was not an extroverted one. But the composition class itself was a lot of fun.' Carr's contemporaries at the Cambridge school included composers Robert Burch, David Farquhar, Dorothea Franchi, Larry Pruden and Ronald Tremain. 'We were all so musical, and everything was so new.'

Inspired by English conductor Eugene Goossens, whom he had heard conducting the National Orchestra in its first year of performances, Carr travelled to England in 1948 with the intention of studying conducting, composition and piano. When he got to London he applied for a New Zealand government bursary, but found he could be eligible only if he were enrolled in a college. 'I had wanted to study composition with Alan Rawsthorne or William Walton, but neither were teaching, so I let it lapse for a while.' Then he heard that English composer Benjamin Frankel was teaching at the Guildhall School of Music. 'He didn't want to accept me at first because he thought I was too young, and hadn't gone far enough. I begged him to let me come along for a couple of lessons and show him what I could do. It worked out perfectly: he accepted me as a student just in time for me to be eligible for a government bursary.'

Carr's decision to further his composition studies was quickly vindicated: his overture *Mardi Gras*[3] won first prize at the Auckland Festival Competition in 1950. The overture was to be performed by the National Orchestra the same year, but after a single read-through conductor Michael Bowles withdrew it from the programme, declaring the work 'unplayable'.[4] Carr puts the local hostility down to musical conservatism.

> It shocked people. They were used to very Teutonic ideas about music, and I was all French and Russian and English. It was too much fun: this bubbly little overture lasted five and a half minutes and went *pffst* over their heads. They rose up to their two inches of height, and I got all sorts of funny criticisms – that it was flimsy, that it lacked melodic beauty. They misunderstood it entirely.

The work found readier audiences in the UK. *Mardi Gras* was first performed at the Festival Hall's Royal Tour Concert of 1953, played by the Royal Philharmonic Orchestra under Charles Mackerras. The following year it was recorded by the BBC Scottish Symphony Orchestra – the first of Carr's many works to be recorded. New Zealand audiences did not hear the overture until 1956.

Carr's compositional technique matured under Frankel's strict discipline. 'Ben taught me how to work hard. He had enormously high expectations of himself, and of his students.' Frankel was particularly emphatic about clarity of musical intention, and instrumentation. 'He insisted that we understand each instrument's capabilities, and its ability to be heard in particular contexts.' Other works from Carr's London years include his *Symphony for String Orchestra* (1951), *A Blake Cantata* (1952) for choir and orchestra, and Suite No. 1 (1953) for two pianos. These works brim with the young composer's enthusiasm for Stravinsky and Walton, and with his delight at finding himself immersed in a vibrant musical culture – London agreed with him, professionally and personally. 'I felt my musical personality expand, because there was no inhibition. Responses were immediate and honest.' Carr counted among his London friends New Zealanders Robert Burch, David Farquhar and Larry Pruden, all of whom had followed him to Frankel's classes. He drank at the Ordnance Arms with pianists Richard Farrell and Gordon Watson, and shared a love of new music with then ballet dancer and commercial photographer Ken Russell, who completed several portraits of the young composer.

After four years with Frankel, Carr was awarded a British Council scholarship to study with Goffredo Petrassi at the Conservatorio di Santa Cecilia in Rome. The approaches of his two teachers were very different.

> Whereas Frankel had immersed us in the whole body of music – he'd take one aspect of composition, like cadential extensions, and examine the principle through many composers and a variety of styles – Petrassi's style was cool and finely wrought. With him I refined everything I knew. He taught me detachment, and I think made me more musically self-aware.

Carr spent his two Roman summers at the Accademia Chigiana, an annual residential school in Siena. There he met Dutch singer Sandra Baumeester, who introduced him to Italian dancers Kiki and Pepe Urbani. The Urbanis were in the process of forming a new ballet company with Iranian director and choreographer Grant Mouradoff, and in 1955 invited Carr to join Il Nuovo Balletto d'Italia as musical director. 'We recruited New York pianist Joe Giardino as second piano and attracted some first-rate dancers.' Carr's highly developed rhythmic sense as a composer and his ability as a pianist made him a great asset to the young company: during his brief association with Il Nuovo Balletto d'Italia he composed two new works of his own – *Cacciati dal Paradiso* and *Electra* – and arranged many others. '*Electra* was put together in a most unusual way. Mouradoff had been thinking about the choreography for years, so I had to compose music to fit his conception.' Section by section, Carr would take down Mouradoff's steps in the dance notation he had invented, and then rush to an adjoining room to compose. 'I think the creation of this ballet – backwards, with music fitted to action – must have been unique. The effect in performance was hair-raising. It created a sensation wherever we took it.'

Following an altercation over finances, Carr left the company later in 1955 and moved to Munich to further his piano and composition studies at the Hochschule für Musik. 'I went to Germany to find out why I had such a revulsion for the German race, and for German music: I wanted to know how German music had come to such a decadent end with the likes of Strauss, Berg and Webern, after such a solid and magnificent background.' Carr didn't see much of his composition teacher, Carl Orff. 'He never came in to the Hochschule. I had to go out to him – by train. I only went twice. I was so bored in Germany. To live in a place with no sense of humour was very difficult for me.'

In 1957 Carr had received his first commission from the New Zealand Broadcasting Service: *Nightmusic* was to be premiered by the National Orchestra at the Auckland Festival of 1958, conducted by the newly appointed John Hopkins. Carr decided to return for the occasion but, even though *Nightmusic* was received warmly,[5] he found he couldn't stay in New Zealand for long. 'I was bewildered. I'd been away for ten years, and it was a great cultural shock. Everything here was so pale and shadowy and colourless compared to all the richness I had experienced in Europe.' After two disconsolate years in Auckland, he left for Sydney and spent 1960 saving for his return to England, working as a copyist and arranger for the Australian Broadcasting Commission (ABC).

On his return to England, Carr taught for two years at the Suffolk Rural Music School in Ipswich and then returned to London where he spent the following ten. The first success of his second period overseas was with his First Piano Sonata (1955), written in Siena some years previously for Australian pianist Gordon Watson. 'He was renowned as an interpreter of new music and his career was at its peak.' Carr gave Watson the sonata on his return to London. 'He was rather taken with it. He included it in his recitals and recorded it for the BBC.' Ricordi published the sonata shortly afterwards, and commissioned another work from Carr. The result was the *Edith Sitwell Song Cycle* for mezzo-soprano, oboe and piano (1966). 'Edith Sitwell was notoriously difficult when it came to giving permission for her poems to be set, but she was a great friend of Gordon Watson, and Gordon recommended me.' Watson also wanted to introduce his two friends – Sitwell had enjoyed Carr's piano sonata – but the meeting was not to be. 'Edith had been looking forward to attending the first performance of the song cycle at Wigmore Hall. I rang to tell her the work was finished and confirm the date of the première, but the person who answered the phone told me she had died about an hour before.'

Other English works included the ballet *The Snow Maiden* (1963), written for the pupils of Highbury Quadrant School in north-east London, and the opera *Nastasya* (1969–72), which Carr regards as his greatest achievement. Based on Dostoevsky's novel *The Idiot*, the three-act opera had its beginnings in the late 1950s, when Carr asked Wellington writer Edward Hill for a libretto. Carr describes Myshkin (the idiot of the book's title) as a Christ-like figure whose purity of soul precipitates tragedy all around him. 'All I said to Hill was that Myshkin would not quite make an operatic hero, and that the focus of attention should be Nastasya, the heroine. She's a sort of kept woman, and the drama centres on her emotional confusion.' Hill produced the libretto in 1963 but Carr was not able to turn his full attention to the score until 1970, when, with the assistance of a British Arts Council grant, he spent a year working on the opera in Hill's Wellington home. The orchestral score was completed in England in 1972, and in 1973 the work was recorded and broadcast by the NZBC. That *Nastasya* has still not received a stage production is a major source of disappointment for the composer.

Carr's *Aubade* for clarinet and piano was also completed in Wellington in 1970.[6] 'That year I had the chance to conduct the NZBC SymphonyOrchestra, so I orchestrated the *Aubade* for Frank Gurr, and dedicated it to him.' *Aubade* is an excellent example of Carr's approach to his musical materials.

> Although it's twelve-tone – and I've used basically serial techniques since 1961 – it's processed. You've got to be able to see the harmonic possibilities of the row you're using, so I simplify it to make it more interesting and more accessible – and I don't avoid diatonic and modal associations. Neither does one need rules for every parameter: Boulez and Messiaen used intellectually complicated procedures, and I think they made a terrible mess of it.

Carr next returned to New Zealand in 1973 to take up the two-year Mozart Fellowship at the University of Otago. In Dunedin he completed the vocal score and piano reduction of *Nastasya*, wrote *Four Short Concert Studies* for piano, composed the song cycle *Out of Dark* for Honor McKellar, and completed *Seven Medieval Lyrics* for choir and orchestra for the Cambridge Music School of 1974.

The largest work to come out of the Otago residency was *The Twelve Signs: an Astrological Entertainment* (1974), commissioned by the NZBC Symphony Orchestra and scored for woodwind, brass, harp and percussion – including a typewriter. A single twelve-note row, never obviously stated, provides the structure for the twelve sections of this pungent, colourful piece. 'It all began with a dream I had of crabs scuttling across mudflats, making their strange clicking sounds. Then came a lion, a goat, a fish and an archer, so it's programme music of a sort.' Leo, the creator, opens the work. 'It's the sign I was born under, so I start with myself. After all, I created the work.' [CD Track 3] Next comes a sarabande for the Vestal Virgins. 'Virgo is also the celestial secretary, so she gets on with her typing between the sections of the dance.' The music for Scorpio is mysterious and passionate, Aries is war-like and martial. 'Cancer is tenacious, melancholy and steady, so there's a pedal note going through the whole section – and there's also a quick bassoon figure like a crab walking.'

The Twelve Signs was premiered by the NZBC Symphony Orchestra in Wellington in July 1974, with the composer conducting. Critical response was mixed. The *Evening Post* noted the work's kaleidoscopic colours and Carr's skilful craftsmanship,[7] but the *Dominon* gave an example of the kind of criticism that perhaps fuelled Carr's growing feeling that he was still not receiving an intelligent hearing in New Zealand:

> The twelve short pieces offer many points of interest, but obviously a single hearing could not provide the answer to just how many beans make twelve. The composer conducted what sounded like an authoritative performance,

> though later, listening to Strauss's animal noises and other oddities, I could hardly help wondering if Strauss, without the benefit of serial technique, had not said it all last century.[8]

At the end of his tenure in Otago, Carr again found he was unable to stay in New Zealand. 'I wasn't getting enough feedback from people. There was no profession outside the universities, and I didn't want universities any more than they wanted me. I felt like a fish out of water.' He spent the next ten years in Sydney, teaching privately and at the Conservatorium of New South Wales. 'The conservatorium was a wonderful outlet. I taught composition, orchestration, conducting and musicology, and also coached language at the opera school: my European background was wide-ranging by Australian standards, so I was quite useful.' As well as his teaching commitments, Carr conducted all the ABC orchestras and recorded his own works with the Queensland, Sydney and Melbourne symphony orchestras. In Sydney he also produced his Second Sonata for piano (1975), *Five Wolfskehl Songs* for baritone and piano (1977), *Seven Elizabethan Lyrics* for chorus and orchestra (1978) and a string quartet (1978). Orchestral works included his *Sinfonietta* (1979) and his Symphony No. 1 (1981), commissioned by the New Zealand Symphony Orchestra (NZSO) to commemorate the centenary of Stravinsky's birth.[9] The première was conducted by Carr's old friend John Matheson. Although the work is a homage to Stravinsky, the work is very much Carr's own. 'At its first performance it was readily apparent from the reactions of both audience and orchestra that this symphony was an important and welcome addition to the repertoire. Carr's desire to communicate is apparent from the very first bar.'[10]

Carr returned to New Zealand in 1984. 'I'd worked very hard in Sydney, teaching up to forty-five hours a week, and for the first time in my life I'd made some money, so I went to live in Taupo. I needed tranquillity in which to write some music.' His Symphony No. 2, begun in Sydney and completed in Taupo, was premiered by John Matheson and the NZSO in 1985. Subtitled 'The Exile', the symphony commemorates Karl Wolfskehl, the German Jewish poet who fled Nazism in 1938 and spent his last years in Auckland.

> When I wrote it I thought it was just about him, but I suppose it's about both of us. Although exile was a choice for me, and I'm happy with my life, I've probably missed out on certain things that go with settling down. The idea of settling down has always filled me with dread. I could never do it.

In 1991 Carr was on the move again. Chilled by the Taupo winters, he moved to Waiheke Island, taking his house with him. He feels he has come full circle, back to the sunny Auckland beaches of his early childhood. Carr's parting gift to Taupo was *Taupo-te-ao-marama: Eye of the World* (1990), a symphonic cantata for soprano, choir and orchestra, written for soprano Deborah Wai Kapohe. Wai Kapohe's talents also inspired *Ariki Nui* (1996) for soprano, orchestra and piano. Carr and writer Witi Ihimaera had long planned a collaboration, and Wai Kapohe's voice was the stimulus they needed. Ihimaera's text takes as its subject four aspects of womanhood. 'Kiwi Pacific were immediately interested in recording the work, even before a première performance, and applied to Creative New Zealand for funds to do it. But they let us all down with a firm refusal.' The work remains unperformed.

If moving has been one constant in Carr's life, another has been his need to write music for people who want to perform it. Since returning to New Zealand, he has written his Second Piano Concerto (1985) for Australian pianist Sally Mays; his *Pacific Festival Overture* opened the first International Festival of the Arts in Wellington in 1986; in 1987 the Auckland Philharmonia commissioned Symphony No. 3, and his 'symphonic cantata' *Song of Solomon* premiered in Christchurch in 1989. The initial inspiration for *Song of Solomon* had come from actor Louise Petherbridge during Carr's Mozart Fellowship, and Petherbridge took the role of the Speaker at the first performance. The following year saw the première of the *Gaudeamus* overture, a commission commemorating the 125th anniversary of Carr's *alma mater*, Otago Boys' High School.

The last major work completed before his move to Waiheke was Symphony No. 4 (1991), again commissioned by the NZSO.[11] Next came *Ten Concert Studies* for piano (1994–95)[12] written for then twenty-year-old Tahu Matheson – John's eldest son – and in 1997 the NZSO gave Carr 'a smallish commission' for an orchestral work. *The End of the Golden Weather*, 'a ten-minute orchestral soundscape', premiered at the Bruce Mason Theatre in Takapuna.

> Bruce and I were at the same primary school, but he was a little older than me. I only knew his name because it was painted in gold on the school honours board: he was Dux of the school in 1934 when I was in Standard 2. I didn't actually meet him until I returned to New Zealand in 1958, and then again when he performed *The End of the Golden Weather* in Dunedin.

Carr's childhood memories of North Shore beaches give the work its simple programme. Picnickers emerge on the beach; in the distance a portable gramophone plays a few phrases of a jazz tune and a tango. The afternoon light mellows and a haze appears at the far end of the beach. The tide ripples out and a chill wind rises. Slowly darkness falls and Rangitoto merges into the evening. For critic Heath Lees, the work's simple conception was its greatest strength. 'All the old and abiding musical values are there: tunefulness, growth, solo opportunities, ensemble effects and an unashamedly cyclical form. That this work drew the evening's best playing attests to its quality.'[13]

Waiheke Island has proved salutary for the composer. The year 2000 saw the premiere of *Akarana*, a four-section 'symphonic sketch' for large orchestra commissioned by the Auckland Philharmonia, and in 2001 the Waiheke Choral Society commissioned *Seven Waiheke Lyrics*, settings of poems by Waiheke writers, to commemorate the choir's twenty-fifth anniversary. The same year, the NZSO marked Carr's seventy-fifth birthday with a commission for a piano concerto: pianist Richard Mapp premiered this work, *Concerto Ballabile*, in a programme of Russian music including *The Firebird* by Carr's beloved Stravinsky. In his note to the dance-inspired concerto, Carr speaks his mind about the shortcomings of much contemporary music. 'Looking back on the musical tendencies of the second half of the 20th century, I find it depressing that there is so much abstract and profoundly ugly music written. Perhaps a fresh look at the possibilities of dance rhythms will lead composers into a more enlivening attitude to their creations.'

If Carr's opinions appear conservative, it is the unashamed conservatism of a composer who for over fifty years has aimed to write what he describes as 'accessible' music: music he hopes will please people. 'Music must have a solid technical background, but it must also be an expressive organism, so it must never be abstract. Your music must express not only you, but your generation, your race, your everything. It's a delicate balance: composers must not kowtow to the public, but they must realise they are part of something beyond themselves.' Carr holds that many younger New Zealand composers are talking only to each other.

> Many avant-garde university people are not part of anything except a university. They've given contemporary music a bad name. They aren't interested in making their music accessible, and they're not interested in developing their own personality in their music. To do those things you need technique, and you need a knowledge of twentieth-century music. And that takes a lot of study. It took me thirteen years to feel I was on the right track. These composers pass their exams and think they're composers because they can make funny noises that are supposed to be avant-garde.

Carr's views about contemporary interest in the music of Asia and the Pacific are equally firmly held. 'You can't just borrow music from other places and blend it into our heritage. That's nonsense. A student of mine once expressed a wonderful attitude to all this. He said, "You don't plunder the temples." I think that says it all.'

Carr is equally convinced of the decadence of much Western music since World War I – 'the period of disintegration up until our own time'. He finds symptoms of this decadence in a breakdown of the composer's need for harmonic, melodic and formal clarity, stemming in turn from the desperate pursuit of novelty at the expense of 'expressivity and cohesive communication'.[14] He believes New Zealand and Australia have escaped the worst excesses of European decay, and therefore have the potential to make a fresh start by going back to 'musical verities' of harmony, melody and form.

> What's needed is severe discipline of those elements. Of course you have to study them first, to see how they evolved in classical music, and in the twentieth century – in Haydn, Beethoven and Schubert, and of course in Sibelius, Debussy and Stravinsky. Then we need to go back to our musical heritage and choose what's worthwhile and what's meaningful in the present moment. That takes a lot of thought, and you've hardly got enough time in a lifetime to make those choices. You've got to take over from someone who's already digested a lot of it. That's why someone like Ben Frankel was so important. He was able to accumulate all this, digest it and see to it that his students had attitudes to their work that were really genuine and fruitful.

In Carr's case, those attitudes have made him impatient with what he regards as the narrow nationalism of his nearest contemporaries. 'I was never part of the movement where New Zealanders were very consciously trying to be New Zealanders, and trying to produce things that were nothing but New Zealand. It was too self-conscious.' He is none the less profoundly conscious of being a New Zealander, even if this consciousness is more than a little ambivalent.

> I've lived in London, Rome, Munich and Sydney, and there are wonderful things about all of these places, but no other country comes close to New Zealand's beauty. It's so inspiring. But I don't fit in here, because it's a philistine society. There's this awful schism between who I really am – what my background is – which is absolutely European, and my physical self, which is a New Zealander. How do you solve that? I don't know.

1 Conductor John Matheson (born 1928) graduated in music from Otago University and studied piano, composition and conducting at the Royal College of Music. He made his conducting début with the Sadler's Wells Opera in 1953 and the same year he joined the Royal Opera at Covent Garden, remaining there until 1960. From 1961 to 1971 he was a staff conductor with Sadler's Wells, and after that regularly worked there and with the Royal Opera. Matheson also gained distinction as a conductor in Austria, Germany and Australia.

2 English-born Dr V. E. Galway was appointed to a lectureship in music at the University of Otago in 1925, and in 1939 became Blair Professor of Music.

3 Edwin Carr, *Orchestral Music: Mardi Gras, Aubade, The Twelve Signs, Five Wolfskehl Songs, Nightmusic* (Kiwi Pacific CD, SLD 101, 1995).

4 'New Carr Work to be Sung', *Auckland Star*, 24 Nov. 1966.

5 'Immensely competent music this, with fresh and scintillating orchestral sounds. I hope we will hear it again soon. Mr. Carr has developed tremendously during his ten years abroad.' Ronald Tremain, 'Auckland Festival Music', *Landfall* 47, Sept. 1958, pp.271-3.

6 Edwin Carr, *Aubade* (Chesham, Buckinghamshire: Ricordi, 1972).

7 'Top League', *Evening Post*, 15 July 1974.

8 Russell Bond, '"Quixote" Impressive', *Dominion*, 15 July 1974.

9 Edwin Carr, *Symphony* (Wellington: Waiteata Music Press, 1983); Edwin Carr, *Three Orchestral Works: Gaudeamus Overture, Symphony No. 1, Symphony No. 2: The Exile* (Corellia CD, CRA 1005, 1995).

10 John Pattinson, 'Communicating Music – The Symphony', *NZ Listener*, 24 Apr. 1982.

11 Edwin Carr, *Symphony No. 4, Promenade, Sinfonietta, Pacific Festival Overture* (Continuum CD, CCD 1077, 1997).

12 Edwin Carr, *Ten Concert Studies* (Kiwi Pacific CD, SLD 98, 1997). Carr completed a further ten studies in 1999.

13 Heath Lees, 'Boyish Pianist Belies Age', *NZ Herald*, 7 Oct. 1997.

14 Edwin Carr, *Music or Musicology* (1996 Massey University Composer Address) (Palmerston North: Massey University Music, 1996), p.4.

GEOFFREY SMITH

Donald McIntyre : Mastersinger

Opera must be relevant – both to the time of the composer, and to the audience sitting out there watching. Obviously you've got to achieve other things as well, but if you can achieve that relevance, you're in business. The audience must feel they're involved with the problems on stage, especially in Wagner. I think that's absolutely essential.

For over two decades, the world's great opera houses acclaimed Donald McIntyre (born 1934) as the pre-eminent Wagnerian bass-baritone of his generation, and, although he has occasionally returned to perform and teach, McIntyre has not lived in New Zealand since 1958. None the less, he has always been conscious of being a New Zealander, and his formative years as a singer are inextricably linked to the country of his birth. 'I'd often take myself off to the Coromandel Peninsula and walk along the beaches, singing to the mountains, hearing the voice bouncing and echoing all over the place. Singers need to know what it feels like to fill up a lot of space with the voice, and if you're only singing in your teacher's studio you never have that experience. You need space. And New Zealand certainly gave that to me.'

Until World War I, Donald's father, George, worked as a carpenter, building houses in the Waikato with his three brothers. The four young men enlisted together, and three of them returned at the end of the war to rehab farms near Morrinsville. But for George McIntyre, who had lost an arm at Gallipoli, farming was out of the question. 'He couldn't return to carpentry either, so he was out of work a lot of the time during the Depression.' While recuperating in England, George had met and married the young English violinist Hermyn Conroy, and the couple settled in Auckland. During the lean years, Hermyn helped support her husband and two young daughters by teaching violin and piano at their Mt Eden home, and playing in cinema orchestras. Along with the easing of family circumstances after the Depression came a much younger little brother for June and Betty McIntyre.

Hermyn taught her son the violin, but, although he eventually led the school orchestra at Mt Albert Grammar, McIntyre claims he never took to the instrument. 'I think my mother was a bit disappointed: for generations, the youngest child in her family had played the violin.' Donald's treble voice, however, more than made up for his reluctance as a violinist. Performances of 'Cherry Ripe' and 'Oh, for the Wings of a Dove' attracted much local attention, and Donald was often asked to sing at weddings and church socials. Although Hermyn arranged for him to have a few lessons, she kept a careful eye on the number of engagements he accepted. 'She believed voices could be damaged if they were trained much before seventeen. I think it was very wise of her.'

McIntyre stopped singing when his voice broke, but was too interested in sport to take much notice: winter Saturdays would be spent playing rugby and soccer, and summers were taken up with tennis and swimming. 'Sometimes we'd swim out into the middle of the harbour and laze about all afternoon, dodging the ferries.'

After his voice had settled down, Hermyn found him another teacher and paid for eight lessons in advance. After five lessons, however, the teacher declared McIntyre unteachable and refunded the fees. 'He didn't think I had a lot of talent.' For McIntyre, the unsuccessful interlude now demonstrates the problems facing any young singer and their teacher:

> Starting off can be very frustrating, because you're trying to acquire a technique, and technique is all to do with sensations. Until you've experienced certain sensations yourself, it's nearly impossible to have them explained to you. It's like trying to explain the colour blue to a blind person. When you do get it right, the teacher needs to tell you to remember that sensation so you can reproduce it. You gradually build up your technique that way. It takes quite a long time.

McIntyre's next teacher was the burly Scottish bass-baritone James Leighton. 'He helped me a lot. He was short-sighted and used to stand up very close, and every time he thought I wasn't supporting firmly enough he would whack me in the stomach with his fist. I soon learned that I could never stop supporting, or he'd wind me.' When Leighton returned to Scotland for six months, leaving him without a teacher, McIntyre approached the tenor Hubert Milverton-

Carta. 'I got on very well with him. He was a real showman and taught me quite a few tricks of the trade, but he also had a lot to offer technically.' Milverton-Carta helped McIntyre extend his low and narrow range upwards – 'I had to look for things like "O Isis and Osiris" that didn't take me higher than a C' – and emphasised the importance of articulation. 'It's a crashing bore for an audience if they don't understand every word you sing.' Milverton-Carta's most lasting legacy, however, was his boundless enthusiasm. 'He showed me what fun music could be, and what a source of pleasure. He was a truly inspiring teacher.'

Although a career in singing was already becoming a distinct possibility, McIntyre made a pragmatic decision to attend teachers' training college. 'I wanted a career in singing, but I also felt I needed an insurance policy in case it didn't work out, so I decided to train as a primary teacher.' After gaining his teacher's certificate, McIntyre taught for a year at Mt Roskill Intermediate, and then went relief teaching. 'I was doing a lot of singing at the time, and it seemed fairest not to spend too much time with one class while I was pre-occupied with another interest that took precedence over schoolteaching.'

Ray Wilson, the director of the Auckland Choral Society, had quickly recognised McIntyre's potential and engaged him to sing as a soloist with his choir. Mozart's *Requiem* was followed by a Bach cantata, the *St John Passion* and *St Matthew Passion* and the B Minor Mass, plus Handel's *Messiah*. His last work with the choir before leaving for England was Haydn's *Creation*. By the time he was twenty-one, McIntyre had acquired a large repertoire of cantatas and oratorios, and gained valuable experience performing with orchestras: he made his début with the National Orchestra in 1956, singing the part of Polyphemus in Handel's *Acis and Galatea*. The same year he won the aria prize in the Auckland competitions.

McIntyre had his first taste of performing staged opera at training college, when Harry Luscombe[1] cast him in a production of Vaughan Williams's *Hugh the Drover*, and gave him a couple of small roles in Stanford's *Shamus O'Brien*. 'I think he must have been talking to James Robertson about me, because Roberston turned up at one of those performances.'[2] Impressed, the conductor asked to meet the young bass. 'He asked me if I was interested in carrying on with singing. I told him I was, and he suggested I apply for a New Zealand government bursary, which supplied £400 a year for two years, to study overseas.' McIntyre went through the preliminary auditions in Auckland, but didn't make it to the final round. 'I don't think I did very well on the sight-reading, but I think James Robertson intervened and told them to send me down to Wellington anyway. I must have done a bit better there, because they gave me the bursary.'

Within six months McIntyre was on his way to England. He was accepted by the Guildhall School of Music and Drama, and assigned a teacher. 'Ellis Keeler was a very nice man, but half of each lesson was taken up with polite prefaces, and I couldn't be bothered with that. I like people who are more direct: if someone thinks you're singing like a cow, they should come straight out and tell you. He wasn't that sort.' McIntyre attended classes in languages, harmony, opera and lieder, but he quickly outgrew the Guildhall: at twenty-three he was considerably older than the other students and he found it did not meet his growing professional needs. He lasted just over a year. 'I already had more experience in New Zealand than they could possibly offer at the Guildhall, so I began to look for outside work. That didn't go down well with the school. I was firmly asked to pack my bags.'

McIntyre made his UK début with the Welsh National Opera in October 1959, while still a student. Dunedin-born Warwick Braithwaite was then conducting the Welsh National Opera in Cardiff. McIntyre auditioned for him, and was offered the bass role of the priest Zaccaria in Verdi's *Nabucco*. 'This was just before the summer holidays. I expected rehearsals to start a few weeks before the first night, so I went off to Germany for a month.' He returned on 10 July, to find a letter telling him that rehearsals had been brought forward, and would take place on 5, 7 and 8 July. 'I thought I'd blown my first big opportunity.' McIntyre rang Braithwaite and explained what had happened. 'He was very curt. He said, "Of course you know the part, don't you?" I gulped and said I did, but I hadn't even looked at it.' Braithwaite told McIntyre to come to Wales the following week for a run-through. 'I went over the road and sat in Kensington Gardens and stared at one spot in the grass for about an hour, kicking myself. Finally I said, "To hell with it. I'll do it if it's the last thing I do."' He crammed the role in a week. 'I think I rather surprised them at the first rehearsal: I'm sure they were expecting me to blow it. They let me start off with the first act, and I got right through it without a single blue. After that they were very helpful and supportive.'

The success of *Nabucco* quickly led to further work. The following year McIntyre was invited to audition for the Sadler's Wells Opera and at the Royal Opera House at Covent Garden. He sang the aria he had performed at the Auckland competitions, which he has used in auditions ever since: 'Schweig, Schweig' from *Der Freischütz* by Weber. 'It's short, it's showy, and it shows what the voice can do.' As it turned out, the two offers came almost simultaneously, but both were for chorus contracts. 'I turned them down. I told them I wanted to be singing roles, and if they couldn't give them to me I'd try somewhere else.' Both then offered him junior principal contracts – in effect, junior soloist positions. 'I looked at the two offers and thought Sadler's Wells would be best, because I felt I'd get lost at Covent Garden with all the international singers coming in. I think it was the best decision.' At Sadler's Wells McIntyre found himself working alongside other New Zealanders, including Inia Te Wiata, Noel Mangin, Denis Dowling and Heather Begg. In that highly professional and supportive environment, he consolidated his technique and built up a substantial repertoire without the added pressure of international attention.

McIntyre made his Sadler's Wells début as Biterolf in Wagner's *Tannhaüser* on 6 October 1960. Other small roles followed: the Baron in *La Traviata,* Ferrando in *Il Trovatore* and the baritone role of Monterone in *Rigoletto*. Musical director Colin Davis had recently appointed Glen Byam Shaw[3] as head of production and the young singer blossomed as an actor under his experienced direction. 'I was very lucky to be there then. Glen Byam Shaw taught me how to act, really.' McIntyre soon graduated to principal parts: in his seven years as principal bass at Sadler's Wells he built up a repertoire of some twenty-five roles sung in the English language, including Mozart's Figaro, the title role in Verdi's *Attila*, Wagner's Dutchman, Guglielmo (*Cosi fan Tutte*), Mephistopheles (Gounod's *Faust*), Caspar (*Der Freischütz*), Pizarro (*Fidelio*) and Pennybank Bill in the first British staging of *Mahagonny*. The position also brought financial security, and in July 1961 McIntyre married English schoolteacher Jill Redington, whom he had met at a dance at London University not long after his arrival in England.

McIntyre's contract at Sadler's Wells permitted him a degree of professional flexibility. 'They had a very tight budget, and didn't seem to mind people accepting outside work. If you went away for a week they'd just dock a week's pay.' In 1965 he sang the role of Pater Profundus in a performance of Mahler's Eighth Symphony which opened that year's Edinburgh Festival, and appeared with the Harmonic Society of Christchurch in Walton's *Belshazzar's Feast* when the choir performed at the Royal Festival Hall, London, during the Commonwealth Festival of the Arts. In 1966 he sang the role of Hunding (*Die Walküre*) – his first role in German – for the Scottish National Opera, and made his New York début in Mendelssohn's *Elijah*.

The following year McIntyre made his Covent Garden début. The Royal Opera House's musical director, Georg Solti, wanted to revive Richard Strauss's

Die Frau ohne Schatten but was having difficulty casting the role of Barak the Dyer. He asked McIntyre to audition. 'Barak is a lovely, lovely role, but it's very demanding. It lies quite high, and has a very big range. At the time there were not many people around who could do it.' Solti offered McIntyre not only Barak, but the role of Pizarro in a revival of Beethoven's *Fidelio*, due to open early in 1967. He made his début in *Fidelio* on 1 February, but it was his performance as Barak in June that launched his international career. While opera critic Harold Rosenthal had reservations about some aspects of the production, he had no doubt about McIntyre's 'world class' contribution.[4] Reviewing the production for *Music and Musicians*, Alan Jefferson hailed McIntyre as 'one of the most important baritone acquisitions to the opera stage in the last ten years'.[5] McIntyre's estimation of his performance is characteristically self-effacing. 'I was very lucky to get that role. It was a huge success as a production, and it did more to put me on the map in Britain than the *Fidelio* had done. The part suited me very well: I thought I was better at more sympathetic characters than the other type.'

McIntyre was given the opportunity to portray 'the other type' not long afterwards: his second major international début of 1967 was at Bayreuth, where he appeared as the villain Telramund in a new production of Wagner's *Lohengrin*. It was the beginning of a long association: McIntyre sang at every Bayreuth festival until 1981 and made his final appearance at the Festspielhaus in 1988.

McIntyre's relationship with Bayreuth had begun rather on the back foot. Wieland Wagner, Richard's grandson, and director of the Festspielhaus from its reopening after the war in 1951 until his death in 1966, had come to hear of the young singer and invited him to audition, but had died before this could happen. On his brother's death, Wolfgang Wagner took over as director and issued his own invitation, summoning McIntyre to audition for his new production of *Lohengrin*. 'I went and sang the part of Telramund. Wolfgang Wagner kept on saying something I didn't understand, and I tried to bluff my way through it by saying "Ja" or "Nein" whenever I thought it was appropriate.' McIntyre returned home, and was singing in Oxford when his wife sent him a cable telling him he had been given the part of Telramund for the 1967 production.

> Years later Wolfgang took me aside and asked if I remembered the audition. I told him I did, and confessed I'd been bluffing. He said, 'Yes, I know.' It turned out that he had asked me to prepare the much smaller role of the Herald, but the message

> had gone astray. He couldn't understand why I was singing the much harder part of Telramund, and was asking when I was going to sing the role they'd asked me to prepare – and I'd kept on saying 'Yes' and 'No'! He told me later he'd given me the part as revenge. It's frightfully difficult – it's the biggest voice-killer of all time.

McIntyre attributes his vocal survival in that production partly to Bayreuth musical director Rudolf Kempe. 'I didn't fully realise the difficulty of that role until I came to sing it at the Met, years later. *Lohengrin* has probably the loudest orchestral music of any Wagner opera, and to fill that vast auditorium the conductor has to get the orchestra to produce a very solid body of sound, which puts a great strain on the singers.' Those problems never arose at Bayreuth. 'Kempe was wonderful at graduating the orchestra – keeping them down, and just letting out the parts that really mattered. He really played *pianissimo* when it was written. It made life a lot easier.' McIntyre's triumph as Telramund ensured his future at Bayreuth. German writers commended his 'majestic, never roaring, expressive Telramund baritone', hailing him as 'an ideal embodiment of the passionate diabolical' and 'the discovery of the evening'.[6]

Over the next few years McIntyre established himself as the great Wagnerian baritone of the day. His Bayreuth roles included Telramund (1967–68), the Dutchman (1969–71, 1981), Klingsor (*Parsifal*: 1968, 1972, 1979), Wotan (*Die Walküre*: 1971), Amfortas (*Parsifal*: 1981, 1987–88), Kurwenal (*Tristan und Isolde*: 1974), the Wanderer (*Siegfried*: 1973–80) and Wotan/Wanderer in complete cycles of *Der Ring des Nibelungen* from 1975 to 1980.

McIntyre's *Ring* cycles at Bayreuth perhaps mark the pinnacle of his career. His first complete cycle was in 1975 – the final year of Wolfgang Wagner's production, staged annually since 1970.

> Wolfgang's production was the last of its generation, really. Wieland had cut out all the unthinking paraphernalia that had grown up before the war, and brought the cycle back to its basic, simple essentials. It was like doing oratorio, really – it was very static, there was no realistic scenery, and the atmosphere was created with very subtle and expressive lighting effects. Wolfgang's conception was fairly abstract as well – it was set on a huge round daïs, which represented the whole world. It cracked into various parts as the opera went on. I think it was the best thing I saw him do, but that style of production had reached its sell-by date.

East German director Götz Friedrich went some way towards renovating the *Ring* at Covent Garden in 1974, but it would take the young French director

Patrice Chéreau to complete the job. Chéreau's hugely controversial Bayreuth centennial production of 1976 would become the most talked-about event in McIntyre's career. 'Wolfgang wanted Pierre Boulez to conduct, and Boulez brought in Chéreau. He was about twenty-seven at the time, and he'd never seen a Wagner opera on stage.' Chéreau, the then *enfant terrible* of the Paris stage, had directed only two operas previously: Rossini's *L'Italiana in Algeri* at Spoleto, and Offenbach's *Les Contes d'Hoffmann* in Paris. 'Chéreau had very few preconceptions about the cycle, except that he was suspicious of Wagner, as most people are when they don't know much about it. So he picked people's brains.' McIntyre and Chéreau met in Bayreuth in 1975 and discussed the cycle at length.

> I suggested he bring the production right up close to the audience, so people could see and hear: that way it has the greatest impact. The idea must have appealed to him, because he ended up bringing it close to the audience in all sorts of ways. He not only brought it right down to the front of the stage but he brought it closer in time as well: instead of setting it in some vague mythical time, he set it more or less at the time of the first complete production in 1876.

Chéreau also wanted to bring his Bayreuth audience face to face with the political dilemmas at the heart of the cycle. 'The *Ring* is about power, and what happens when people desire absolute power. This was during the oil crisis, so he set the first act of *Das Rheingold* on a rusting hydro-electric dam. The Rhinemaidens were flitting about more or less like prostitutes.' Incensed by Chéreau's irreverence, audiences erupted in storms of booing. Street vendors handed out triller whistles as patrons filed into the auditorium. Police ringed the theatre because of threatened violence. 'Wagner societies around the world threatened to withdraw their financial support. Books and newspaper articles were written against it. Threats were even made against Chéreau's life. I think of all the operatic bosses in the world, only Wolfgang would have had the guts to support Chéreau in the face of all that.'

McIntyre too was convinced of the significance of Chéreau's *Ring*. Following the first performance of *Das Rheingold* he was asked to join a radio discussion panel about the production. 'The others – a critic and a Wagner expert – gave it the thumbs-down, and when I said I thought it would go down as a milestone in the history of operatic production they almost lynched me. But if at any time in my career I've been proved right it was then. I'm quite proud of that. I think it was the significant production of its generation.'

During their summers in Bayreuth, the McIntyres occupied a flat in Haus Siegfried, built by Wagner's son Siegfried in the grounds of his father's Villa Wahnfried. The rest of Haus Siegfried was occupied by Siegfried's English widow, Winifred Wagner.

> She was my landlady for about five years. She was an extraordinary woman. A bit of an old Nazi – there was a story that Hitler wrote *Mein Kampf* on her notepaper. She was very attached to him. She kept the festival going during the war and Hitler attended performances and stayed in her house. I used to work in her study – it was lined with photographs of Hitler, with her at his side. I'd get a funny feeling seeing my daughters sitting on her knee, and her singing nursery rhymes to them. To give her her due, though, she ran the opera house single-handedly from the time Siegfried died in 1930 right through until 1944, and apparently used her influence with Hitler to get some Jewish singers out of Germany, in the early stages. She was certainly about the most interesting person I ever met, even though I found her political beliefs and prejudices quite distasteful. More than distasteful – revolting, really. But there was more to her than that. It's like when you play villains in opera: they don't really ring true unless there's more than one side to them.

At Bayreuth, McIntyre sang roles ranging from Hunding (bass) and Wotan (bass-baritone) to the higher baritone roles of Telramund and Amfortas. 'Wotan, Amfortas and Telramund – and I suppose Hans Sachs – are really *heldenbariton* parts. They're bass-baritone parts, but the *heldenbariton* quality is like a bass singing in the baritone register, a third higher. It gives you an extra dramatic quality which comes from putting pressure on the voice.' However, McIntyre has never categorised himself as a baritone or a bass-baritone. 'I've sung everything from Scarpia and the Count in *Figaro*, which I suppose are lyric baritone roles, to Sarastro and Rocco, which are real bass roles.' He is less interested in how a role is categorised than in what he can find within himself to bring to the role.

> To make musical sense of anything I need to get to the centre of the character first. That's why I don't listen to other singers while I'm learning a role. I have to find characters for myself. When I was at Covent Garden in the early years, Sir David Webster[7] offered to send me to work on the role of Wotan with Hans Hotter, who was the great Wotan of the day. I said, 'No, thank you', which shocked him. I turned it down because I felt he would have been too much of an influence on my own interpretation. Hotter was a wonderful Wotan, but studying with him wouldn't have been a helpful way of me finding my own Wotan.

McIntyre claims that for a similar reason he has never been entirely satisfied with his Scarpia. 'I saw Tito Gobbi in *Tosca* about fifteen times at Covent Garden, and worked on the role with him as well. I couldn't get him out of my mind: I was so overwhelmed with his personality, and his interpretation, that I could never quite find it for myself.'

With the completion of the Chéreau *Ring* in 1980 and Brian Large's historic film of the production the following year,[8] it was time for McIntyre to put down Wotan's spear at Bayreuth. 'I'd had a pretty fair crack of the whip, really. They have quite a quick turnover of productions – each one runs for only four or five years. You move through the productions, and when you've run out of operas it's time to be going somewhere else.'

McIntyre's Bayreuth festivals were to some extent a busman's holiday. At the same time he continued to expand his repertoire, performing with some of the great names of the opera world.

> I suppose I did at least a hundred performances with Birgit Nilsson, at Covent Garden and at the Met. I particularly remember Richard Strauss's *Elektra*, where she sang the recognition scene in my arms. I could look right down her throat and watch everything that was going on – all the technique, and that incredible voice coming out. Standing right next to her it didn't sound like a particularly big voice, and yet when you were out in the theatre it used to ricochet off the walls. It used to spin around the whole theatre. I could never quite work out how she did it, but I know it was to do with focus, not volume.

Otto Klemperer also made a profound impression. 'I admired him perhaps more than any conductor I've ever worked with.' McIntyre was unable to put his finger on the basis for his admiration until someone asked the German émigré conductor why he stayed in Britain. 'All he said was, "English law requires you to tell the truth, the whole truth and nothing but the truth." To me that is the essence of what we should be doing.'

McIntyre's association with Wagner, and particularly the Chéreau *Ring*, has perhaps overshadowed his commitment to twentieth-century repertoire. In 1970 he created the role of Axel Heyst in the Royal Opera's production of *Victory*, newly commissioned from Richard Rodney Bennett. He has also given noted performances in the title role of Hindemith's *Cardillac* in Munich (1985), as Balstrode in Benjamin Britten's *Peter Grimes* (Covent Garden, 1989) and the Doctor in Alban Berg's *Wozzeck*, first at Covent Garden and later at the Met. In February 1989 he shouldered his most demanding contemporary role to date, singing the part of Prospero in the Royal Opera's production of Luciano Berio's new *Un re in ascolto*.

> It was an enormous part. It really carried the opera from beginning to end. It was also fiendishly difficult – completely atonal. Just singing the right notes was a feat in itself. I couldn't make head or tail of it to start with. It begins with Shakespeare's *Tempest*, and I'm Prospero, but then it all gets mixed up, and Prospero becomes a kind of impresario, auditioning various women for parts in a production of *The Tempest*. Prospero thoroughly disapproves of everything going on – the stage producer, the sets, the girls flitting in and out. At the end of the first act he has a heart attack and spends the whole second act dying.

McIntyre initially had difficulty imagining how it would make an interesting opera. 'In the end I found something to latch on to, and it was Klemperer's comment about "the whole truth". That's what Prospero was searching for, among all that confusion.' McIntyre's committed performance in this difficult new work drew praise from critics and audiences alike.

There was one great role that McIntyre was deliberately keeping on hold.

> I came to Hans Sachs very late in life, although Solti asked me to do it at Covent Garden, very early on. At the time I said no: although my German was good enough for *Die Frau ohne Schatten* I knew it wasn't good enough for Hans Sachs. *Die Meistersinger* is written using speech rhythms, even more than the *Ring* or *Lohengrin*, so the text really has to trip off your tongue.

He finally sang the role of Hans Sachs for the first time in December 1984 in a production celebrating the opening of the newly refurbished Zurich Opernhaus. By then the same age as the warm and worldly Sachs, McIntyre could bring his own maturity to bear on a role he still regards as one of his favourites. 'Ever since I first played Telramund I've been a little bit tied up with villains, and there are a lot of them for bass-baritone. But I really feel that I do my best work in roles like Hans Sachs, and Barak, and Rocco in *Fidelio*. I think they suit me particularly well.'

Hans Sachs's humane tolerance particularly appeals to McIntyre.

> The German word *Wahn* can't really be translated into English, but it means something like the obsessive force that drives people onwards. Although Wagner named his home in Bayreuth Haus Wahnfried, which means something like 'freedom from craziness', *Wahn* can be either creative or destructive: it's the very

> essence of creativity, but it can also lead to destruction. Hans Sachs is quite aware that this has been a big human problem throughout history, but he doesn't fully understand *Wahn* – nobody does. But he tries his best to use it in a positive way. [CD Track 4]

The West German Republic's bicentennial gift to the people of Australia had been a production of *Die Meistersinger von Nürnberg*. This production – complete with a Sachs who 'commanded the stage like a gentle giant'[9] – was bought for the Wellington International Festival of the Arts in 1990. Wellington festival director Christopher Doig had been singing the tenor role of David in the Sydney production. 'We were sitting on Bondi Beach, and Chris said, "Wouldn't it be great to do this in New Zealand?" I thought it would be impossible because of the lack of a suitable venue, but he'd organised it within three months.'

Wellington's Michael Fowler Centre was not designed for opera. Sets were suspended on weighted pulleys and the NZSO spread out just below the level of the stage. Despite these improvisations, it was the triumph of the festival. 'New Zealanders had been pretty well cut off from Wagner, and were very suspicious of it. Before opening night they just couldn't sell it. After the opening you couldn't get a ticket for love or money.' McIntyre believes two factors in particular contributed to the success of the Wellington production.

> Chris Doig chose not only the best singers he could get, but singers who could speak German fluently, even for the smaller parts. In opera, and in that opera especially, everything springs from the words: the style, the meaning, the drama, everything. Unless you know what you're trying to express, all of that is lost. The other reason was the conductor. Heinz Wallberg got to the absolute core of the music. The whole thing lived with vitality. I can't think of anyone I'd rather have done it with.

McIntyre's next major production in New Zealand was *Der Fliegende Holländer* for Auckland Opera in October 1992. He had already performed the Dutchman in some forty previous productions, but was at pains to keep his tormented wanderer fresh and alive. 'Every time I perform a role I know well I try to find some fresh aspect to the character. I go on each night thinking of just one little thing – even a grain of an idea – that's different. It can lead you along all sorts of paths you didn't expect. Wagner himself said, "*Schaffet etwas Neues.*" It means create new things, basically.'

On a subsequent visit to Auckland, the mastersinger's life was disrupted by near tragedy. In 1993 and 1994 the University of Auckland had brought Sir Donald and Lady McIntyre to New Zealand to give a series of masterclasses for performing arts students. In 1994, disoriented by an adverse reaction to anti-depressants, Jill McIntyre fell from the fourth-floor window of their inner-city apartment. Months in hospital in New Zealand and later in England still resulted in the loss of a leg and confinement to a wheelchair. 'It certainly quietened things down for a while, because I needed to be with her for some time, but things returned to normal eventually. She's writing a book about it. I've put in a couple of chapters covering the parts she doesn't remember.'

McIntyre's contribution to the world opera stage has been widely honoured. In 1977 he was awarded an OBE, and honoured as only the sixth singer ever to have given 100 performances at Bayreuth. He received a CBE in 1985, and in 1989 he was awarded the prestigious Fidelio Medal, bestowed by the International Association of Opera Directors/Intendants, at the instigation of the management of Covent Garden. His citation reads: 'The Royal Opera House has great pleasure in nominating Donald McIntyre for the Fidelio Medal because of his outstanding service to the House since 1967, and his worldwide contributions to the opera repertory, particularly as one of the great Wotans of our day.' He was knighted for his services to music in 1992.

Despite his distinguished career, McIntyre is under-represented in recording catalogues.

> At the time when I might have been doing a lot of recording there wasn't much activity. Digital technology was just coming in, and the big companies were being very cautious – it was very expensive, and they weren't making many new recordings. By the time the new technology was firmly established, I'd already done a lot of my main work, so I rather missed out on that.

McIntyre is now easing himself towards retirement. 'I've started to wind my career down a bit. I'm still working quite hard, but I've cut down the number of performances I do, and the size of the roles. I'd like to fizzle out rather than stop suddenly. That would be the nicest way of doing things.' Perhaps ironically, this means he is still adding roles to his repertoire: in 1998, for example, he sang Arkel in *Pelléas et Mélisande* for the first time. 'I used to sing the role of Golaud – Arkel is Golaud's grandfather. They are completely different: Arkel is much more poetic, and understands all sorts of things that Golaud has no comprehension of whatsoever. All the drama rests with Golaud, but there's not a tremendous amount of poetic imagination in him.' He has recently sung Count Waldner in Strauss's *Arabella*, and the Old Prisoner in Shostakovich's *Lady Macbeth of Mtsensk*, and in 2002 he revisited the roles of Rocco (Welsh National Opera) and Hunding (New National Theatre, Tokyo). McIntyre has also begun teaching a few hand-picked students, sometimes helping needy singers by giving free tuition in exchange for work on the farm in Kent which is now home to the McIntyres.

> I'd like to build up my teaching a bit before I retire. I enjoy working with young singers. They don't have to be very far advanced, as long as they respond well. But it's not enough to sit in a room with a teacher. Young singers have to get out and sing as soon as they can, and then take it back to the drawing board. Singing in the bath won't do it: you need to get up in front of an audience to find out what works and what doesn't.

Although he may have had some regrets about leaving his family and the open air life he loved in New Zealand – 'the fishing, the bush, and the beach at Piha' – McIntyre still maintains the physical lifestyle he enjoyed as a teenager in Auckland.

> I like to keep the muscles going. I've got a friend with a tennis court and we've had fours in tennis games for about twenty-five years. Before Jill had her accident we used to walk a lot together, but I push her wheelchair now. We've got a swimming pool on the farm, too, and a lake I swim in. We swim on holiday, as well. I did a scuba diving course in Fiji and later in the Maldives. Jill likes snorkelling, but I tell her she'd better make sure a shark doesn't take off her other leg.

The farm also keeps him fit. 'We have 107 acres of arable land and woods in a lovely valley close to London. A tenant farmer does the serious business, but I get out and do a bit of fencing and things – chop a tree down if it's blown over. That sort of thing.'

On the phone in Amsterdam, putting on his shoes and socks prior to a rehearsal of Stravinsky's *The Rake's Progress*, McIntyre displays the patience and lack of pretension which have endeared him to colleagues around the world. He analyses his own success with the modesty befitting a good Kiwi bloke. 'I've always taken my opportunities as they've arisen. I think that's worked quite well. My success, if you see it as that, has been a combination of hard work, and having the knack of saying yes and no at the right time.'

1 Born in Otago, Henry Charles Luscombe (1901–61) taught music at King's College in Auckland and at St Peter's School in Cambridge. He was appointed lecturer in music at Auckland Teachers' College in 1939 and conducted the Auckland Dorian Choir for twenty years from 1940.

2 Englishman James Robertson (1912–91) was resident conductor of the National Orchestra 1954–57, principal conductor of the New Zealand Opera Company from 1955 and resident conductor of the NZBC Concert Orchestra in 1962–63.

3 Glen Byam Shaw (1904–86) already had vast experience as an actor, teacher and director when he was appointed co-director of the Shakespeare Memorial Theatre at Stratford-on-Avon in 1952. Sole director from 1956 until 1960, he resigned to pursue a freelance career and was appointed director of productions at Sadler's Wells in 1962.

4 Harold Rosenthal, review of *Die Frau ohne Schatten*, *Opera* 688, Aug. 1967, p.690.

5 Alan Jefferson, 'Magic for the Ear', *Music and Musicians*, 15 Aug. 1967, pp.28-9.

6 *Süddeutsche Zeitung*, Munich; *Fränkische Presse*; *Kölner Stadt-Anzeiger*.

7 British musical administrator Sir David Webster (1903–71) was general administrator of Covent Garden from 1945 to 1970 and of the London Opera Centre from 1962 to 1970. 'He was largely responsible for making Covent Garden one of the world's leading opera houses.' (Grove)

8 *Der Ring des Nibelungen*, dir. Brian Large (Philips Classics 070-407-3, 1981).

9 Brian Hoad, 'The Gift Worth Having', *Bulletin*, 11 Oct. 1988, pp.136-7.

Jenny McLeod : Child of Her Time

If I ever thought about it in those terms I suppose I'd say that music was my vocation – and if it's not, it's a bit late for anything else. But I've never really thought of it that way. I've just been getting on with my life, taking one step after another, and music has always been the thing that's come to me.

Jenny McLeod (born 1941) returned from study in Europe in 1966 and quickly became a household name. Her music drama *Earth and Sky* (1968) caused an immediate sensation; in his review of the even more grandly conceived *Under the Sun* (1971) critic Bruce Mason took McLeod's achievement as a sign that New Zealand had 'ceased forever to be a provincial society'.[1] McLeod's star was also rising in the academy: in 1970, at the age of twenty-nine, she was appointed professor of music at Victoria University of Wellington, and announced her intention to include the study of popular and non-Western musics in the curriculum. The headlines soon read rather differently, however: in 1976 McLeod gave it all away to work for the Divine Light Mission. She emerged from almost total musical obscurity in the early 1980s and began accepting commissions again, but her functional and community-based approach to music still makes her reluctant to describe herself as a composer. 'I've been saying for years that I'm not a composer, but nobody believes me. I'm just a human being, and music happens to be close to me.'

Although she claims to have been no child prodigy, reading music came to McLeod 'as naturally as a mother tongue'. Music was an important part of home and school life, but despite her extensive involvement in community music-making in Levin – from organist at the local Methodist church to school pianist at Horowhenua College to playing at dances in the three-piece band she formed with her brothers – music was not a professional aspiration during her teenage years. Following a year as an AFS scholar in Illinois she worked as a research assistant at the Horticultural Research Station in Levin, 'getting out on the land, being all nostalgic and romantic', and taking extramural papers towards an arts degree at Massey University.

McLeod's first Cambridge summer school was a revelation. A friend who had been studying music at Canterbury University told McLeod she was going to Cambridge with some other music students. 'They were all going to camp out in the grounds of St Peter's, and she asked me if I wanted to go with them. I said, "You bet!" That summer blew the doors wide open for me. I don't think I'd heard any twentieth-century music until then – most of what I'd played and listened to had been fairly light.' Webern's Op. 27 *Variations* for piano, performed from memory by Wellington composition student Robin Maconie,[2] issued a special challenge. 'I thought he was making it up until I heard him playing it again. It was just the same, so I realised it must have been written down. It left a huge question-mark dangling in the air.'

Inspired by her Cambridge experience, McLeod enrolled in a music degree at Victoria University. Just before she started university, she heard a recording of Douglas Lilburn's *Festival Overture*. 'I'd thought all serious composers were dead. It was quite a shock to realise that there was a real composer living sixty miles down the road, and I was going to meet him.' At Victoria, Frederick Page encouraged her keyboard skills and Douglas Lilburn encouraged her composition: as an undergraduate she completed several chamber works, and two larger pieces – *Cambridge Suite* (1962) and *Little Symphony* (1963) – both for the Cambridge summer school orchestra. 'There wasn't anything you could call an orchestra at Vic in those days, so I used to write things during the year, knowing that there'd be an orchestra at Cambridge where they'd be tried out.' The *Little Symphony*[3] was first performed at Cambridge in 1964, conducted by Cambridge composition tutor Larry Pruden. At the time of the work's first broadcast, McLeod commented to the *Listener* that the first and last movements use the classical sonata form. In a further, perhaps wry, acknowledgement of the work's neo-classical antecedents, she said, 'I can cheerfully state that this piece is of no significance whatever in the contemporary scene.'[4]

McLeod's relationship with the contemporary scene was about to be lifted to another level. English cellist John Kennedy had visited Cambridge in the summer of 1963, bringing with him a recording of Olivier Messiaen's *Quartuor pour la fin du temps*, which he played to the interested few who gathered in the gym at St Peter's School. It was the first time Messiaen's music had ever been heard in New Zealand, and was a turning-point for McLeod. 'I'd never heard a note of Messiaen before. It was like music from another world. I was stunned. I knew the next thing I had to do was get myself to Paris, and get to this man.' In the meantime she returned to her final year of study, and ordered a copy of Messiaen's piano work *Cantéyodjayâ* (1948). 'I worked like a demon, and it was really beyond me, but I bluffed my way through it.' At an International Society for Contemporary Music concert in Wellington in 1963, McLeod performed the first live Messiaen work heard in New Zealand.

She graduated from Victoria with first-class honours in 1964, and headed for the Paris Conservatoire. Every year Messiaen devised a different way to test prospective students; her friend Robin Maconie had arrived the previous year to find Messiaen testing fugue, and warned McLeod what to expect.

> The trip was about six weeks by sea in those days. I thought I'd give myself a course in Conservatoire fugue, so I got hold of a copy of the standard French text: André Gédalge's *L'Art de la fugue* – a great thick book, all in French. I began to read this bloody book and my heart sank further and further. It was unbearably academic. I thought if that was what I had to do to get into Messiaen's class I'd never make it. So about three weeks out of Auckland I heaved it over the side. It was a wonderful feeling. It's resting where it deserves: at the bottom of the Indian Ocean.

As it happened, Messiaen decided to test aural skills in McLeod's year. 'Those ear tests were completely appalling. I couldn't do any of it, so I resorted to rather a low tactic. He was asking people questions at random, so whenever I knew the answer I gave it, whether he asked me or not. It probably didn't escape him, but I got in.'

McLeod was accepted as one of five international students in Messiaen's class at the Conservatoire. 'He really opened my ears, and completely changed my perception of music – resonance, colour, texture, rhythmic cells, accentuation, Gregorian chant, Greek rhythms, all interspersed with constant references to poetry and music. It was a whole new world, and I lapped it up.'[5] Messiaen's influence came to extend well beyond the immediate impact of his classes.

> Although he certainly taught me things about music, the most important lessons weren't to do with music at all – they were to do with life. That didn't dawn on me until a long time afterwards. My teachers taught me how I would like to be, or how I would like not to be, and I had never met a more charitable, kindly, humble, utterly transparent soul.

Within a year, however, McLeod had begun to share her classmates' view that Messiaen was 'too old-fashioned', and had transferred her musical allegiance to Pierre Boulez. She followed Boulez to Darmstadt and to his summer conducting course in Basel, and went on to spend most of her second year in Europe studying in Cologne with Stockhausen, Henri Pousseur and Luciano Berio. In Cologne she completed her most ambitious work to date. The ferociously difficult *For Seven* (1965),[6] for flute, clarinet, violin, viola, cello, piano and marimba/vibraphone, premiered at the conclusion of Stockhausen's course in 1966, and later the same year was performed at the Berlin Festival by the Stockhausen Ensemble conducted by Bruno Maderna.

For Seven subdivides into three main parts, each comprising several shorter sections, most of which feature a substantial solo for one or two of the instruments. Relationships between the work's foreground (solo) and background, and its overall proportions, are based on a network of numerical ratios. The same ratios form the basis for lines of composed *accelerandi* and *ritardandi*.

> At the time, I was thinking of the music mostly in fairly abstract terms. Only years later did it dawn on me that the piece is actually full of 'insect life' and the sounds of the bush. The manic woodwind 'bird-song' was certainly conscious, but not what I now hear as sudden little chatterings and flurries of insects, wings, or leaves, or the microscopic detail that for me now evokes the intense activity of the forest floor, as studied close at hand, say, from some meditative seat on a fallen punga log. Clearly Gondwana was asserting itself despite the black depths of Cologne (which I hated).[7]

The seeds of her next major work were sown during that dark Cologne winter. McLeod had travelled with a copy of Allen Curnow's *Penguin Book of New Zealand Verse* – the only non-musical text she had taken with her to Europe – and found herself returning again and again to Richard Taylor's translation of the Maori creation narrative. Not long before her return to New Zealand in 1966, she submitted a report to the Queen Elizabeth II Arts Council, whose travel bursary she had been holding, foreshadowing her next undertaking. 'I have in mind a project that interests me very much – a work based on some of the Maori poetry for the Creation, set in some kind of "explosive" fashion for choir and orchestra of strings, flutes, clarinets, trombones and percussion.'[8]

McLeod returned to Wellington in 1966, to a part-time lecturing position at Victoria University. Around the same time, the Wairarapa Branch of the New Zealand Educational Institute had mounted a successful school production of Britten's *Noye's Fludde*, and was looking for another work that lay within the competence of 300 primary school children. McLeod's idea of a large-scale work based on Maori mythology fitted their specifications, and *Earth and Sky* – 'music theatre in three acts' – began to take shape.[9] McLeod devised her own text, based on the Taylor translations, and turned again to the numerical principles which had structured *For Seven*: 'I was obsessed by symmetries – Webern had enhanced this for me – and in *Earth and Sky* symmetry plays a part on all sorts of levels: symmetrical chords, the whole first piece is symmetrical in terms of the bar structure, in one place the melody mirrors itself underneath, and so on.'

Scored for three massed choirs, double small choir, two woodwind, brass and percussion orchestras, two pianos, electronic organ and taped narration, *Earth and Sky* drew on the pupils of ten local schools and utilised all of Masterton's musical resources. The critical and popular response was ecstatic. 'Not since Stravinsky conducted his *Firebird* in Wellington have I experienced the same raw thrill as I did during the "Invocation to Io" scene in Act 1.'[10] 'A remarkable fusion of Maori-Pakeha thought.'[11] 'Such was the impact of this work that the event could better be described as a blast-off.'[12] News of the triumph reached as far as London. '*Earth and Sky* must surely be one of the most ambitious works ever written for children. . . . One was aware that a new force has come into New Zealand music.'[13]

Productions of *Earth and Sky* were also mounted in Tauranga and Christchurch, and the Mercury Theatre mounted a new production for the Auckland Festival of 1970, under the direction of Ian Mune. The interest the work had already generated – combined with the fact that Queen Elizabeth II would attend a gala performance at the Mercury – meant that the demand for tickets reached fever pitch. Two thousand people applied for seats in the 700-seat auditorium: the *New Zealand Herald* announced that applications would be 'sorted out by computer'. The lucky applicants were doubtless pleased that ticket prices for the royal performance would be no higher than they had been for the rest of the season: 'the best seats should cost about $2'.[14]

McLeod's next project was on an even larger scale than *Earth and Sky*. Described in its publicity as 'a total musical happening', *Under the Sun* (1971) – commissioned by the Palmerston North City Council for the city's centenary celebrations – attempted nothing less than the history of the world from its creation to its ultimate destruction with the death of the sun. Also devised for amateur performance and children, *Under the Sun* was written partly in rock idiom and called for a cast of 600, including four massed choirs, four orchestras, double chamber choir and a rock band. The critical response was mixed:

while all commended the boldness of McLeod's conception, many found the work structurally flawed – the climax of the two and a half hour work came at the end of the fourth act, leaving the fifth and final act to flag somewhat. McLeod herself regards this work unsentimentally. 'You can't repeat yourself. In my supreme cocksureness I decided if you don't think big you'll never do anything big, and so I just sailed in. But I really didn't have the technique to cope with something that big and the players couldn't cope. I'm dissatisfied with a lot of the music in it, because it's so primitive, organisationally and rhythmically.'

The lyrics of 'Shadow People', the pop song which formed the climax of the fourth act of *Under the Sun*, show how closely McLeod was attuned to the spirit of the age:

> Leave your mind hanging in the closet,
> the world will not refund your deposit,
> the management advises all cities
> that stocks are short, especially on pity.
> Compassion sold out ages ago,
> supplies of tolerance are low,
> in fact we're short on all that stuff
> and love's so scarce we can't get enough.

McLeod's exploration of the 'rock opera' format confirmed her increasing frustration with what she felt to be the conservatism and Eurocentrism of the professional musical establishment. As she put it at the time, 'What percentage of the world's population has ever heard of Beethoven? or Bach? or any of the others? How much credence can we give to the increasing band of thoughtful people who see the future of music in terms of non-western practice, some aspects of the European avant-garde, and pop music?'[15] She began to look towards popular music and non-Western musics as a means of escaping what she regarded as an élitist, abstract and alienating musical 'high' culture. 'It started with *Under the Sun*. There was a rock group in it, and one night we got into a jam session. This was something I'd never done before. I'd *never* improvised. We went on until three, four in the morning and when I came out of there I felt completely refreshed – renewed, in a way.'

From the early 70s on, McLeod began to see her musical and spiritual development moving in step. 'I'd never asked myself what I was doing. I'd spent so many years concentrating on the written note, and with rock it was like starting all over again. I found there was a whole natural and spontaneous side of myself that had got lost, or had never been there because I'd never improvised.' Drugs and alcohol helped her on her journey of self-discovery. 'Then I began to read Hindu and Buddhist philosophy and it was almost as if I knew it all already in some odd way.' McLeod had also read about the teaching of the Guru Maharaji and the Divine Light Mission.[16] 'One of the Indians came to talk at the Tasman Street Indian Association Hall in Newtown. We bowled along, and I just got zapped.'

By that time McLeod had stopped writing in what she described as 'conventional' idioms, turning her attention instead to rock music and the study of Indian drumming. After her initiation into the Divine Light, her only compositions were 'devotional soft rock songs' written for 'The Divine Light Missionaries', with whom she played keyboard and guitar. McLeod spent her sabbatical in 1974 exploring the 'international musical idiom' of rock, which she regarded as the mirror image of Western classical music – counterposed to everything it represented – and touring beach resorts with another Divine Light band, 'The Light Brigade'. She later recalled that her intellectual life was becoming increasingly remote from what was happening in her classroom. 'I'd begun to introduce things that I'm sure left everybody miles behind. I was losing touch with my teaching, and things developed spiritually to a point where I realised that I needed something else.' Yearning to escape the academic scene, amd with her brief marriage to pianist Bruce Greenfield over, McLeod gave her house and car to the mission, resigned from the university and moved to Auckland, where she nursed her elderly father and worked as an instructor for new converts.

For the next five years she worked as a volunteer for the Divine Light movement in Auckland, Australia and the United States, but disillusionment eventually set in. 'In the States I met the spiritual scene head on, and was pretty disgusted by it. I was being really dragged down by them, so at that point I waved goodbye.' She returned to New Zealand in 1981 and settled in Pukerua Bay, where she still lives.

Soon after her return to New Zealand, choral conductor Roy Tankersley commissioned McLeod to write a piece for Wellington's Bach Choir, and she responded with *Childhood* (1981), a setting of eleven of her own poems for a cappella choir.[17] Although McLeod herself is not entirely satisfied with these engaging and often-performed works – 'I felt I'd taken an intuitive approach, and I felt I couldn't keep on doing that' – colleagues greeted their appearance with some relief. Music writer and educator Elizabeth Kerr later remarked to

McLeod, 'to those of us in the world you'd left, it seemed that writing the *Childhood* songs represented a return to "serious" composition'.[18]

After *Childhood*, commissions started coming thick and fast. 'At that stage I saw a composer's function as being a binding force in society. I wanted to unite people – performers and audience – in a common experience.' The graphic score *Piece for Wall* (1982) – 'it's more of a joke than a "piece"' – was commissioned by the Alexander Turnbull Library for an exhibition of New Zealand scores. *Through the World*, for mezzo and piano, was completed the same year, and in 1983 the Wellington City Council commissioned music for the Wellington Sun Festival, an outdoor extravaganza staged in and around Oriental Bay. McLeod contributed processional music, eight choral works for groups of children and electro-acoustic music to accompany the climactic fireworks display; not long afterwards she arranged the choral works into *Sun Festival Carols* (1983) for children's voices and piano. At the same time she was at work on the soundtrack for *The Silent One*, adapted from Joy Cowley's novel. It was her first work for feature film, and earned her the Best Film Soundtrack award in the 1984 New Zealand Music Awards.

McLeod was making a living as a composer, writing for film and television, and for specific occasions and individuals – 'I've done that most of my life. I've never had a strong urge to do anything myself.' But she had also begun to pay the price – 'the price a mother pays of just keeping on giving herself until she runs dry'. She had often turned to popular music for inspiration, most successfully in her two rock sonatas for piano (1987), but her search for a new classical idiom incorporating rock values was starting to feel like a deadend.

> I had big problems to confront. I'd spent all those years on a popular language, finding ultimately that it didn't permit me to say certain things. I finally couldn't go on using it: as a musical language it had very limited expressive potential and it was almost impossible to use it to say anything of real depth. But I still needed to find a rationale so that my music would make sense, at least to me. I was in a complete quandary.

A fortuitous meeting in 1987 showed McLeod the way out of her predicament. In August that year she was one of several international composers invited to attend a ten-day contemporary music festival celebrating the fiftieth anniversary of the Louisville Orchestra in Kentucky. Also present were Swedish composer Jan Carlstedt, Sofia Gubaidulina from the then USSR, Julio Martin Viera from Argentina, and the Dutch composer Peter Schat.

> I knew Peter Schat was some kind of serial theorist, and was prepared to dislike his ideas from the outset: serialism was a complete no-no for me – I'd been there, done that. We started off by arguing furiously, but then I began to pay more attention to what he was saying, and found he wasn't talking about serialism at all: he was talking about an entirely new system of tonality.

Schat's 'Tone Clock' theory offered McLeod a wholly fresh approach to the organisation of pitch material, which she expanded into her own pitch classification system. 'The Tone Clock permits you to think of some very easy ways of creating harmonic fields, which you can then compose with. It's also a way of thinking about virtually any music, provided it uses equal-tempered notes.' Tone clock theory derives from Schat's observation that within a twelve-note chromatic scale there are twelve possible combinations of triads – 'not just the major and minor triads, but every other possible one'. He further discovered that when each triad is transposed three times it fits exactly into the chromatic scale, thereby accounting for every degree of the scale. Each of the twelve triads (or 'hours'), and their inversions, become harmonic fields in their own right, with their own particular properties and colours defined by the intervals between each of the three notes of the original triad.

> The tone clock hours turned out to have marvellous symmetries and chordal combinations and colours which really struck my ear. There's wonderful colour in Messiaen's language, but I never felt able to use his modes – you'd end up sounding just like him. They were too personal. The tone clock hours work like a tonal language as well, and a multi-coloured one like Messiaen's, but it's much less personal.

She has since translated a volume of Schat's essays on the tone clock from their original Dutch,[19] but her own work on tone clock theory still awaits publication.

McLeod's first work using the new language was a piece for piano based on the 9th hour (C-D-G) written for composer David Farquhar's sixtieth birthday in 1988 [CD Track 5]. She finished a further six pieces and then refused all further commissions: at the time, she felt the tone clock pieces were as close as she had come to finding her 'true and original voice', and she needed time to come to terms with that.[20] 'I had to excuse myself from my large commitments, and pay back the two advance payments I'd had from the Arts Council for *The Clio Legacy*, which was to have been a major work with Witi Ihimaera. For the first time in my life I felt like I was composing through an inner necessity, rather than responding to what someone else had asked me to do.' Indirectly, Olivier Messiaen had made this luxury possible. 'His glowing reference had got me the chair at Victoria when Freddy Page retired. Although I moved on from there, it ended up providing sufficient resources for me now not to have to worry about an income.'

An opportunity for further personal and musical growth came early in the winter of 1993. Having lost touch with Maori friends made at secondary school in Levin, McLeod was puzzled by a vivid dream of paddling a canoe with some Maori people. 'Within a week of that dream, one of my old friends phoned me out of the blue, and I'd embarked on a new choral piece for Maori and Pakeha choirs.' The first performance of *He Iwi Kotahi Tatou*, written at the request of the New Zealand Choral Federation, took place at the federation's second triennial festival, held at Ruapehu College, Ohakune, over Labour weekend 1993. The 'Sing Aotearoa' festival had been conceived as a bicultural event, and McLeod took this as her brief for *He Iwi*, which she scored for large choir, chamber choir, Maori choir, marae singers and two pianos. 'The federation asked for a piece that had Maori and Pakeha singers in it, and I thought it was an opportunity to put the local tangata whenua in it as well.' The title of the work comes from words spoken by Governor Hobson at the signing of the Treaty of Waitangi, and the order of events on a marae determines the overall structure of the seven-section work. The central movement is an ancient waiata tangi belonging to Ngati Rangi, the tangata whenua of the Maungarongo marae at Ohakune. McLeod wrote the text for the other six movements. 'I tried to learn enough Maori so I could make it a dialogue between Maori and Pakeha. The text is very simple and full of mistakes, but it's from my heart.'

The writing of *He Iwi* was the beginning of an increasingly close association with the people of Maungarongo marae. While McLeod was working on the 'Sing Aotearoa' piece she had formed a close friendship with kuia Joan Akapita, and in January 1994 Akapita invited McLeod to join the iwi's annual canoe trip down the Whanganui river. 'The Tira Hoe Waka – "coming together to paddle" – is open only to members of the river tribe, and I felt very privileged to be there. It's a wananga, for spiritual learning. The rules are strict, and strictly observed: no drugs, no alcohol, and no radios or tape recorders.' McLeod was the only Pakeha among the 110 paddlers who set off from Taumarunui for the 234-kilometre trip downstream to Wanganui. 'When I wrote *Earth and Sky*, I didn't know there *was* a Maori culture. I'd been at school with Maori, and had some good Maori friends, but I didn't realise the extent of the Maori world.' She experienced the trip as an ideal of community, tolerance and co-operation. 'The Maori will always give you time – to express yourself if you're shy or hesitant, to show them who you really are. This is what they love, what they most want you to be, and what they're most interested in finding out. So they're wonderful listeners and, when you're sincere, very slow to pass judgement.'

The trip brought other revelations. Although she was aware that the version of the creation poetry she had used in *Earth and Sky* came originally from the upper Whanganui – 'that was one important reason I needed to make the trip' – she had not realised that the poetry was still alive, and still being sung. 'When I heard it on that trip I nearly died of shock. Most nights we stayed way up on marae, in the back of beyond, and every night there were karakia. It was all in Maori, so I would just have this nice feeling because I couldn't understand a word of it, and then suddenly one night I recognised the words. It was the ancient creation poetry.' McLeod was sitting next to her friend Joan. 'She leaned over and said, "This is very ancient."' McLeod realised she had a problem.

> I knew that a lot of the material I used in *Earth and Sky* had come via Richard Taylor, who'd been the first Anglican missionary – the first missionary of any denomination – on the river, and of course my whanau knew Richard Taylor. We'd been past his mission in our canoes. How was I going to tell them that I used the creation poetry in *Earth and Sky*? When I wrote it, I didn't think of it as drawing on Maori culture – we didn't think like that back then. I thought I was bringing it back to life, and I'd just discovered it had been alive all along.

Joan Akapita died before McLeod could tell her what she'd done, but soon after she had another opportunity to 'come clean'. 'A group from Waipukurau wanted to do *Earth and Sky*, and I realised that it couldn't be performed again without telling the Whanganui elders what I'd done, and getting their blessing: they said they had to make sure that none of the words were too sacred to be used.' McLeod handed over the libretto with some apprehension.

> I was dealing with the nightmare of having to find another word with the same number of syllables that meant roughly the same thing, but it was all alright in the end. These days I'd never dream of just taking something that isn't mine and using it – that magpie Western European thing, with no understanding that it belongs to a people, and it is their means of identifying themselves. It's sacred. It's not mine to touch. You can only do it by becoming a part of the culture.

McLeod's friendships within Maungarongo blossomed to the extent that she has become an adopted whanau member and honorary kaumatua of Ngati Rangi. 'For ages I felt quite conspicuous in the Maori world, and barely made a squeak. I would just sit quiet. Now I can say things without worrying that I might be offending their cultural consciousness, because I'm family. I know there are two worlds, but I'm at home in both of them.'

McLeod's relationship with the devoutly Marist Catholic Maungarongo has not been all one way. Not long before Joan Akapita died she suggested to the whanau that they invite McLeod to become the permanent judge of the choral section of the Maori Katorika Hui Aranga, the annual Easter hui and choral competition held by the Maori Catholics of New Zealand. The offer gave McLeod the chance to do something in return, and also an 'excuse' for a permanent connection with Maungarongo. 'I was kind of family by then anyway, but I was glad I went in there with Joan's mana behind me: the group at the hui was much bigger than the one I already knew – there were several thousand people there. There's a very strong Maori Catholic presence on the Whanganui, dating back from Mother Aubert's time.'

McLeod's first hui was in 1994. Every year subsequently she has composed a four-part hymn for the competing a cappella choirs. 'The hymns have to be completely tonal because the Maori choirs can't read music. Their conductors have to teach it to them, but a lot of them can't read music either, so I send them a tape where I sing all the parts, one after the other. I started by multi-tracking the parts, but it sounded like a sick cow when it was mixed.' McLeod writes the texts to the hymns herself. 'I've tried to get them to write some words, but they always say they want the tune first, so I've ended up writing my own words, or snitching them from somewhere. I'd started learning Maori when I was working on *He Iwi*, but I didn't know it would be so hard. I'm living the kind of life where I learn a lot.'

McLeod now sees even life's hardest lessons as part of a larger plan. In 1996, cancer brought her close to death.

> Getting sick was one of the best things that has happened to me. That was the first time I experienced the power of other people's prayers. I couldn't communicate directly with God myself – I was too out of it. All I could do was ask other people to pray for me. Messiaen had died, and Joan had died. They were both strong Christians, so I sent them messages asking them to have a word on my behalf. I called on every power I knew. Then it happened. It was like an almighty hand coming down out of the sky, picking me up.

Although she had already come to feel enfolded within the spirituality of Maungarongo – 'I liked being around their services – karakia and everything – and I particularly liked not understanding a word of it' – the apotheosis of her life-long quest for spiritual connectedness didn't come until some months into her recuperation.

> For years I used to have my TV on at night. I'd often go to sleep with it on. If something vaguely interesting came on it would penetrate my sleep and I'd cock an ear and roll over. There were two TV evangelists I particularly liked – Joyce Meyer at five in the morning, and Benny Hinn at 5.30. I didn't listen to what they were saying – I just listened to their tone of voice, and whether they were enjoying themselves. They sounded fun. Then gradually I became aware of what they were saying. I don't really know how it happened, but I do know that I'm a born again, baptised in the Holy Spirit Christian, and it all happened in my bedroom.

McLeod's commitment to a spiritual community once again dominates her life.

> I felt no real desire to go anywhere near a Pakeha church, and I've never even set foot in one of those charismatic churches, so eventually I wandered up the road to the combined Methodist and Presbyterian church. I was brought up a Methodist, so I thought I'd see what it was like. It was tiny – about the size of the Maori church I'm used to – and it was full of Cook Islanders, and elderly Pakeha who'd been going there for donkey's years.

She felt at home at once, and before long found herself returning to her teenage role of church organist, playing two services a day on many Sundays.

> Once they found out who I was it didn't take long for them to start dropping broad hints. I'd have been quite happy not to do it – I was really enjoying not having to worry about that side of it – but in the end I felt I should offer to help. We've got one of those stupid electronic organs with some notes missing. There are two manuals – three and a half octaves, with F on the bottom, C at the top. The pedals start on C, so the notes between that C and the manual F are just not on the instrument. I can't believe anybody could have designed an instrument like that. You've had it if you want to play a fugue from Bach's 48 Preludes and Fugues where the bass voice always goes down to C, so I just transpose them up. It sounds ridiculous for a few beats, but then it's all right.

McLeod also writes for the church when the occasion arises.

> I'd been to church one morning at the beginning of Advent, to find that the altar had completely disappeared. One old lady had done all the decoration – a black cloth with stars on it, a cardboard box with a little crèche in it, all in lovely colours. Up above she'd put a strip of brown paper with verses on it – her own verses, which she'd lettered herself. The whole thing was folk art. It was lovely. She told me she'd been doing it for fifteen years, changing the words periodically. I asked her if there was any music for those words, and she said there wasn't, so I told her I'd write a song for them.

McLeod finished the carol that afternoon, and took it back in time for the evening service. 'They loved it. We sang it for weeks on end.' She has since completed many hymns and sacred songs, often in a popular idiom, but has not discounted the idea of writing more 'serious' music: 'I'll just see where I'm led.'

Although there have been times in her life when she has desperately needed to listen to new music, McLeod's needs are now more simply met. 'I walk every morning, with an empty mind. I love empty mind.' Her route takes her up through the pohutukawas at the back of her beloved garden, and down a zig-zag path to the beach. 'Until I started walking I never noticed the seasons – their different smells, and the way the plants change – or where the wind's coming from, or if it's going to rain today. And then there are the people with their dogs – you get to know all the dogs. It's great. It gives you a feeling for the place, and for the people. It's always changing. I love it.'

Her awareness of change in the natural world also encompasses her own life's path. 'People looking from the outside probably think I've gone like a blinking zig-zag, backwards and forwards my whole life long. I don't care what they think. It looks different from the inside.'

1 Bruce Mason, 'After *Under the Sun* New Zealand Ceases Forever to be a Provincial Society', *NZ Listener*, 21 June 1971, pp.5-7.

2 Composer, writer and teacher Robin Maconie (born Auckland 1942) completed an MA at Victoria University and studied in Paris under Messiaen and in Cologne under Zimmermann, Stockhausen and Pousseur. Maconie's *The Works of Karlheinz Stockhausen* (1976, 1990) and *Stockhausen on Music* (1988) are standard works of reference. He has lived in England since 1969.

3 Jenny McLeod, 'Little Symphony', *New Zealand Composers: McLeod, Farquhar, Pruden, Carr* (Continuum CD, CCD 1073-2, 1995).

4 'Unashamedly Tonal', *NZ Listener*, 14 May 1964.
5 Jenny McLeod, 'Messiaen Through the Eyes of a Small Pupil', *Canzona* 14: 35 (1992), pp.3-14.
6 Jenny McLeod, *For Seven* (Wellington: Waiteata Music Press, 1967, 1990).
7 'The Composer Speaks: Jenny McLeod on *For Seven*', *Music in New Zealand*, Spring 1992, pp.28-31.
8 Mervyn Cull, 'An Explosive Kind of Fashion', *Ascent* 1: 3 (Apr. 1969), pp.30-4.
9 Jenny McLeod, *Earth and Sky* (Philips LP, 6503001, 1970).
10 Cameron Hill, '*Earth and Sky*', *NZ Listener*, 4 Oct. 1968.
11 Owen Jensen, '*Earth and Sky* has Great Impact', *Theme* 1968, p.11.
12 L. C. M. Saunders, '*Earth and Sky* Outstanding', *NZ Herald*, 8 Sept. 1969.
13 Frederick Page, 'New Zealand', *Musical Times* 110: 1511 (Jan. 1969), p.64.
14 '2000 Apply for *Earth and Sky*', *NZ Herald*, 25 Feb. 1970.
15 Jenny McLeod, 'Progress?', *Arts and Community* 7: 2 (Feb. 1971), p.1.
16 The Divine Light Mission, now known as Elan Vital, was founded in India in 1960 and in the United States in 1971. Hailed by his followers as 'the Lord of the Universe', spiritual leader Guru Maharaji offered his disciples an experience called 'Knowledge' – an awareness of the primordial energy of the universe manifest within each individual. This knowledge was experienced through service and mediation, and contemplation of Maharaji's teachings. Accused in the 1980s of exploiting his followers to amass a vast personal fortune, Maharaji and his mission now maintain a low international profile.
17 Jenny McLeod, *Childhood* (Wellington: Waiteata Music Press, 1988).
18 Elizabeth Kerr, 'Jenny McLeod Talks to *Music in New Zealand*', *Music in New Zealand*, Spring 1988, pp.7-13, 40.
19 Peter Schat, *The Tone Clock*, translated from the Dutch and introduced by Jenny McLeod (Switzerland: Harwood Academic Publishers, 1993).
20 McLeod wrote a further four 'Tone Clock' pieces for Douglas Lilburn's eighieth birthday in 1995. The pieces were published together as *Eleven Tone Clock Pieces* (Wellington: Waiteata Music Press, 1997).

Malvina Major : A Cross to Bear

When I was quite young my father and I shared an ambition that I'd go to New York to train, and have a career in song and dance. That's what I wanted, and that's where I believed I was going. It was my mother who really pushed me into the classical side of music, and I resented it. I really resented it.

The course of Malvina Major's career is legendary. Barely a year after her international début at the 1968 Salzburg Festival, Major (born 1943) returned to New Zealand to settle on the Taranaki dairy farm where she and her husband Winston had decided to raise their children. After nearly fifteen years of rural exile, however, Major resumed the international stage, commuting between the family farm at Oaonui and opera houses around the world. Then personal tragedy struck: her husband died suddenly in September 1990. Shock triggered a career-threatening vocal crisis, and Malvina fought her way back to health and further international acclaim. But beneath the story of the dairy-farming diva runs a rather less familiar narrative of conflict and compromise, ambition and sacrifice. 'My father and I never actually sat down and talked about it: it was simply a foregone conclusion that I'd train for a career on Broadway. I was incredibly versatile – I could play the piano, I could sing, I could dance – but from the age of sixteen I had to learn all about opera. It was the right thing to do, of course – it *is* an operatic voice, and has all the qualities necessary for opera singing – but it took me into a field I didn't understand, and that's what I resented most.'

Eva Major wanted an unusual name for her seventh child and fourth daughter. 'Dad was reading the paper one morning and called out that he'd found one: apparently Mrs Roosevelt's secretary was called Malvina. My mum said, "That's a nice name. It'll do."' Music was an integral part of life for the strictly Presbyterian family, and Malvina's talent soon declared itself. Eva didn't allow alcohol in the house so the family entertained visitors with singing and dancing, and everyone played a musical instrument. 'My oldest sister, Betty, taught me the ukulele, and how to yodel. She also sang beautifully.' Seventeen-year-old Betty and nine-year-old Donald formed a duo. Malvina joined them before she turned three, and not long after they sang at the opening of the local radio station in Hamilton. 'I had to stand on a chair to reach the microphone.' The Major Trio – with Betty on guitar, Donald on banjo and a pint-sized Malvina on ukulele – featured regularly on Station 1XH, and performed for returned servicemen, church groups and weddings.

Railway worker Dick Hunt had come to live with the Major family in Hamilton East after his fiancée had been killed horse-riding. 'He had his own piano, and played marvellously. He encouraged me to start with, but then paid for me to have proper lessons.' Hunt also bought Malvina her first piano accordion. 'My mother disapproved a bit – she thought I should stick to piano – but we formed another band, with Dick on piano, me on accordion and my younger brother Daryl on drums. By the time I was ten we were playing all over the Waikato.' By then the family had moved to the north Waikato dairy farming community of Te Kowhai, where Vincent Major ran a small dairy herd.

Although a physically strong child and 'a fairly rugged tomboy', Malvina was sheltered into late adolescence by her highly protective mother. 'My sisters were much older than me, and the two oldest had already married divorced men. It had upset my mother terribly, and she wasn't going to have it happen to her youngest daughter, so she protected me from a lot of things.' The strait-laced Eva was, however, a physically remote figure.

> She never kissed me or hugged me. I remember when I was about nine I was supposed to be going on a week's holiday to Waihi with my piano teacher, Mrs Bateman. Mum kissed me goodbye, and I went over to the beach convinced she was going to die and she was sending me away because she didn't want to tell me. It was so unusual for her to kiss me. I was so upset that they had to bring me home two days later.

As much as Malvina loved her mother, the relationship continued to have its difficulties. 'She'd come to all my music lessons, and to school dances, and on every date I ever had. It didn't bother me much until I was about seventeen, when I began to resent the hold she had over me. From then on things began to deteriorate.' Eva Major's plans for her talented daughter didn't involve the distractions of boys and dancing: having had her own talent stifled by marriage and family, she refused to see Malvina forced into the same decision. 'My mother sang and danced, and had once been offered a job travelling with a vaudeville show, but her mother wouldn't let her go – it just wasn't done in those days. So her great ambition was to see her own children on the stage.'

Despite her own religious convictions, Eva believed that Malvina 'would do best with the nuns' and sent her to the convent at Ngaruawahia for piano lessons. Singing lessons quickly took priority over the piano, and annual competition successes encouraged Eva to steer Malvina towards a career in opera. 'When I started winning singing competitions in the Waikato, the judges told my mother I was singing arias I wasn't ready for and, unless she sent me up to Sister Mary Leo in Auckland, they'd take me out of her hands and send me themselves.'

Major auditioned for Sister Mary Leo in 1959, and spent the next four years travelling to St Mary's College in Auckland for weekly lessons.[1] 'Sister Leo was very warm, but an absolute disciplinarian. During my first year with her she wouldn't let me sing any of the songs I knew, or perform in public.' Although she resented it at the time, Major also understood the need to learn new habits. 'She taught me how to stand, how to support the sound, and how to make the sound and the word – two separate things – blend together like pearls on a string. Nobody has ever been able to fault the technique and breathing control she gave me.'

Major's years with Sister Mary Leo culminated in triumph in the 1963 New Zealand Mobil Song Quest. The finals that year were held in Hamilton and judged by James Robertson, then musical director of the New Zealand Opera Company. 'I think one of the reasons I won was because I remembered Sister's advice that it was a radio contest. She had instilled in us that we were to perform to the microphone rather than to the audience: the judges were sitting a couple of miles away in the radio studio, listening to the live broadcast.' Cyril Brown, Song Quest organiser from 1961 to 1977, also advised 1963 finalist Kiri Te Kanawa to sing to the microphone:

> Of course she took no notice. She let it rip, and the audience just lapped it up. When the judges got back to the theatre with the list of winners, everyone was horrified, saying things like, 'You can't do this! Kiri should win!' But if you listen

> to the tapes, there is no doubt about it: Malvina sang better on the night. Kiri realised this and was very happy with second. It gave her the spur to work harder and win it next time.[2]

The Song Quest success propelled Major – already somewhat ambivalent about the direction her life was taking – into the next phase of her career. 'Sister Leo told me I needed to move on, and that I should go to Australia.' The prospect filled her with panic. 'I'd never left home, and I'd met Winston, but off I went to the Sydney *Sun* aria competition.' Sister Leo's order gave her permission to join her pupils Pettine-Ann Croul, Hannah Tatana and Major in Australia, where she helped them prepare for the competition. Croul won in Sydney, with Major a close second. Dispirited and homesick, Major travelled to Ballarat to compete for a place in the 1964 Melbourne *Sun* aria competition. 'I won in Ballarat, so we went on to Melbourne. Once we got there Sister didn't leave me alone. She badgered me, and pulled everything I did to pieces in ways she had never done before. I got so angry that I vowed I would never go back to her.' When Major came off the stage after her win had been announced, Sister Leo was standing in the wings. 'She put her arms around me and said how sorry she was she'd had to do it to me, but that it had paid off.' Sister Leo had realised that Major needed to be goaded out of her emotional slump. 'She deliberately went out to provoke me: she knew that if she could make me angry enough I'd perform.'

Major had met Taranaki-born farmer Winston Fleming while he was working at the Te Kowhai dairy factory. Eva Major made a habit of welcoming young visitors to the family dinner-table, and the romance blossomed under her unsuspecting nose. In the face of Eva's rage and disappointment, Malvina and Winston married in January 1965. 'She thought he would stop me singing, and the last straw for her was the fact that he was Catholic. But I would have become a Catholic whether I'd met Winston or not.' Major had first contemplated conversion in Ngaruawahia. 'Tension was already growing between me and my mother, and the serenity of the nuns and the tranquillity of the convent captivated my imagination.' In Auckland, she asked Sister Mary Leo if she could become a nun. 'She said we'd talk about it again when I was twenty-one, but by then I'd met Winston, so I converted when we married.' Eva Major did not attend the wedding. 'I visited her on my wedding day, but she would have nothing to do with me. I didn't want to lose her, so when I went to London I wrote to her, and she wrote to me, but she never acknowledged that I was married.'

Mother and daughter were not reunited until shortly before Eva's death. In September 1967 Malvina had been in New Zealand singing in the Hamilton Amateur Operatic Society's production of *The Sound of Music*. 'My mother was in hospital, and my eldest brother rang me and told me I'd better go and see her. I had Andrew with me, who was two, and she clung to me for only the second time in her life. She said she had prayed that we would come to visit her. That was the tragedy: she really did want to see us.' Eva died two weeks later, by which time Malvina was back in London. 'When she died, I remember standing on a street-corner in Lewisham, crying my eyes out, having a real hate-session with her. I asked her why she'd pushed me into this horrible career, and why it was a sin not to use my talent. There I was, stuck in this dreadful place singing things I didn't want to sing, and I couldn't go back.' It would be many more years before Malvina was reconciled to the accuracy – and inevitability – of Eva's vision of her daughter's talent.

The newly-weds had set out for London with the Melbourne prize of £1200, £300 from the Mobil Song Quest and £100 from the Hamilton West branch of Rotary. 'Sister Leo had written to James Roberston asking his advice about where I should go, and he told her to send me to the London Opera Centre. He was musical director of the centre and he told her he would take care of me, which he did.' At the Opera Centre – 'really an operatic finishing school, and workshop-cum-rehearsal space for the Royal Opera' – Major studied movement, stagecraft and languages, and learned repertoire with the help of conductor and composer Gerald Gover. As the centre did not retain its own staff of vocal coaches, Major studied singing with Professor Ruth Packer of the Royal College of Music, paying her out of precious grant money.

Major found herself in demand for mezzo and soprano roles in student productions, but Packer agreed with James Robertson and Sister Mary Leo that she should be steered towards the lyric soprano repertoire. 'Madame Packer recognised that the voice had a very low mezzo quality at the bottom and a boy soprano quality at the top. It changed somewhere about E, F and G in the middle of the range, so she helped me even it out by taking a little of the weight from the bottom and adding it to the top. Yodelling had been a great exercise, because it drops the voice right down onto the vocal cords. As a result the bottom of the voice was very well formed, but I was never a mezzo.'

Major had been at the Opera Centre for eighteen months when Gerald Gover offered her the soprano role of Matilde in Rossini's *Elisabetta, Regina d'Inghilterra*, which he was to conduct for the Camden Festival at the Euston

Road Town Hall in February 1968. Major's performance as the fictitious daughter of Mary Queen of Scots attracted enough critical attention to launch her international career.[3] 'It wasn't a huge part, but I really loved it. Matilde is the secret wife of Elizabeth's beloved Leicester. She's smuggled into the court dressed as a page-boy, and of course the queen discovers her. It's a great drama, as well as wonderful music.' Word of Major's success reached conductor Claudio Abbado, who had talent scouts in London looking for a Rosina to replace the pregnant Riri Grist in the 1968 Salzburg Festival production of Rossini's *Il Barbiere di Siviglia.* She auditioned for Abbado at La Scala. 'He offered me the role of Rosina, which is usually sung by a mezzo, but with soprano coloratura. I remember Abbado's argument with the opera house hierarchy to this day. They told him I was a soprano, and reminded him that he needed a mezzo for Rosina. He wanted the role to be sung by a mezzo as Rossini had intended – without any soprano coloratura – and kept telling them that I had the mezzo quality he wanted. He won, and I went to Salzburg.'

There Major joined Jean-Pierre Ponnelle's young cast for his new festival production of *Il Barbiere di Siviglia*.[4] Abbado had corrected the score against Rossini's original, reinstating Rosina's original mezzo-soprano coloratura. The production was a triumph for Major. 'Sung by a mezzo-soprano, the coquettish chatterbox becomes a resolute young lady and a real character. It is not easy, of course, to find singers with a real low G sharp and an effortless top C in their voices, who combine a round fullness of voice with coloratura agility and who also look as alluring as Malvina Major. This New Zealander, little known on the Continent up to now, was a brilliant discovery for Salzburg.'[5] [CD Track 6] In the wake of her Salzburg acclaim, Major won a contract with EMI and recorded a recital of songs at the Abbey Road studios in September 1968 with pianist Gerald Moore. Possibly because of her sudden departure from London the following year, EMI delayed a commercial release and the recording languished until 1998, when it was released together with a long-forgotten audition tape recorded in March 1968, at the time of her Camden success.[6]

Despite this promising start to her career, Major had already begun to experience some of the frustrations that would eventually lead to her decision to return home. Ponnelle's 1968 production of *Il Barbiere di Siviglia* was repeated in Salzburg the following year, but the growing critical opinion suggesting she was miscast as a mezzo – and Abbado's continued insistence that her voice *was* suited to the lower roles – had begun to unsettle her.

> Abbado tried his best to turn me into a mezzo. He offered me *The Barber of Seville* and *La Cenerentola* at La Scala, but I finally told him I couldn't do the mezzo roles. It was just too hard to push the voice out across the orchestra, when the top of my voice carried so easily. I knew in my heart I was a soprano. If I'd gone the way he wanted me to, I would have pushed the voice in the wrong direction and probably lost it.

Major's mentor James Robertson confirmed her own intuition and suggested she pass up the mezzo offers, but also advised her to turn down the offer of an American tour with the D'Oyly Carte company. 'He said "authentic" opera companies would never take me seriously again, but it would have been a wonderful acting opportunity. My entire life might have been different if I'd taken it.' Then Robertson vetoed a season of *Don Giovanni* at Glyndebourne. 'Much as I wanted to do it, he believed the part of Donna Anna was too big for me, and that I would force my voice.'

More disappointment came early in 1969. When she arrived in London it had been her greatest aspiration to sing at Covent Garden, and, following the success of the first *Barbiere* in Salzburg, the Royal Opera invited her to sing the part of Rosina in their own production. But then the offer was withdrawn. 'I got a letter from the management saying they could no longer afford to cast Rosina outside the company. I was devastated. I thought if they weren't even going to take me in as a company member, then I may as well go back to New Zealand.'

In addition, the personal cost of her career was mounting. Even though Winston gave her all the practical help he could, including taking an active role in caring for Andrew, his inability to come to terms with her professional life had begun to put a strain on their relationship.

> He hated me acting, and he hated me going away. We both saw other marriages split up because people couldn't separate their lives on stage and their personal lives, and I was constantly trying to prove to him that I wasn't that sort of person. He wanted me to be successful, but at the same time he couldn't handle it. It became a real problem, and eventually he couldn't cope with it at all.

Malvina chose to save her marriage. 'Winston wanted to be a farmer, and I wanted to sing and have more children. I thought, "Let's go back to New Zealand, if that's going to make him happy. I can sing for the New Zealand Opera Company, and be a mother. It doesn't matter about this side of life." So at that point, which was near enough the end of 1969, I gave it all away.'

The family moved back to Taranaki. Winston took sharemilking jobs, first on his family's farm at Oaonui, and later at Pihama, south of Opunake. Malvina looked set to realise her dream of combining work and family: in 1970 she appeared as Rosina in the New Zealand Opera Company's production of *The Barber of Seville*, and her daughter Alethea was born. The dream receded somewhat with the collapse of the New Zealand Opera Company the following year, and with the expansion of her duties as a farming wife and mother: Lorraine was born in 1971, and the Flemings bought the family farm at Oaonui in 1975. 'From the time we went farming, and for the next eleven years, I milked night and morning. We started off milking 112 cows on 104 acres, but as we brought in more land we had closer to 200 cows. We had 300 pigs as well.'

Contrary to the popular mythology which still rather affronts her, she did not vanish into the cowshed: although she was out of the international limelight, she remained in demand around her region, and around the country. 'Once a month or so I did an hour's cabaret for a big hotel in New Plymouth. I entertained for the National Party, and for the music society in Wanganui, and helped with fundraising for the New Plymouth branch of Rotary. I never forgot that Rotary had given me the last £100 we needed to get to London.' Between returning to New Zealand and her first vocal crisis in the early 1980s, she appeared in oratorios and recorded for radio, sang Mimi in *La Bohème* (Auckland) and Cio-Cio-San in *Madama Butterfly* (Auckland, Wellington and Christchurch), recorded *Tosca* and *Die Entführung aus dem Serail* with the NZSO, starred in the Hamilton Operatic Society's production of *The Merry Widow*, and in January 1981 hosted her own television show.

Meanwhile, she had begun the charity work for which, with her services to music, she was awarded a DBE in 1991. 'I'd left a high-profile career behind me in England, and suddenly I found myself on a farm with three babies. I knew if I didn't keep my standard up I wouldn't be able to sing.' It was partly the need to perform that led her to enquire about what she could do for music at the local primary school.

> I found myself organising pantomimes. I wrote them myself because I wanted to use everyone who wanted to be involved, and some of them weren't very musical. We made all the costumes, a man in Opunake made the scenery, and we toured these shows all around Taranaki. We ended up doing shows with the Lions Club for World Vision, and adopting a child who was the same age as my daughter Lorraine – about five or six. We supported him right through until he got a job.

The double life took its toll. 'I had problems with tonsillitis, sinusitis and asthma, I lost weight, and finally my health broke down completely. I'd gone down to under seven stone, and ended up in hospital in New Plymouth. I was absolutely exhausted. I thought I'd never sing again.' The problem turned out to be stress, exacerbated by a debilitating allergy to dairy produce. 'The doctor put me on a strict dairy-free diet, and I couldn't have gone to the cowshed if I'd been chained to the tractor. That was the end of work in the cowshed for me. Although I did help from time to time after that, it became extremely stressful.' She was ill for over two years.

> Although I was getting better physically, I was depressed. I shut the lid of the piano. I never wanted to touch it again. Whenever I'd sung there'd been a trauma – first with my mother, and then with Winston – and I'd had enough of it. My mother would tell me I had to get on stage and sing, and I'd tell her I didn't want to. Then she'd give me all the reasons why I had to do it. That started when I was eight or nine. Winston never liked me going away, even once we got home. So there'd always been a row, and I decided I didn't want it any more. I sank very low, and Winston became very worried. The doctor told him he'd better encourage me to sing, so we went off to look at the Australian Opera. I didn't want to sing in Australia. What would I want to do that for? I didn't even want to lift the lid of the piano.

John Matheson, then a resident conductor with the Royal Opera at Covent Garden, had heard Major sing in London in the 1960s, and had conducted her in a 1982 performance of Verdi's *Requiem* with Heather Begg, Donald McIntyre and Anthony Benfell. 'John was in New Zealand again in about 1984. I was ill at the time, but he told the NZSO he wanted to hear me at Covent Garden.' The orchestra wrote to her and suggested she audition. 'Winston pushed for it as well – he thought it would help me get better – so I went and did all these auditions in England and in Europe. I still wasn't well, and for me it was a disaster but out of it came the offer of work with the Belgian National Opera at the Théâtre de la Monnaie in Brussels. I had to take it up. I couldn't let it go.'

Her performance as Arminda in Mozart's youthful *La Finta Giardiniera* in Brussels in 1986 launched her second international career. In the two years following, Karl-Ernst Hermann's production toured to Vienna, Amsterdam, Salzburg, East Berlin and Antwerp, each time with Major as Arminda. Critics and opera house directors were delighted that her voice had lost none of its bloom in the years she had been away from the limelight. 'People were quite surprised that my voice was still fresh. It all went towards people employing me again.' An invitation to sing with the Drottningholm Court Theatre Company in their 1987 Brighton Festival production of *Don Giovanni* was a direct result of *La Finta Giardiniera*'s success, and the production, although presented only three times, created much interest. The year also saw the beginning of her association with the Australian Opera: only months after her Drottningholm Donna Elvira, Major sang Donna Anna in a revival of George Ogilvie's 1978 production of *Don Giovanni*. 'Singing the two roles so close together was quite a challenge. It was terribly tempting to come in at the wrong moment, or sing the wrong line.' The production toured Australia for over a year.

Major also maintained her New Zealand ties. In 1988 she sang Constanze in Wellington City Opera's *Die Entführung aus dem Serail*, and Richard Strauss's *Four Last Songs* with the NZSO; returning to her Waikato roots, she appeared as Rosalinde in the Hamilton Operatic Society's production of *Die Fledermaus*. Later that year she returned to Wellington for her first *Lucia Di Lammermoor*: since she was finding herself more and more drawn to coloratura roles, Wellington City Opera mounted the production partly at her suggestion. 'I'd been a Mozart specialist, so when I did *Lucia* for the Wellington City Opera I expected it to be the most difficult role I'd ever attempted. I waited for it to be difficult, but it didn't happen. It was as if it was written for me.' Her Edgardo, tenor Richard Greager, then working across the Tasman, reported her triumph to the Australian Opera: Joan Sutherland's retirement was imminent, and the Australian company had begun searching for a singer to replace her in the bel canto roles over which she had towered for thirty years.

Major's Australian début as Lucia took place in May 1990 in a revival of a production created in 1980 especially for Dame Joan, and Australian critics immediately hailed her as Sutherland's successor.

> I knew when I went there I'd be compared to Joan Sutherland, but the truth is I don't compare to her at all. I think the secret of my success in that role was that I'm an actress, and I don't think Dame Joan was: she never had to be. I was determined to do the part the way I saw it – as a woman who was used despicably by her husband. When it came to the coloratura that Dame Joan was famous for, I didn't follow her interpretation at all. So people saw the part in a totally new context, and it worked.

On the crest of a wave, Major took part in the sesquicentennial gala concert, 'New Zealand at Covent Garden', on 8 July 1990. Three weeks later, the Royal Opera issued the long-awaited invitation. Joan Sutherland had just announced her retirement and Covent Garden engaged Major to replace La Stupenda in the January 1991 performances of *Die Fledermaus*.

Malvina did not have long to savour her situation. On 10 September 1990, at the age of forty-six, Winston died of a heart attack. 'There'd been no warning. One morning I saw him limping back to the house from the milking shed, and I went out to meet him. He told me he had pains in his chest. Half an hour later he was dead.'

The shock robbed her of her voice for several weeks.

> I couldn't sing at all. I could barely speak. About three weeks after he died I was supposed to be singing in a concert. I knew that wallowing in self-pity was bad for me, so I had to get back to work. I started to work on my singing, but there was no voice there. One Saturday night a friend came round, and she had to bang on the window of the music room to make me hear her. I was crying, playing the piano, trying to sing, and it just wouldn't happen.

However, in the months between her husband's death and her departure for England, Major honoured charity commitments in Tauranga and Hamilton.

> I was barely able to hold myself together. It wasn't just the death: it was the responsibility for the business, and the children, and the trauma of adjusting to a completely different way of life. When I got to Covent Garden I was still breaking into uncontrollable tears for no reason. My concentration had gone right down to nil. And then they asked me to sing the 'Csárdás' in Hungarian. I couldn't even memorise the English, but I did it.

The circumstances surrounding Major's two Covent Garden performances were hardly auspicious. She was aware that she was struggling vocally, and that many of the audience would have booked to hear Sutherland. 'The first act went all right, but I was over-singing to compensate for how I felt, and missed my top note at the end of the act, which threw me into a panic. I just couldn't get myself into gear. I felt I had let everybody down. I just wanted to crawl into a hole and hide.' Max Cryer, in the audience for Major's début, remembers differently: 'Covent Garden forbids the presentation of flowers on stage except on special gala occasions. A début in the middle of a run (another soprano had opened in the role of Rosalinde the week before) is not a gala occasion. But this time the management must have thought otherwise. At curtain-call Major was nearly buried in bouquets.'[7]

Major's daughters had come to London to hear her sing. Seeing them off on the plane back to New Zealand, she was struck by another wave of grief.

> I looked at these two teenage girls leaving the airport, and I thought to myself that they didn't need me any more. I'd been made redundant. I remember thinking they were self-sufficient, and I didn't have a purpose in life any more. It took me a long time to realise that they did need me, and that my ability to sing was important to people, and that as a human being I was necessary to somebody.

Although she kept working – other 1991 engagements included a *Madama Butterfly* for Canterbury Opera in May, a Mozart *Requiem* in Brisbane in June, and a *Le Nozze di Figaro* in Brussels at Christmas – she became increasingly worried about her voice. 'For nearly two years I was really scared. When you lose your voice through emotions you compensate by using the muscles of the throat for support, but the moment you start doing that you get into trouble. At the time I had no idea what I was doing. I just knew that I was choking.' One night during a concert in Hastings she actually choked. 'I had broken a tiny blood vessel and the blood had spread across my vocal cords. The public didn't realise what had happened, but when I walked off that stage I thought I'd never sing again.'

Major was about to announce her retirement, but was persuaded against it by English conductor Brian Law, who had moved to Christchurch from Canada in 1991. Law had taken up the musical directorship of the Christchurch City Choir, and was conducting Canterbury Opera's 1992 season of *Don Giovanni*, with Major in the role of Donna Anna. 'He said to me, "It's not your voice that's gone, it's you." He explained that the problem was with my emotions and not my voice, which had been my greatest fear.' It took New York teacher Carolina Segrera – one of Pavarotti's first vocal coaches, by then in her nineties – to isolate the trouble.

> She made me understand that I had started to use the muscles of the throat to *make* the sound, and I'd started lifting the back of my tongue, which made me feel like I was choking. That tension was also affecting the natural vibrato in the voice. I was trying to hammer the notes home without any vibrato, so she'd

> walk around me shaking my body, making the note shake. I needed to be reminded not to put too much pressure on the note – just enough to give it a certain natural vibrato, like the fingers of a violin player.

Major visited Segrera every day when she was in New York, and the problems started to come right. 'It took a long time – maybe three years – but as my emotional state began to improve I began to relax.'

In her own teaching, however, Major doesn't emphasise vocal anatomy.

> I don't *want* to know what the muscles of my throat are. I don't *want* to know how they work. All I want to know is that if I pass the air – with good breathing technique – over the vocal cords, and put the voice into the mask of the face, it will all take care of itself. It's like a baby crying for the first time: it doesn't have to be told how to scream. It just does it.

She is, however, emphatic about breath support.

> Without proper support, the muscles of the throat try to bring the two vocal cords together to make the sound. Those little muscles can't sustain it. They get tired and start to shake, and a quiver comes into the voice. If you go on singing right on the vocal cords, without proper support, you can do terrible damage: the vocal cords redden and thicken, and eventually they form nodules to stop the vibrations and stop the pain. It's the vocal cords trying to protect themselves.

Major's own experience of vocal problems has given her a practical insight into problems facing other singers. Adjunct professorships at the University of Waikato from 1998 to 2000 and at the University of Canterbury since 2001 have given her the flexibility to continue her own career while helping young performers, and the Dame Malvina Major Foundation, launched in 1992 in conjunction with Rotary West New Plymouth, supports the education and training of New Zealanders in the performing arts. The Dame Malvina Major Emerging Artist Programme, run within the structure of the NBR New Zealand Opera and partly funded by the foundation, offers up to six young singers at a time a year of practical assistance and experience. 'The programme aims to equip them with some of the skills they will need to develop into professional performers. The focus is on vocal and dramatic training, but career advice comes into it as well. Overall we aim to provide an environment that offers the support necessary to move into the professional world of opera, so they can approach the future with confidence.'

If Major's voice has brought her professional triumph and, more recently, personal fulfilment – in 1997 she moved to Christchurch to be closer to her partner Brian Law – it has also been the source of private suffering.

> People are constantly telling me my life has been like a fairytale, but my voice has many times been the cross I had to bear. Sometimes I've found myself standing in the wings with a cold, or a headache, thinking, 'What am I *doing* here?' People have no *idea* what you go through. They think it looks easy. They don't know that you don't talk beforehand, you don't socialise beforehand, you don't eat too much beforehand, or that you actually have to practise. It is hard work and can be very lonely at times. But I have to do it. There is no question in my mind that my voice is a gift from God.

1 Dame Sister Mary Leo (1895–1989) taught singing at St Mary's College of the Sisters of Mercy in Auckland from 1930 and into her late eighties. She taught three consecutive winners of the Melbourne *Sun* Aria Competition, and between 1959 and 1972 taught six consecutive winners of the Mobil Song Quest, two runners-up and more finalists. Former pupils who went on to international careers include Heather Begg, Lynne Cantlon, Pettine-Ann Croul, Elisabeth Hellawell, Patricia House, Dame Kiri Te Kanawa, Dame Malvina Major, Patricia Price, Mary O'Brien, Anne Rasmussen, Hannah Tatana, Nicola Waite and Patricia Wright.

2 Roger Joyce, quoted in 'The Mobil Song Quest 1956–1991', *Music in New Zealand*, Autumn 1992, pp.45-51.

3 Desmond Shawe-Taylor, 'Salute to a Young Singer', review of *Elisabetta, Regina d'Inghilterra* in *Sunday Times*, 3 Mar. 1968; Winton Dean, 'Rossini's Elisabetta', *Musical Times*, Apr. 1968, pp.353-4; Harold Rosenthal, 'Elisabetta, Regina d'Inghilterra', *Opera*, Apr. 1968, pp.334-5; Alan Blyth, 'Gloriana alla Rossini', *Music and Musicians*, May 1968, pp.40-1.

4 Jean-Pierre Ponnelle (1932–88) always worked as both designer and director, initially in Germany and then on the world's great opera stages from Bayreuth and Salzburg to La Scala, San Francisco and Covent Garden. 'His work was always innovative, animated and beautiful to view.' (Grove)

5 Kurt Honolka, '*Il Barbiere di Siviglia*', *Opera Festival Volume*, Autumn 1968, pp.54-5.

6 *Malvina Major: Recital 1968 with Gerald Moore* (EMI Classics CD, 7243-5-56724-2-1, 1998).

7 Max Cryer, 'A Successor Worthy of Joan Sutherland's Mantle', *NZ Listener*, 4 Mar. 1991, pp.52-53.

Jack Body : Active Listener

I carry a little tape recorder around with me when I travel, as other people might carry a camera. For a musician it's logical to use a tape recorder in the same way, simply to record environments or sounds that one comes across.

Jack Body (born 1944) is a tireless advocate for New Zealand music. When he is not working on his own scores or teaching composition, he is likely to be found producing recordings of other New Zealand composers, raising funds for supporting guest musicians, or planning a concert series to promote the work of younger composers. Body's quiet speech and self-effacing manner belie his enormous tenacity: when funding for his opera *Alley* (1998) collapsed at the last minute, it seemed that ten years' work would be in vain. 'It was all there, ready. If it had been necessary to commit murder, maybe I could have done it.' Fortunately, there was no need for bloodshed: instead, Body's huge fundraising effort secured sponsors for *Alley* within the private sector. Nothing daunted by this near disaster, he is now planning even larger multimedia works. 'I am convinced of an essential fact of life: the more labour invested, the greater the reward.'

Jack Body grew up in the Waikato. Both his parents came from farming backgrounds. 'My mother was very intelligent and artistic, but she never went to secondary school – she had to stay home on the farm and help her mother bring up the younger kids.' Body's maternal grandfather sired six children and then wandered off. 'He quite liked it in England, so he stayed. My grandmother had to bring up the family by herself.' Body's father, Stan, grew up on a farm near Te Aroha. 'He and his brother were sent away to boarding school, but when my grandfather died my father came back to farm. Eventually, my uncle took over the family farm and my father bought another one, which is where my sisters and I were born.' Before Jack was a year old, however, his father decided he was tired of milking. The family moved to just outside Te Aroha township, where Stan Body went into business as an earth-moving contractor.

Although Jack's parents had little interest in music, they encouraged their daughters to learn the piano. Hearing his sisters playing, he asked if he could have lessons too. 'I was a solitary child – there weren't many playmates around, and my sisters were rather older than I was – so it was an ideal interest for me. There was plenty of time to practise.' Body's first teacher was William Cranna.[1] 'I adored him, and what he represented. He only taught part-time – he worked at the power board during the day – but he still managed to organise end-of-year concerts for his pupils in a local church hall.' One year, Jack played his own compositions. 'I'd taken some little excerpts from the Royal Schools grade exercises – the ones where they give you a couple of bars to identify a cadence – and continued them. Even though the inspiration didn't last for more than a few bars, I knew I was onto something pretty exciting: it was such an incredible thing, to be able to write notes down and play them.'

As a boarder at King's College in Auckland, Body found his solitary ways – and his passion for painting and music – helped create something of a personal mystique in a highly conformist environment.

> I started to develop little eccentricities. I would suddenly say things that had no connection to what was being discussed. I would impose a code of silence on myself for a day or two at a time. As I got older I became a night owl. I used to love practising the organ alone in the chapel at night, or painting at night in the art room.

Even though Body enjoyed cultivating the image of an artistic odd-ball, the dynamism of music master L. C. M. Saunders[2] meant that music was in fact a central part of school life. Body credits Saunders with some of his most significant early musical experiences. 'The annual *Messiah*s and *St Matthew Passion*s could be pretty rugged at times, but Saunders was able to engage some very high-calibre soloists. My strongest memory is of the glorious rolling resonance of Noel Mangin's voice.' Body also cherished a personal friendship with his teacher. 'I took private piano and organ lessons with him, and quite often he would have two tickets for concerts. If his wife wasn't interested, he'd invite me to go instead.'

In his final year at King's, Body completed the preliminary examination for Elam School of Fine Arts, but opted instead to study music at the University of Auckland. 'I found painting relatively easy, while my efforts at composing were painfully slow and difficult. In fact that was part of the reason composition attracted me. It was such a complex and exacting art. I wanted to rise to the challenge.' For a young man who wanted to compose, the challenge included completing a degree in music without studying composition. 'Only when you had studied harmony, counterpoint, aural perception and music history were you allowed to go on and do your master's in composition. But I remember writing things, even in my first year.' Works completed as an undergraduate include *People Look East* (1965), *Ave Maria Gratia Plena* (1965), and music for a production of the York nativity play, all written for the choir of St Mary's Cathedral, Parnell. 'Peter Godfrey taught me organ for a few years, and insisted I join the cathedral choir, which was a marvellous music education. He was very supportive and encouraging.'[3] Body's high Anglican musical education stood him in good stead when, as a third-year university student, he was appointed organist and choirmaster at St Aidan's Church in Remuera.

Body began his master's degree in 1966, studying composition with Ronald Tremain.[4] 'He was a profound inspiration. He showed us that music could be created and experienced in the here and now.' As founding president of the Auckland chapter of the International Society for Contemporary Music, Tremain organised performances of Boulez, Stockhausen and Dallapiccola, as well as Serocki, Skalkottas, Davidovsky, Earle Brown, Hans Otte, Lou Harrison, Maxwell Davies and Roberto Gerhard. 'By sharing his enthusiasms and seeing how these influenced his own thinking, I realised that as a composer one learned most from the music of one's contemporaries.'[5]

Tremain left the university in 1967 and Body completed his MMus under the supervision of Robin Maconie, who had recently returned from his own studies in Europe. In his final year at university Body also attended teachers' training college – 'I'd taken out a studentship when I started university, and that was one of the conditions' – and took over as president of the ISCM.

> Until then, we'd had concerts in the Art Gallery – quite formal, with small audiences, and we'd play seriously avant-garde music. When I took over, being young and foolish, we organised a three-day festival called Aucklanders and the Arts. There was mime, and an exhibition of paintings, and some mad improvisations. We took over the Student Union building as an unconventional

> and inexpensive venue. Nobody could see *anything*. It was probably a bit unprofessional, but we wanted to make our own statement.

In 1968, Body's *Turtle Time* [CD track 7], a setting of a text by Russell Haley for piano, harp, harpsichord, organ and speaker, premiered at an ISCM concert. 'It was a piece which reflected well the youthful spirit of the times, with its challenge of authority and its drug-enhanced striving for some kind of liberation.' Body's friend and colleague Noel Sanders regards this work as a watershed, noting that its overlapping layers of sustained keyboard sound look backwards towards the capacities of the organ – Body's own instrument – and forwards towards his involvement with gamelan.[6]

An energetic avant-garde scene revolved around Body's flat at 27 Birdwood Crescent, Parnell. 'It was an expansive house, down in the gully in Parnell. It was fun – it had a great history.' In March 1969 he collaborated with poet Ian Wedde, kinetic sculptor Leon Narby, lighting designer Keir Volkerling and painter David Armitage on a 'total ceremony' of the Stations of the Cross, presented at the university's Maclaurin Chapel. 'None of us were particularly religious, I think: it was just an excuse to enjoy ourselves.' Wedde based his text on fragments of the Catholic missal and the Bible; Body had assembled his *musique concrète* sound-image in Douglas Lilburn's Electronic Music Studio at Victoria University in Wellington. 'Although it would probably look terribly naïve from today's perspective, it was a big event for all of us.'

Partly as a way of postponing the inevitability of entering the classroom, Body took up an Arts Council grant to study in Europe in 1969. 'Originally I applied to go to North American universities – Michigan, particularly – but it would have meant enrolling for another degree, and being in an institution. The European system was more open: you studied something because you were interested in it, not because you wanted a piece of paper.' Body's first stop was Mauricio Kagel's Ferienkurs für Neue Musik in Cologne. The major project during his four-month stay was an experimental video of short, apparently arbitrarily juxtaposed sequences of Dada-inspired music theatre.

> It was fascinating to take part in. There was one section in a bare studio where they choreographed the cameramen filming each other. The soundtrack was a tape recording of a child crying and a dog barking. Then they released a live goose in the middle of the studio. The director of the television studio was furious. He said he'd never seen such amateurism. His argument with Kagel went on for hours. Kagel finished by declaring it was the most imaginative television production he'd seen in years.

With his grant extended into 1970, Body's next stop was the Institute of Sonology in Utrecht, where Gottfried Michael Koenig had begun using the computer program Project II as an adjunct to composition. 'Cologne had been cold and a bit miserable, and although Kagel was an inspirational figure he'd also been rather remote. The six months I spent in Utrecht were much more congenial. The teaching was done in English, and the course was very well-organised: we had to do practical work in the studio, and learn programming.' While in Utrecht, Body began work on *23 Pages* (1971) for large orchestra, commissioned by the New Zealand Broadcasting Corporation for the twenty-fifth anniversary of its Symphony Orchestra.

Body returned home overland through the Eastern Mediterranean and Asia. Listening to a short-wave radio on a beach in Greece inspired the electro-acoustic piece *Kryptophones* (1973)[7] – 'suddenly music and voices from all of Europe, Africa and the Middle East flooded in, the airwaves filled with a whirlwind of sound' – and the singing of the Tibetan monks in Bodhgaya in North India became one of the inspirations for the choral work *Pater Noster* (1973). Although the trip through Asia was short, it began a love affair which remains one of Body's most abiding musical and personal passions. 'I'd allowed myself a twenty-four-hour stopover in Jakarta, but that glimpse of Indonesia left me with an image of harmonious sensuality I could not forget.'

He spent the first few months after his return at Waihi Beach. 'I knew I'd have to go teaching when I got home, but I avoided it for a while: I hid away at my parents' beach house and tried to be a composer by the seaside.' After finishing *23 Pages* he found he had run dry.

> I had a crisis of sorts. I didn't really know what to write, or why. You can't write just because you feel like writing a piece one weekend, or even because someone asks you to write something. Each piece has to have its own reason: it might be for a performer, or for an ensemble, or it might start with a concept. But I always have to have a strong reason to write, and I didn't have one.

The Department of Education caught up with Body in the end and, after a couple of false starts in Auckland schools, he accepted a position at Tawa College. 'That brought me to Wellington, and I've been here ever since.' Although Tawa College treated him well – including giving him six weeks off in the middle of the year to tour with Gaylene Sciascia's dance company New Dance '73 – he had resigned before the year was out. 'I enjoyed working with kids, and when schoolteaching worked it was very rewarding, but it was also utterly exhausting. What struck me was the anarchic energy of adolescence. You were doomed if you tried to make them sit still and learn. You just had to join in the anarchy.' In an article about his classroom experience written for *Islands* magazine, Body displays his obvious enthusiasm for teaching as well as revealing why he may have found it so exhausting:

> SHEEPDOG GAME: the Dog leaves the room. the Shepherd nominates what the Dog will do (crouch under a chair, place a hand on a certain spot). Dog re-enters. Shepherd gives the instructions: high whistle (or hum) turn and move to the left, low to the right. (the piano also proved satisfactory for signalling). Important: move only for the duration of the signal. Example: very short high followed by sustained low produced a forward motion (from the original position). always working against the clock. Refinement: finger clicking signifies up, clapping down. i was asked to be the Dog. i find myself climbing on to the desktops and out a high window. but there's a rubbish bin out there i complain. out of deference to age (?) i am redirected along the tabletops to the next window. no rubbish bin here. halfwayout and the whole class erupts outside to watch the landing.
> – mr body, did the music room door jam yesterday?[8]

Even before resigning to devote himself to composition, Body had found time for his own projects. While teaching in Auckland he had been involved with dance classes in movement and theatre with Jennifer Shennan, and completed scores for theatre and mime productions. Body also conducted an ambitious programme of music theatre for the 1972 University Arts Festival, in which his own multimedia work *Sexus: Everyman's Guide to Christian Living* formed half of a double bill with Stockhausen's *Kurzwellen*.

Working freelance, and with his reputation as a musical organiser steadily growing, Body was able to devote even more of his energy to multimedia events. In March 1974 he co-ordinated New Zealand's first Sonic Circus, commissioned by the NZBC and the New Zealand Students' Arts Council. Although the idea itself was not new – John Cage had mounted a Music Circus in the Round House in London in 1972 – Body's innovation was to devote the whole programme to New Zealand music. The event featured the work of seventeen New Zealand composers and took place over six hours, in eight separate venues in Victoria University's Student Union building. Audience members were encouraged to select and structure their own programmes, circulating around the venues as their interest dictated. 'It was the spirit of the times, really: all in and all free.'

Later in 1974 Body made a four-month trip to Bali and Java. 'I thought it was paradise on earth. I went to a local music school and told them I'd like to stay for a while, and asked if they could sponsor me if I could get funding from New Zealand.' The Akademi Musik Indonesia in Yogyakarta invited Body to return in 1976 as a guest lecturer, but he did not waste the intervening year. TV One planned a new drama series for 1975 and Body was commissioned to write the theme music. '*Close to Home* made me famous, really. People seemed to like it, and to recognise it. The money was nice, too. Until then, I'd been getting a couple of hundred dollars a year in royalties from all my music, but suddenly I was getting a thousand dollars a year.'

Carol to St Stephen was another of the year's successes.[9] Commissioned by Wellington's Bach Choir, and now a standard text for study in New Zealand secondary schools, it is a 'deconstruction/recomposition' of a fifteenth-century carol for three soloists and choir. The year 1975 also saw the realisation of the electro-acoustic work *Musik Dari Jalan*. While in Indonesia, Body had been fascinated by the calls of the street sellers and sounds of the street. *Musik Dari Jalan*, based on the field recordings of ethnomusicologist Allan Thomas, was awarded first prize in the prestigious International Festival of Electro-acoustic Music, held in Bourges, France, in 1976. 'I was in Indonesia by then, and Douglas Lilburn entered my piece. So it was a dead surprise when I got news of the win through the post.' John Rimmer's *Where Sea Meets Sky* was selected for honourable mention in the same competition; of the eighty-four composers from twenty-three countries who had submitted entries, two of the ten finalists were New Zealanders. 'I remember Douglas remarking on it some time later, and saying that if it had been football it would have been splashed all over the papers, but it hardly got a mention.' In the year prior to his departure for Indonesia, Body also found time to design a second Sonic Circus, and produce a three-LP set of New Zealand electro-acoustic music,[10] realised in Douglas Lilburn's Electronic Music Studio. 'At that stage there'd only been two public performances of New Zealand electro-acoustic music. Larry Sitsky told me later that when the boxed set arrived in Australia they'd been quite taken aback: I think we were quite a long way ahead of the game.'

Body returned to Indonesia supported by a living allowance from New Zealand's Ministry of Foreign Affairs. 'The Akademi Musik Indonesia was a state academy, but it taught basically Western music. It was a kind of colonial hangover: Western music was the sort of music you *learn*. You didn't learn traditional music in the same way. It was much more part of the whole cultural pattern. The academy gave me a base, really, from which to try to understand the lifestyles and cultures in a broad sense.' Although he spent some time studying gamelan, he quickly became more interested in village music traditions virtually unknown outside their local area. He was just as fascinated by environmental sounds:

> Even traffic noise had a quality different from what I had been used to. There was a predominance of big vehicles (buses and trucks) and small vehicles (motor-bikes, bicycles and various animal-drawn conveyances), but not many cars. The engines of the motorised vehicles tended to be at least twenty-five years old and that too contributed a particular sonority which was quite different from what we'd hear in a New Zealand city street. Early in the morning or in the late evening when the motorised traffic would be lighter I'd frequently hear the asymmetrical rhythms of a particular bell – a pair of bells in fact – that would signal the passing of a cart hauled by two oxen. I discovered that these brass bells with wooden clappers varied in size and would be chosen according to the relative size of the beast. Since the oxen were always in pairs one would always hear a pair of bells, and from the tempo of the sounds be able to judge whether the cart was loaded or empty.[11]

Body met his partner Yono Sukarno at the end of his first year in Yogyakarta. 'We began a project together, recording street musicians. I got a big fat tape recorder – a Nakamichi, which was the state of the art in its time – and whenever a street musician passed by, or we met somebody, we rushed out and recorded them. Travelling around we discovered an extraordinary richness in regional musics, some of which are very rare. I became fascinated by collecting and recording.'

Although he was highly attuned to his sensory environment, the political environment of Indonesia in the 1970s made little impact.

> People in Java knew absolutely nothing about the invasion of East Timor. There was complete control of the media, so it was not an issue. When Yono first came back to New Zealand people asked him about Timor, but nobody could have known what it was like. Stories would come back to Indonesia from people who'd been in the army in East Timor saying they were the only person left in their battalion. Everyone else had been slaughtered. None of this was able to be published at the time. People were not permitted to talk about it.

Body chooses to make his political statements indirectly. In Indonesia he had seen how music's many traditional functions helped provide a sense of social cohesion, and he began to see his activities as a composer as 'rather meaningless and elitist' in comparison. 'I began to question the values I'd been brought up with, and whether I could continue with my view of musical composition as a meaningful and productive activity. Suddenly I felt my music needed to relate to the immediate circumstances I saw around me.'[12] A series of electro-acoustic pieces based on recordings made in Indonesia sprang from this dual impulse: an ethnomusicological desire to record an environment in which music and everyday life were inseparable, and his desire as a composer to pay tribute to the music, musicians and culture with which he had felt so grateful to come in contact.[13]

Later works have been more overtly political. Body's *Little Elegies* (1985), commissioned by the NZSO, was intended to commemorate the twenty-fifth anniversary of television broadcasting in New Zealand. 'I had just seen the film *The Killing Fields*, and found it shocking, and very moving. I asked myself what unique contribution television had made to our culture. To me, the answer was the news – events worldwide brought to our living rooms within hours, packaged and presented as entertainment in the 6 pm news slot, sanitised so as not to put us off our food.' Body wanted to convey his sense of outrage at this trivialisation of human tragedy, while pointing out that even the most anguished protest is insignificant in the face of such suffering. 'It's a very sombre piece. I don't know if it was appreciated: I got paid, but nobody particularly thanked me. Maybe if I'd quoted all the TV theme tunes current at the time they would have been happy, but I felt as an artist I had a right and a duty to use the occasion to express what I really felt.'

Jack and Yono returned to Wellington at the end of 1977. 'When we got back we were living on The Terrace, pretty much hand to mouth. I was picking up a little bit of tutoring at the university and at polytech, and doing workshops in schools. I felt a bit contemptuous of people who worked in universities. I wanted to write. Working freelance seemed a good way to live.' Douglas Lilburn was due to retire in January 1980, and suggested Body apply for the vacant position. 'Originally I applied jointly with Gillian Whitehead and Lyell Cresswell. We were going to do it year about. I was to be first up, but then it turned out the other two weren't that serious about it: Lyell had his career in Scotland, and Gillian also had other commitments. So I had the job for a year, and then another year, and it 1982 it was made permanent.'

At the same time, Lilburn had retired as editor of Waiteata Press Music Editions, which he had established in 1967 under the umbrella of Victoria University's Wai-te-ata Press.[14] Since 1967, Lilburn had produced three facsimile editions of contemporary New Zealand scores: ten titles appeared in 1967, five in 1969 (including Body's *Four Stabiles for Piano*) and a further five in 1972, including *Turtle Time*. 'When Douglas left university in 1980 he suggested I reactivate the Music Press. I did, and got carried away for some time. We brought all the old issues back in, so we've got about 180 scores now, and growing.' Waiteata also produces promotional CDs of scores published by the press. 'We distribute the CDs free to international radio stations, performers and orchestras. The idea is that when people hear the music they want to play it. We provide the scores, and the royalties come back to the composers.' Waiteata Music Press receives a small annual grant from the Lilburn Trust.[15] 'Other than that we have no regular funding, so we have to ask for the rest. There's lots of letter-writing.'

If Body's early pleasure in capturing music on the page finds its contemporary parallel in his music publishing, his love – and mastery – of music transcription might well have its origins in the same delighted impulse.

> I've turned to transcription [of indigenous musics] when I've been unable to focus on original composition – as Ravel is supposed to have turned to orchestration in similar circumstances. I like to transcribe music in which I sense a particular quality – melodic, perhaps, or rhythmic – which my ears find attractive but which I have difficulty deciphering. I want to understand what is happening in this music to give it this special quality. My ideal is to learn something that I might be able to apply in my own composition.

In practice, however, Body's transcriptions – made with the help of an old-fashioned variable-speed dictaphone – have become considerably more than additions to his stylistic toolbox. In a process he calls 'double-transcription' he first tries to capture the 'essentials' of a new and often unfamiliar sound phenomenon, and then translates those into a form playable by Western musicians.[16] 'I try to recreate the music I'm transcribing in another form, with the intention of transmitting at least something of those qualities to which I first responded. Some people construe this as cultural exploitation. It's a tricky area: while it's foolish to suggest that intercultural exchange isn't universal, one must still respect one's material.' To that end, Body uses recordings he has made himself wherever possible – 'this means I have some knowledge of the social and cultural context in which the music belongs' – and presents the original music in its entirety, even when it has been translated into another musical form.

His first major exercise in transcription was *Melodies for Orchestra*, commissioned by the NZSO to celebrate the centenary of the University of Auckland in 1983. For this he chose three unrelated pieces of music: the Horos Serra, a fast Greek dance played on a two-stringed fiddle, a flute melody from West Sumatra, and a recording from Pune, India, of a street band playing film music themes. 'The choice was quite arbitrary: these were pieces I had been listening to at the time – music that caught my ear and fired my curiosity.' Each transcription was as literal as Body could make it. 'After that, the task was to find the right glue to stick the three sections together, and maybe provide something more – but still wholly derived from the original. The originals are still there, intact.'

The impetus for the next major transcription project came in the form of an invitation from the Kronos Quartet. 'At that stage they weren't very famous. They were doing gigs on campuses, and when they were visiting Vassar College they asked Annea Lockwood about New Zealand composers.[17] She told them about me, and they wrote and asked if I had anything for string quartet. I said that I didn't, but I soon would!' *Three Transcriptions* premiered at the International Festival of the Arts in Wellington in February 1988. The first transcription comes from a recording of the *long-ge*, a multiple jew's harp from Southern China. The second movement uses a *valiha*, a bamboo tube zither from Madagascar, and the third movement is a *ratchenitsa* – a wild dance in 7/8 time from Bulgaria. 'The *Three Transcriptions* were a hit for the Kronos Quartet. They hadn't really got into transcriptions or ethnic music at that stage – mine was one of the first, and I think they remember that.'[18] The following year Body completed *Epicycle* for the Kronos Quartet – 'they thought it was one of the most difficult works they had ever played' – and *Arum Manis* followed in 1991. 'They'd accept another piece, too, when I can find the time. It's interesting, really: several New Zealand composers have had a big break with an international artist or group. Kronos was mine, Evelyn Glennie gave John Psathas and Gareth Farr theirs, and Douglas Lilburn's, perhaps, was the Boyd Neel String Orchestra. The heavens smile at least once in one's lifetime.'

Body's interest in non-Western music is often audible in pieces which are entirely his own. In *Five Melodies for Piano*, written in 1982 for Margaret Nielsen, he set out to explore 'different types of melody'. In the first movement the pianist is required to dampen specified pitches with the left hand while playing running semiquavers with the right, producing the effect of a melody within a melody. The second movement features ornamentation inspired by bagpipe music, and the third makes extensive use of the harmonics which result when the strings are stopped at pre-determined points: 'I had in mind the ancient Chinese zither, the *gu-qin,* an instrument from which the player elicits a range of exquisite, subtle sounds using both hands.' The fourth movement sets a wide-leaping melody against a two-note drone, and the fifth movement's delicate bell sounds evoke the tonal qualities and subtle melodic shifts of the gamelan.[19]

In 1987, Body's interest in Asian music took him on his first field trip to China. Recording the music of the minority tribes of Gansu province – where Rewi Alley ran his industrial school for boys – Body gained some insight into the forces which shaped the life of that extraordinary man. 'Alley had obviously connected with something: a temperament, and a culture with a recorded history of three thousand years. Although Indonesia is a different experience altogether, I began to identify some of my own responses and to link them with what might have motivated this man, a New Zealander, to devote sixty years of his life to China.' Alley's story presented itself as a perfect subject for an opera. Working with Alley's biographer, Geoff Chapple, as co-librettist,[20] Body began transcribing folk songs recorded in Gansu. The goal was to complete the work by 1998, the centennial of Alley's birth: the Wellington International Festival of the Arts had undertaken to produce it that year. Body engaged Gansu folk singers Ji Zheng-Zhu and Li Gui-Zhou; Beijing's Huaxia Chamber Ensemble would join a small orchestra of New Zealand musicians. The production would be directed by the New York-based actor, choreographer and opera singer Chen Shi-Zheng, who had left China in 1989 after the Tiananmen Square massacre. Chen would also take the role of Yen Wang, the Chinese judge of the dead. Actor Martyn Sanderson would play the old Alley, and Australian baritone Lyndon Terracini would play Alley as a young man.

The opera begins with the old Alley slumped in his chair. It is the hour of his death. He is haunted by disturbing, fragmentary images from the past. Yen Wang, the Chinese god of death, enters and begins a scrutiny of the old man's life, which brushes past the titles and honours gained in sixty years' work inside China. The examination evokes Alley's younger self, and the determinants of his life in China: the suffering, the strength and the individual beauty of the youth of the Chinese masses. 'What is your name? Who are you? Where did you come from?' Yen Wang asks. The enquiry unlocks the past and, as Alley looks back on the defining moments of his life, Yen Wang forces him to relinquish his dreams. 'If he dreams of industrial co-ops, the god would show how futile it was in view of later events. If he believes in youth taking power, the god shows him the Cultural Revolution. In a sense he's smashing down Alley's dreams in order that he can die.'

Body's own dream itself came close to foundering. *Alley* had been commissioned by the Festival of the Arts and was to be its biggest production of 1998, but a funding débâcle saw a substantial grant from Creative New Zealand reallocated to other projects. Six months before the première, and half-way through pre-production, *Alley* had no funding at all. 'To have an opera accepted by the festival would be the dream of every composer in the country, and that chance would only come once in a lifetime. *Alley* was my chance, and it was ripped out of my grasp. I was just so angry and powerless.' A passionate newspaper article by Geoff Chapple focused public attention on the issue.[21] 'Miraculously, Geoff's plea produced an overwhelming response. Against all odds, we were suddenly back on track.' Supported by a raft of private individuals and trusts, *Alley* was premiered on 27 February 1998.

Although audiences and critics were enthusiastic, Body regards *Alley* as a qualified success. Funding had already broken down when he returned to China in June 1997 to collect more *houzi* – the rhythmic call-and-response songs of Chinese work teams – and to rehearse the folk singers and the Huaxia ensemble. 'At that time the whole production had collapsed, so I'd lost heart and didn't really take advantage of the possibilities of working with those musicians, as I had planned to do. Some of the finest musicians in China were in that ensemble. They could have done much more marvellous things than what I'd written for them.' Body is keen to mount a revised *Alley,* this time with the planned dream-like film component (abandoned for financial reasons) and possibly with surtitles: Body and Chapple both felt that the directorial decision not to have surtitles meant that much of the richness of the text was lost to the audience.[22]

While revisiting *Alley* may be a possibility, Body is not given to dwelling on the past. *Carmen*, his current project, is a celebration of the life and works of Wellington's famed drag queen.

> It's to do with gender and power. In a way, mankind's first gods were female, and the most potent force is the power of reproduction, which belongs to women. So if a man really wants to have power, maybe he becomes a woman. It's also about musical kitsch. A dancer would dance seductively as Carmen would have danced in her cabaret: a Hawaiian hula, an African snake dance, Matahari's dance, Salome's dance, and Carmen's flamenco. The music to accompany it would be gorgeous 1950s kitsch – like Mantovani, but much bigger: beyond kitsch and into the

> sublime. There'd be a symphony orchestra, a guitar soloist who plays the ukulele and the Hawaiian guitar, and singers: a Maori kuia, a flamenco singer and a male soprano – all powerful figures representing a kind of yin-yang cross-over. The singing and the orchestral music will be quite serious and dark – all the texts are incredibly powerful poems by women – but then suddenly it would turn a corner, and you'd be in the midst of all this kitsch. The exact opposite of the deadly serious stuff. Delicious.

Body is not fazed by accusations of exoticism. 'I believe one of the functions of art is to be outrageous, to be provocative, to be politically incorrect. As an artist, one has to be learning new lessons all the time. For instance, one has to learn not to become an embittered, grumpy old man. There's a few of those around. I hope that I can grow old joyful and unrepentant.'

1 Born in Scotland in 1923, William Cranna trained at the Royal Scottish Academy of Music, Glasgow. He taught piano in Te Aroha until 1957, and thereafter in Morrinsville and at St Paul's Collegiate, Hamilton, until his retirement in 1988.

2 L. C. M. Saunders (1908–95) was music master at King's College from 1936 to 1974 and reviewed music for the *NZ Herald* from 1940 to 1993.

3 English choral conductor and organist Peter Godfrey (born 1922) was appointed to the staff of the University of Auckland in 1958 and retired as Professor Emeritus in 1982. He was director of music at Auckland Anglican Cathedral from 1958 to 1974 and director of music at Wellington Cathedral from 1983 to 1989.

4 Composer Ronald Tremain (1923–98) attended Douglas Lilburn's composition classes at the Cambridge Music School and studied piano, conducting and composition at the Royal College of Music, London. He studied composition with Goffredo Petrassi at the Conservatorio Santa Cecilia, Rome, and conducting at the Accademia Chigiana, Siena. Tremain lectured in music at the University of Auckland from 1957 to 1967 and from 1970 until his retirement in 1989 was professor of music at Brock University, Ontario, Canada.

5 Jack Body, 'Tributes for Ron Tremain', *Canzona* 16: 37 (1994), p.30.

6 Noel Sanders, 'Convocations, Evocations and Invocations: Jack Body and his Calling(s)', *Music in New Zealand*, Summer 1994-95) pp.20-4.

7 Jack Body, *Kryptophones* (Kiwi-Pacific LP, SLD 46, 1973).
8 Jack Body, 'Diary of a School Music Teacher', *Islands* 2 (Summer 1973), pp.385-90.
9 Jack Body, *Carol to St Stephen* (Wellington: Waiteata Music Press, 1997; Ode/Manu CD 1412).
10 *New Zealand Electronic Music* (Kiwi-Pacific LP, SLD 44-46, 1975).
11 Jack Body, 'A New Zealand Composer in Asia', *Landfall* 36: 3 (Sept. 1982), pp.312-17.
12 Jack Body, *Sex, Politics, Religion – And Music* (1999 Massey University Composer Address) (Palmerston North: Massey University Music, 1999), p.12.
13 See Jack Body, *Suara: Environmental Music from Java* (Manu CD, 1380, 1993).
14 The Wai-te-ata Press was established in 1962 by Professor of English Don McKenzie to assist the teaching of aspects of early book production. Wai-te-ata became a small printing and publishing house, and produced first editions of poetry and prose, including volumes by Alistair Campbell, James K. Baxter, Peter Bland, Sam Hunt and Bill Manhire. Waiteata Music Press is now a separate entity under the direction of Jack Body. (*The Oxford Companion to New Zealand Literature* (Auckland: Oxford, 1998), p.561).
15 Douglas Lilburn established the Lilburn Trust in 1984. The objects and purposes of the trust, administered by the Alexander Turnbull Library Endowment Trust Board, are 'such charitable purposes in New Zealand as would tend to foster and promote New Zealand music, the advancement of musical knowledge and appreciation, the support of the musical arts, and the preservation of musical archives'. On his death in 2001 Douglas Lilburn bequeathed the residue of his collection of scores, sound recordings and papers to the Alexander Turnbull Library, and the residue of his estate to the Lilburn Trust.
16 Jack Body, *Pulse* (Rattle CD, RAT D009, 2000) pairs five of Body's transcriptions with the original field recordings.
17 Composer Annea Lockwood (born Christchurch, 1939) studied composition at the Royal College of Music with Peter Racine Fricker. After further study in Europe, she returned to London and freelanced as a composer–performer in Britain and Europe until moving to the US in 1973. She has taught at Vassar College, New York, since 1982.
18 Jack Body, *Three Transcriptions* (Wellington: Waiteata Music Press, 1994); Jack Body, 'Long-ge', in Kronos Quartet, *Early Music* (Nonesuch CD, 7559-79457-2, 1997).
19 Jack Body, 'Five Melodies for Piano', in *You Hit Him, He Cry Out*, Dan Poynton, piano (Rattle CD, RAT D006, 1997).
20 Geoff Chapple, *Rewi Alley of China* (Auckland: Hodder & Stoughton, 1980).
21 Geoff Chapple, 'Crisis Threatens Festival Flagship', *Dominion*, 28 June 1997.
22 Jack Body, 'From the Alley Scrapbook: The before and after of an opera production', *Canzona* (1998), pp.4-8.

Diedre Irons: Sharing a Language

I believe everyone has a place in the world, and I believe it's my place to play music, which I do to the best of my ability. The people who listen to music have their place, too, which includes making sure that music does not die. We are all just cogs, really – parts of the same machine – and I'm quite happy about that. It's unrealistic to see yourself as anything but part of everything.

Diedre Irons (born 1945) always knew her life would be devoted to the piano. Hailed as a prodigy in her native Winnipeg, she played her first concerto at the age of seven, won a national concerto competition at twelve and at eighteen made her 'official' concerto début as a soloist with the Winnipeg Symphony Orchestra. Further study in the United States followed and, although Irons was enjoying a growing reputation as a soloist, she happily enough followed her first husband to New Zealand when he accepted a position in the New Zealand Symphony Orchestra. Since settling here in 1977, Irons has endeared herself to audiences up and down the country and has maintained an international profile as a soloist, but she is always glad to return to the country she now calls home. 'New Zealand has got a freshness about it, and an unused feeling. I love it, and I love coming home to it. I'm not particularly patriotic, but I absolutely feel like a New Zealander now.'

By the age of two, Irons was picking out Christmas carols on the piano and by four she was begging for lessons. Alice Matthews, her maternal grandmother and the local church organist, was her first teacher. 'I'd listen to "Kindergarten of the Air" on the radio, and after that I'd do my fifteen minutes' practice, and sometimes I'd do it two or three times a day. All I wanted to do was play the piano.' Irons's parents, themselves musical, soon discovered their younger daughter had perfect pitch. 'One day I said to my mother, "Uncle John's coming to visit." She asked how I knew, and I told her that his brakes always squeaked on C sharp.' Every birthday and Christmas the little girl would ask for a grand piano. Her parents explained that it wasn't possible, and one year made the mistake of giving her a toy grand piano, which she took into the kitchen and dismantled. The arrival of the real thing, when she was about ten, produced a rather different response. 'I went off to my lesson one Saturday morning and came home to find moving men in the living room putting the legs on a Nordheimer grand piano. I hadn't known a thing about it. I was paralysed with delight.'

James and Celia Irons's faith in their daughter's talent was quickly rewarded. As a schoolgirl she would routinely practise for four hours a day – 'it was possible to do more on holidays, of course' – and at the age of twelve she was invited to play the Schumann piano concerto with the Winnipeg Symphony Orchestra. At about the same time, her playing came to the attention of the colourful émigrée pianist, violinist and composer Sophie-Carmen Eckhardt-Gramatté,[1] who had recently settled in Winnipeg. 'She arrived on the scene and announced that she was a genius, and told all the local music teachers to give her their best pupils. It wasn't received very well.' At that stage, Irons was studying with local teacher Megan Howes. 'She was a lovely, warm, beautiful woman who knew exactly how to foster the love of music I had as a child.'

Notwithstanding Eckhardt-Gramatté's forthright self-promotion, Howes recognised that lessons with the eccentric genius would be a unique opportunity for her talented pupil. 'Madame Eckhardt-Gramatté brought with her the long tradition of Russian pianism: she had studied with her mother, who had herself been a pupil of Anton Rubinstein. She was a real authoritarian and more demanding than anyone I've come across since.' Eckhardt-Gramatté took Irons back to scratch, teaching her the 'natural' piano technique she had developed. 'I realise now that its principles were a combination of several modern approaches to piano technique, involving relaxation and the use of weight and rotation. It worked well for me.' Rotation, Irons says, is like opening a door. 'When you turn a doorknob, you use the weight and the rotating movement of the forearm to assist your hand. The same weight and forearm movement helps the fingers to play the notes.'

Saturdays were set aside for the Eckhardt-Gramatté household. In the mornings, Madame Eckardt-Gramatté would spend three hours teaching the girl she described as her 'master pupil'. Following a lunch during which only German was spoken, Diedre spent the afternoons studying German poetry and lieder with Dr Ferdinand Eckhardt. She also gave evening recitals in the Eckhardt-Gramatté home. 'Madame Eckhardt expected me to dress all in black, with a touch of white at the throat and wrists. I'd perform musical stunts at the piano – her intention was to persuade the wealthy of Winnipeg to fund my lessons.' Eckhardt-Gramatté made clear distinctions between school and music studies. 'I was allowed to play for school assemblies – it had been a kind of job for me since elementary school – but I wasn't allowed to be in school sports or musicals, which I would have loved. Everything had to go towards the piano.' The Eckhardt-Gramatté regime also brought its social hardships. 'She made me wear a Russian fur hat. Nobody else had a fur hat, and I was terribly embarrassed by it. She used to say, "You must keep your head warm, or all the notes will fly out."'

Irons's memories of Madame Eckhardt-Gramatté are more than a little ambivalent. While she has no regrets about the technical foundations laid during those years – 'it's easy to me now: it's a language I speak without any trouble' – Eckhardt-Gramatté's influence as a musician was more problematic:

> Sometimes you learn something because you have to fight something else. Madame Eckhardt was very fiery. She once said to me, 'Stand on your head. Do anything. But do it differently.' She wanted to put her stamp on everything. I couldn't feel more strongly opposed to that now. I look at the music and try to find out what *it's* trying to say. I don't want to put my stamp on things. I want to let the music speak.

Irons realised that, in order to develop her own musical individuality, she would have to break with the woman who had given her so much. 'Madame Eckhardt was planning to take me to Vienna and present me to musical society there. I kept telling her that I couldn't go with her: I wanted to study further, either at Juilliard or Curtis. She just couldn't accept that I wanted to leave her.' A year of bitter confrontation finally came to a head on the telephone. 'In the end, she said, "You are no longer my student," and hung up. That was it. She'd have nothing more to do with me. It must have hurt her so much: she had poured herself into me for six years. It was a very, very difficult break for both of us, I think.'

Irons's first stop was the University of Minnesota, where she studied for six months with Professor Bernard Weiser. She also auditioned for the Juilliard School in New York and the Curtis Institute of Music in Philadelphia, and was offered full scholarships to both. 'I decided to go to Curtis because I wanted to study with Rudolf Serkin. Mieczyslaw Horszowski was there too.

They were very different pianists, but made a good pair: Horszowski was wrapped up in detail, and Serkin was more concerned with huge architectural structures.' Lessons with them taught her to have confidence in her own musicality. 'I remember playing Serkin the Beethoven *Appassionata* sonata. At one point I played quite a violent *sforzando*. He stormed at me, "Why did you do that?" I stormed right back: "Because I *wanted* to do it." Then he quietly said, "You should do *more* things because you want to."'

In Philadelphia, Irons found herself musically extended and personally liberated. 'We covered a huge amount of repertoire – every week we'd prepare something new. I also played a lot of chamber music, and learned to really love it. I was one of the ones who played everything. I remember playing the piano part in Prokofiev's *Romeo and Juliet* ballet, and afterwards running barefoot through the streets of Philadelphia, on such a high from something really very little.' Curtis gave her the freedom she had longed for. 'I'd been very strictly brought up. I wasn't allowed to go out, or be out past a certain time. Then suddenly I was in a big city on the East Coast in the 1960s. Vietnam war protests, Woodstock, the works. I made an escape, and I don't regret any of it.'

Irons graduated from Curtis in 1968. The same year she married double bass player Dale Gold, who had also been studying at Curtis. Together they moved to Atlanta, Georgia, where Gold had accepted a position in the Atlanta Symphony Orchestra. Irons quickly slipped into the expected role of housewife. 'My entire life up to that point had been geared towards becoming a concert pianist, and I didn't even have a piano in Atlanta. After about six months of not playing, I thought I should maybe have a piano, and so I bought an old upright. I learned the Schumann Toccata on it, and a few other things, but it wasn't really very important to me.' When Serkin rang to invite her to teach secondary piano at Curtis she was quite sure where her priorities lay: 'I told him how pleased I was to be asked, but said that my husband had a job in Atlanta, and I couldn't possibly consider it.' Later that day she told Gold what had happened. 'He couldn't believe it. He said, "You told him *what*?"' Gold resigned from his job and together they returned to Philadelphia: he to freelancing, and she to the position at Curtis. 'The secondary piano students were all majoring in another instrument, and had to take piano as a second study. Their main aim during their half-hour lesson was to keep me talking as much as possible so they didn't have to play. That was where I learned how to teach, I think: you learn tricks to make them practise.'

Despite a heavy teaching load – in 1972 she was made head of the secondary piano department at Curtis – Irons still found time for annual appearances as resident pianist at the Grand Teton Music Festival in Wyoming. 'It wasn't a teaching festival – just performance. There was lots of intensive music-making there, interspersed with lots of tramping.' As well as performing a daunting amount of chamber music – including recitals with American violinist Peter Schaffer, who would later become concertmaster of the NZSO – Irons played a concerto every year from 1965 until 1976, and also played orchestral piano in works such as *The Miraculous Mandarin* and *Petrouchka*.

> I worked my head off at those festivals. When I left they replaced me with three pianists. They were gruelling years, actually. My son Jeremy was born in Wyoming in 1972. When he was a week old we drove 2000 miles from the Festival to Philadelphia, and when he was two weeks old I started teaching again. I'd take him in the Snugli pack, leave him with a babysitter in a back room at Curtis and feed him between lessons.

Jeremy was four when Gold accepted a job as principal double bass in the NZSO. Gold arrived at the end of 1976, and Jeremy and Diedre joined him the following year.

> I was very excited about coming to New Zealand, but I'm also quite good at talking myself into being positive about things. When the reality hits I can become quite negative. So I arrived on a great high, and almost immediately plummeted. It's very hard following someone to a job. All my life I'd depended on my playing to give me an identity, and all of a sudden I was reduced to being someone's wife. And I missed my friends terribly. It took quite a long time to adjust.

The transition was eased in part by the friendly atmosphere surrounding the NZSO – 'people took us out in boats, and there were lots of meetings at the '1860' pub in Lambton Quay' – and in part by re-establishing her own musical identity. Peter Schaffer had arrived in New Zealand in June 1976. He suggested they play together again and in 1977 they toured a programme of chamber music for the Music Federation of New Zealand. Shortly after their first concert in July 1977, Irons approached Peter Nisbet, newly appointed as general manager of the NZSO, and inquired about the possibility of playing a concerto with the orchestra. 'In essence his response was, "We thought you'd never ask."' Irons first appeared as soloist with the NZSO in 1978, playing Beethoven's Fourth Piano Concerto under principal guest conductor Michi Inoue. The following year she made her début with the Symphonia of Auckland in a programme of three Mozart concerti. 'Miss Irons gave a thoroughly beautiful account of all three. There is not a trace of affectation in her playing. Instead it is all affection.'[2] Since then she has regularly appeared as a soloist with the NZSO, and with regional and city orchestras throughout the country.

By the time Irons became a New Zealand citizen in 1981, she had begun to feel settled in New Zealand. Her musical identity was once more firmly established. Her marriage to Gold at an end, she had formed a relationship with NZSO principal trumpet player Albert MacKinnon, and their daughter Phoebe was born in 1980. Irons once more found herself practising with a baby in a front-pack, rushing backstage during rehearsal breaks to feed and change her.

When Phoebe was less than a year old, Michi Inoue invited Irons to play the monumental piano part in Messiaen's vast *Turangalîla* symphony. 'I'd enjoyed playing orchestral piano in the Tetons because I liked the anonymity, and being a relatively small part of something. The Messiaen was similar in a way. You became part of a gigantic "happening" that included the audience: people were a little restless to start with, and then they settled into the length and expansiveness of it. It's extremely intense emotionally and spiritually.' The piano part of *Turangalîla* is also extremely difficult. 'It's more like a concerto than playing in an orchestra, except that you get to use the music, and you get to sit in the middle of the orchestra instead of at the front.' Learning the work presented its own challenges.

> There are passages which involve really complicated chords – three-note chords in each hand. I got one particular passage up to the metronome marking and let out a sigh of relief, but then I noticed that I only had it up to quarter-speed: I'd been playing it at about 126 to the semiquaver and it needed to be 126 to the crochet. So I just had to work it up. I guess there's a lot more satisfaction in climbing Everest than in climbing the Rimutaka Hill.

Her achievement won her huge audience ovations, and in 1983 Inoue invited her to perform the work with the New Japan Philharmonic in Tokyo.

Irons had already undertaken several tours for the Music Federation when director Elisabeth Airey asked her to accompany visiting Slovenian violinist Miha Pogacnik[3] on his 1984 visit to New Zealand. 'He was probably the most dynamic musician I had ever worked with. He opened many doors for me, not only musically but philosophically as well. My life – and my whole family's life – was changed for the seven years we travelled together.' Pogacnik had worked in the Rudolf Steiner movement in the United States, performing at Waldorf schools and in the Camp Hill communities.

> He introduced me to anthroposophy. It expanded my consciousness about music and about life, and I found it very liberating. As a child, you do everything spontaneously and unconsciously. As you grow up your consciousness expands and you gradually become aware of everything you do, but sometimes you cripple yourself in the process. Anthroposophy helped me relearn an uncomplicated approach to things. I don't have much to do with it any more, but it's very much part of what I've brought to my playing.

The musical partnership with Pogacnik was electric.

> In retrospect I think he liberated my dark side, musically. When he was here in 1984 we played Enescu's Second Sonata, which was a completely new style for me. I'd been learning it for quite some time, and at our first rehearsal he stopped us after about a page and said, "You won't be insulted if I tell you some things?" From that point, and for about two years, he became like a teacher for me.

Irons feels Pogacnik also liberated her from the obedience and technical refinement she had developed as her way of resisting Eckhardt-Gramatté's insistence that she 'do it differently'. 'He opened up all sorts of possibilities – about freedom to break rules, about not being so uptight and conventional, about playing things "crooked". The communication was very special, too. Sometimes – especially when we played the Bartók First Sonata – it felt like we were one person. It was like being lifted into another sphere.' Critics also noted the chemistry. 'It is difficult to describe the qualities which contribute to the magic of Irons and Pogacnik. One senses in their approach an enormous integrity, a care with the music, a deeply felt involvement with the composers' intentions, with each other and with their audience. They seem to invite the listener to share in an experience both intense and spiritual.'[4]

Pogacnik visited New Zealand frequently between 1984 and 1990, when he and Irons toured for the Music Federation and recorded for Radio New Zealand. The pair also undertook extensive international tours in the interests of the charismatic violinist's contribution to world peace. In 1980, in response to the climate of suspicion and hostility generated by the Cold War, Pogacnik founded IDRIART, the Institute for the Development of Intercultural Relations through the Arts. 'The aim was to raise people's consciousness through the universal language of the arts, thereby gaining the knowledge and understanding necessary for peace. The idea was to promote the exchange of ideas and the exchange of culture.' IDRIART manifested itself as festivals all over the world, including China, Georgia in the former USSR, Hungary, the former Yugoslavia, Czechoslovakia, France, the USA, Australia and New Zealand, which hosted an IDRIART festival in 1985.

> We played together in twenty-five countries. I remember one eight-week tour which began with rehearsals and performances in Iceland. Then we played in Sweden, Denmark, Norway, West Germany, East Germany, and Moscow. Then we flew to the USA and played in Washington and Boston, then Canada, then Michigan. Miha flew to Japan, and I went for a little break to Victoria in Canada, where my parents live. I met up with him in Japan, and then we went to China, Hong Kong, Manila, Australia and home. It was just ridiculous. But I was very fired up by the idealism of it, and was really taken with Miha as a person. I loved playing the concerts, and I loved meeting the people. I'm really glad that I had the energy to do it then. It was an amazing time.

The international touring with Pogacnik came to an end in the early 1990s. 'I cancelled a tour at very short notice, because of the Gulf war – the Iranians were threatening to blow up planes.' Pogacnik was naturally upset, but he understood Irons's predicament – her daughter was still quite young – and replaced her for the tour. 'At that point I realised I wasn't indispensable, and the family was enormously relieved that I wasn't going. In fact, the whole business of me not going was very celebratory for all of us. I went with Miha a couple of times after that, but then gradually stopped. There was so much wear and tear involved.' Ironically, Pogacnik's passion for IDRIART also contributed to the cooling of the musical relationship. Irons became increasingly disenchanted with his focus, which she felt was more on IDRIART than on music. 'I had to make a choice between following him and working on his idealistic project, or being a musician, and I chose the latter.' Pogacnick was in New Zealand again in 1997. 'We played a concert in St Andrews in Wellington and had a brief meeting about IDRIART. He wanted to gauge the amount of interest in New Zealand for resuming the organisation, but it's not a New Zealand thing any more.'

Even at the height of her involvement with Pogacnik, Irons was also developing other musical relationships. Polish violinist Jan Tawroszewicz had arrived in New Zealand in 1985 to join the music department at the University of Canterbury. 'He came backstage after the second concert I played in Christchurch with Miha. We spoke again, and decided to play together.' Irons and Tawroszewicz still keep up a regular programme of concerts and radio broadcasts.

In 1986 Irons and fellow Curtis graduate Michael Houstoun undertook the first of several tours for the Music Federation, and in 1987 they were joined by percussionists Bruce McKinnon and Nicolae Albulescu in a programme which included Bartók's *Sonata for Two Pianos and Percussion* (1937) and Jenny McLeod's *Music for Four* (1986), commissioned for the group by the Queen Elizabeth II Arts Council. Subsequent chamber music partnerships have included flautist Alexa Still and the New Zealand String Quartet, and on her appointment to the staff of the University of Canterbury's music department in 1992, Irons joined Tawroszewicz and cellist Alexander Ivashkin in the university-based Canterbury Trio.[5] 'I enjoy chamber music more than anything else, because you're speaking the language of music with other people. Although you create different characters within solo pieces, playing solo is a monologue in a way. It's much more exciting to have somebody to bounce ideas off.' However, not all musicians speak the language equally fluently. 'When some people rehearse they have to discuss every detail, every nuance. But with others the empathy between the instruments flows like a conversation, without actually needing to talk about it too much. That's where you have to speak the language. It's the spontaneous moment that really makes music.'

Sadly, Irons believes it was the death of her husband, Albert MacKinnon, in 1993 that helped her find the true depth of her love of music. MacKinnon had retired from the NZSO in 1992 and moved to Christchurch with Irons when she took up the lectureship in piano. 'It was very quick – two weeks from going to the GP until he died. It was an enormous shock, and it took a long time to get over: I think it took me about six months to realise he wasn't coming back.' Two weeks after MacKinnon's death, Irons went on tour with the Canterbury Trio, playing Beethoven's Piano Trio Op. 70 No. 1 ('The Ghost'), Charles Ives's *Trio* (1911) and Tchaikovsky's Trio in A minor, Op. 50. 'That was when I fell in love with music, instead of just loving it. I learned to savour it in a much more sensual way than I ever had before. And I could rely on music never to die.'

Irons's commitment to teaching is an extension of her love of communicating through music. 'I was on sabbatical in 1998, which I think helped me strike a balance between playing and teaching. While I was away I visited schools and talked to teachers in Canada and the States. I came back very inspired about teaching. It makes it harder in a way, because I want to do more of both, and there's just not time.' While on leave, Irons also learned how to use the Finale music writing software in order to make her own piano reductions of some Mozart concerti.

> Usually piano reductions take everything possible out of the orchestral score, and condense it onto two staves. They *look* like piano parts, but when you come to play them you find you can't actually play all those 15ths. I tried to reconceive the concerti as piano pieces, more like the sonatas. I'm sure Perlman wouldn't want to use them – he's always got an orchestra – but they should be useful for students who don't have orchestras for exams or auditions.

Irons has always been acutely aware of individual differences between pianists, regardless of their level of experience. 'Although the piano looks simple – you push the key down and the hammer hits the string – people make completely different sounds. It's partly to do with people's fingers – whether they have fleshy pads on the tips of their fingers, or skinny, dry fingers, for example – but also to do with pedal, and all sorts of other things. It's your palette, as a musician.' One of Irons's primary tasks as a teacher is expanding and enriching the range of colours her students have at their disposal. 'You can play a note so many different ways, from striking it with your fingertip, to nudging it with your fingertip, to playing all the way down until you're as flat as Horowitz. Physical things all parallel the sounds that come out of the piano.' Colour must also find its appropriate relation to every other aspect of performance. 'That's really what you have to teach – that with Bach you use a certain type of articulation, and with Mozart it's slightly different, and that the Romantics are quite different from the other two. It's partly touch, but it's also style.' [CD Track 8] Irons maintains that the difference between baroque, classical and romantic style is felt internally.

> When you play classical music, you feel you become that elegant person, and you play elegantly. When you play romantic music you become a wallowing emotional type of being, and when you're playing twentieth-century music perhaps you become an intellect, or, if you're playing Messiaen, you race around the cosmos. It's something you feel inside you as you play.

Irons is not prepared to contemplate the acquisition of style without technique. 'Students should have a reasonable foundation in technique by the time they get to me, but a lot of them don't, so willingness to work is terribly important.' Her own experience has taught her there are no short-cuts. 'Some people have a gift of facility, or of musical comprehension, or with luck both, but you still have to put in the hours – learning physical patterns, memorising pieces, and always paying meticulous attention to detail. It's extremely time-consuming.' Irons advocates a balanced practice routine that combines warm-ups and variety. 'Usually my students are learning the notes of one piece, memorising another, and polishing a third, all in a variety of styles.' She also encourages her students to be aware of the process of learning. 'You can't do it all the day before your lesson. You have to do it on a regular basis, because the sleeps in between are probably as important as the work itself.'

Out of hours, Irons has been developing an interest in jazz.

> I have most of my revelations in the shower. I've always loved singing, and one day I was struck by the realisation that I was meant to be a jazz singer, so I started listening to Sarah Vaughan and Ella Fitzgerald and Billie Holiday. As soon as I understood what they were doing, I realised this was going to be an adventure in appreciation rather than anything else, so I bowed to their enormous gifts and reminded myself that what I can do is play the piano. I've taken to playing jazz chords, and one Gershwin song at a time, trying to find the beautiful harmonies in that idiom. But I haven't yet discovered what the inner feelings are when you're playing jazz.

Irons feels her long immersion in the classical tradition may make the language of jazz difficult to acquire. 'As classical musicians, our whole orientation is to be obedient to a score. People don't learn to improvise any more, although of course in Bach's time, and right through until Liszt, it wasn't like that at all. But give me another forty years, and I'm sure I could be a jazz pianist if I really set my mind to it!'

1 Born in Moscow in 1898, the prodigiously talented Sophie-Carmen Eckhardt-Gramatté (died 1974) began piano studies at the Paris Conservatoire in 1908 and made her début at eleven, playing violin and piano in Paris, Geneva and Berlin. She toured the USA in 1929, performing her own compositions for piano and violin. Eckhardt-Gramatté gave up performing in 1930 to devote herself to composition and in 1934 married art historian Ferdinand Eckhardt. In 1954 the couple settled in Winnipeg, where Eckhardt-Gramatté continued to work relentlessly at her composition. In addition to writing music, she developed the 'Egré Piano Technique' teaching method, based on the use of rotary motion. (Grove.)

2 L. C. M. Saunders, 'Mozart Series Begins with Delight', *NZ Herald*, 2 Mar. 1979.

3 Miha Pogacnik (born 1949) received his musical education in Germany and the USA. Founder of IDRIART and its president since 1983, he has refused all offers to make commercial recordings, preferring to further live communication with audiences.

4 Elizabeth Kerr, 'Magic Rapport', *NZ Listener*, 7 Nov. 1987.

5 German cellist Edith Saltzmann replaced Ivashkin in the trio in 2001, following the latter's departure for England in 1999.

HARLEY-DAVIDSON

William Dart : Hunter and Gatherer

I'm simply obsessed by how little we know about ourselves – and it's artists, writers, composers and musicians who can tell us. They are the ones who can keep alive the stories that touch our hearts, our minds and our souls.

Glance through the programme of any recent concert by the Auckland Philharmonia, and there's a good chance William Dart (born 1947) will have written the programme notes. Turn on the radio and he can be heard introducing anything from Concert FM's Composer of the Week to a new CD by Goodshirt, Pluto or Cloudboy. The *Listener* first carried his idiosyncratic – and sometimes acerbic – music writing in 1977, and he has edited *Art New Zealand* since 1983. Along the way, he has found time to compose scores for music theatre, teach secondary school, contribute a regular film column to *Rip It Up* magazine, amass a legendary collection of peanut butter glasses and hold down a full-time university position. Dart, however, regards *Music in New Zealand*, the magazine he founded in 1988, as his most important achievement. 'I'd seen what *Art New Zealand* had done for the visual arts. It recorded, and it made things accessible. It opened up new eyes and new sensibilities. I wanted to do the same for music.'

William Dart was born in Auckland, and his family moved to Whakatane when he was five. Even as a child, he felt himself to be a misfit in the 'wild, macho territory' of small-town Bay of Plenty. Graham Dart, 'a panel-beater with a taste for Conrad novels' and rather a remote figure, tried to turn his tubby son into a sportsman. 'He gave me all sorts of balls to kick or throw, but they'd always end up displayed as *objets* in my bedroom cupboard, which I'd set up as a sort of art gallery-cum-museum. I wasn't what you'd call a conventional country boy.'

As a teenager, Dart found respite from the 'bullying, harassing' atmosphere of Whakatane High School in music, and, to a lesser degree, in roller skating. 'The school was a battering machine for the oversensitive. I'd ballooned in the third form, and was frequently beaten.' The competition for the Daughters of Empire Trophy epitomised the school's culture of physical brutality. 'The trophy was carried off year after year by subjecting us to arduous and pathetic military drill. These days, tight serge uniforms on hot summer days might seem like a very specialised fetish, but in 1960 it was simply demonic discomfort.' Dart would escape to the skating rink at Ohope beach – 'sadly, now just an old piece of concrete with little tufts of grass growing through it' – and practise alone for hours. He competed at a national level and won a number of championships, including a national men's free-skating title in 1962. Music, however, would prove a more enduring – and rather less solitary – pastime.

There had been music on his mother's side of the family. 'My father wasn't musical at all, but my mother played the piano in a sort of "party" style – Charlie Kunz was one of her culture heroes – and she'd been a secretary at the old 1YA, where she'd come into contact with musicians and radio producers.' Dart's maternal grandparents ran dance bands in Auckland until the 1950s: 'in the early days it was Allan's Dance Band portfolios rather than Bach preludes and fugues lying around the house'. Dart's grandfather George was a piano and sax man; his grandmother Ivy, however, had completed a violin diploma at Auckland University College in 1913, and mysterious volumes of Rode *Caprices* and Kreutzer *Études* could be found among the veletas and gay gordons in her sheet music collection. Like many New Zealand homes in the 1950s, the Dart household resounded with TANZA recordings:[1] 'every time I hear Pat McMinn's mercilessly cheerful vocals in "Opo the Crazy Dolphin" I'm taken straight back to the family bach in the 1950s.' The nearest William got to classical music was a pair of 'rather distressed' volumes of overtures arranged for piano that had somehow been spirited away into the country.

One summer, however, Betty Dart took her eleven-year-old son to meet the local piano teacher, the extraordinary Violet Rucroft. 'Ru had taken herself off to London in the 1920s, got herself an LRAM, and was determined to return to New Zealand and settle in the country: she wanted to give country children a chance for a proper musical education.' Rucroft was also a Forest and Bird Society fanatic, dividing her time between weeding the Ureweras and grilling her students on their Mozart sonatas. Dart recalls her teaching studio as an oasis of high culture. 'She had a pair of Challen pianos, so we could always do two-piano work. There was a complete set of the Grove

Dictionary of Music and Musicians on her shelves, and – significantly for such an ur-feminist – a copy of Christopher St John's biography of Ethel Smyth.' The studio also held a set of Dolmetsch virginals, and an instrument Dart later identified as a bass recorder.

Rucroft bundled her pupils off to concerts whenever she could. 'She took us all around the region to hear visiting pianists. We went to Kawerau to hear the Polish pianist Niedzielski – who travelled with his own Gaveau grand – and to Rotorua to hear a visiting English pianist playing Schumann's *Prophet Bird*. It was a magical experience.' Back in Whakatane, Dart was allowed to play his Purcell hornpipe on Rucroft's virginals, and one day there was a mysterious handing-over of the 1945 Caxton Press edition of Douglas Lilburn's *Four Preludes* for piano, hand-engraved by Leo Bensemann. 'She was an absolute tyrant, but she had real musical values. I think she was a major influence on a lot of people.'

Dart remembers Whakatane High School for more than just the military drill. 'I got caned in the seventh form for mutual thigh-slapping with the boy next to me in Latin. The Latin teacher was also the headmaster, and I think he'd had enough. We all got a belting.' The headmaster would have been Dart's academic nemesis, too, had the maths teacher not intervened on his behalf. 'Maths was my fifth subject in the fifth form, and I got 27% for School Cert. By the end of the sixth form I was getting 2%.' The headmaster told him to straighten up and be a man – only girls were allowed to take history instead of maths – and enrolled him for Scholarship mathematics. 'The maths teacher was getting desperate. He asked me if I'd considered taking music for Scholarship. It had never occurred to me.' Dart approached the headmaster. 'He looked me in the eye and told me music wasn't available. He'd ripped the music pages out of the Scholarship booklet.' The maths master pursued the matter, and found that music was after all an option. 'It obviously wasn't going to be taught at school, so I studied under Rucroft. I'd sit in the maths class and do four-part harmony. I was dux of the school in the end, but it wouldn't have happened with maths as my fifth subject.'

Dart started a degree in music and English at Auckland University in 1965.

> I was rather a strange young man. My grandmother had had a stroke and was living with my mother in the Bay of Plenty, so I went and lived by myself in her old villa in Epsom. I used to play the piano a lot – I'd come home from varsity and play until my back hurt so much I couldn't play any more – and I'd set myself little tasks

> like living for a week on rice and custard and then living for the next week on pumpkin, carrots and cabbage.

His conversion to popular music came in 1967, during his third year of study. 'Someone came to stay and brought some Beatles records. I was the biggest musical snob in the world, but I was converted by *Sgt. Pepper*. Obsession set in and I became a manic record collector.'

He discovered film around the same time.

> I had a bicycle, and every night I'd cycle around the local theatres – to Avondale to see a double feature of Howard Hawks's *I Was a Male War Bride* and John O'Shea's *Runaway*, and to Remuera to see Antonioni's *La Notte*. I was particularly obsessed by *What's New Pussycat?* with its wacky humour and Burt Bacharach score. I must've seen it at least a dozen times. It was billed with Coppola's *Dementia 13*, so I knew that film pretty well too, including the cuts.

Dart's parallel obsession with film censorship culminated in an essay for *Landfall* magazine in which he probed the anomalies of a regime which saw films cut to shreds rather than issued with an appropriate censor's classification.[2] From 1968, Dart was joined in his film-going by poet and painter Ross Fraser.[3] 'He came to live with me in my grandmother's house. We led a delightful hippie existence, going to movies together, and me not finishing whatever I was supposed to be doing at varsity. He was fiercely anti-academic, but he achieved so much without all that degree stuff.'

Dart did, however, finish what he was doing at varsity: postgraduate study in music followed the completion of his BMus in 1967. 'Things really only took fire for me when Robin Maconie came over and deputised for Ron Tremain, who'd left in 1967.' Maconie preached a radicalism that Auckland barely knew existed. 'I remember him pointing to one bar in a Beatles song, 'In My Life', and saying that it was the sum total of Vaughan Williams's influence.' Maconie encouraged Dart when he tackled a twelve-tone setting of Oscar Wilde's 'The Harlot's House' for soprano, piccolo and harmonium. 'Organising a performance for that combination of players, with some of the fearsome lines I wrote, was out of the question in 1968.' Dart also discovered his bent for musicology as a graduate student, writing his MMus thesis on the lieder of Franz Liszt.

The beginning of 1970 found him at rather a loose end. 'I couldn't think of anything better to do, so I decided to go to teachers' college.'

> I was on the committee of a music education series called *Soundscape*, with Jack Body, Sue Rhind – one of the stauncher Auckland music teachers at the time – and Michael Volkerling, who was an editor for Reed publishing. It was a very liberal attempt at doing classroom music. I remember at one committee meeting Jack suggested we use some of the Yoko Ono pieces out of her book *Grapefruit* and ask our pupils to lie on the floor and feel each other's stomachs. Later, through *Art New Zealand*, I met Denys Watkins, who'd done the very hip drawings.

During the year Dart also started his own magazine, called *Contemporary Themes and Music for the Teacher*. 'The problem with popular music was that teachers couldn't get hold of resources, so every three months I'd select ten albums which the teachers then bought for their schools. I'd provide notes and two teaching schemes on each one. It ran for a year: all done on a hired IBM ball typewriter and printed by the local print shop.'

Unfortunately, some 'hideous' classroom experiences during his training college year took the edge off Dart's enthusiasm for schoolteaching, and in 1971 he returned to university. 'I began a doctorate as a strategy of evasion.' None the less, he quickly found himself caught up in the world of English composers Hubert Parry (1848–1918) and Cyril Scott (1879–1970).[4] 'I just adored Parry's music, and there was something of the wild card, the outsider, in Scott that connected for me.' He immersed himself in Scott's writings – from health tracts on the joys of cider vinegar as a cure for obesity to his tales of being driven around Detroit in a Dodge, with a reincarnated Aristotle (who rejoiced in the name of Master Koot Hoomi) at the wheel. 'In fact, when I went to Britain and visited Scott's widow, I was very seriously shown the French doors through which Master K. H. made his entrance.' Scott's major musical text, *Music: Its Secret Influence Through the Ages* (1934) also enthralled him. 'I was fascinated by his tales of the various goblins and fairies, hierarchically arranged in accordance with the music that invoked them, as well as his description of an eternal struggle between the Great White and Black Brotherhoods. If he'd been born later, he'd have made a great scriptwriter for George Lucas.' Notwithstanding his enthusiasm for his post-Victorian composers, Dart's doctorate might well have been on the complexities of progressive rock, had popular music then been treated with any academic seriousness. 'In the early 70s I organised weekly listening sessions downstairs in the old music department, sampling obscurities from the records I was importing from the States. I've always loved finding out-of-the-way things,

things that are a bit weird. It all fitted: Parry and Scott had both been overlooked by mainstream musicologists.'

Three years into his doctoral study, the Department of Education reminded Dart that he still owed it $200 from his bonded year at training college, and he took a job in the music department of Auckland's Edgewater College. Although he found teaching 'hell' at first, he stayed at Edgewater for eight years, eventually becoming head of department. 'There were the usual rigours of School Certificate music, back in the cosy days when it was four-part cadences and eight-bar melodies, but there were also some quirky delights.' Prize-giving ceremonies might be leavened by a few numbers from William Walton's *Façade* suite, with a plucky fifth-former elocuting Edith Sitwell's poems through a homemade megaphone. On one notorious occasion the school orchestra played a Fux *Intrada*, but despite Dart's careful phonetic instructions the headmaster mispronounced the composer's name – 'much to the merriment of all'. 'We even staged the murder-in-the-bath sequence from *Marat-Sade*, with Richard Peaslee's tough little songs. I think it rather startled the handful of unsuspecting parents who'd come along to what they thought was a chamber music concert.'

Dart began writing for *Rip It Up* when Murray Cammick started the popular culture magazine in 1977. His first contribution was a monthly rock column, but he switched to film reviewing a few years later – a function he performed for over twenty years. In 1977, too, the Concert Programme engaged him as a classical record reviewer, and the *Listener* invited him to contribute a fortnightly Auckland concert column.

> It was a different *Listener* back then – different in look, and in attitude. These days one ends up bargaining for a 300-word review on a strictly 'one-off' basis; then one had the luxury of selecting what one thought were the high points of Auckland's concerts for the fortnight. Those could be anything from Joni Mitchell playing at the St James to an enchanting programme of solo clarinet that Peter Scholes presented at the Pumphouse in Takapuna.

Radio meant working in the beautiful old Radio New Zealand building in Durham Lane with Pat Towsey, who, it turned out, had been one of the livelier spirits in the organisation in the early 1940s, when Betty Dart had been a secretary at 1YA. 'During Pat's regnum I was asked to present an introduction to pop music – ten introductory programmes. It ended with a couple of programmes on Punk and New Wave. I could get away with one Stranglers song, but I couldn't get in any Sex Pistols, because of the four-letter words.' The successful pilot series was followed by a regular fortnightly session. 'Pat was a valiant colleague, but, apart from his admiration for Aretha Franklin, he didn't care much for the new breed of musicians I was airing between Bach and Bruckner.'

The format of Dart's *New Horizons* programme has changed since it first went to air in 1980. Initially it was a forty-minute review of recent releases, but when David McCaw took over as producer he suggested Dart occasionally focus on one theme or artist. McCaw also suggested he incorporate interviews into the programme. 'My first interview was a rather lively one with Charles Tumahai and Willie Hona of Herbs – so lively, in fact, that Radio New Zealand extended the running time to an hour to accommodate the material.' Produced by the 'simpatico' Tim Dodd, *New Horizons* now runs to fifty-two minutes fortnightly; Dart ensures that the programme carries a New Zealand content of at least thirty percent. 'It's been great creating interview-based documentaries with musicians like Mahinarangi Tocker, Dave Dobbyn, Greg Malcolm, Matthew Bannister, Chris Knox and Bryce Galloway.'

Radio and writing for the *Listener* were not the only things distracting Dart from the classroom in the late 1970s. Director John Curry had engaged him to provide music for his productions of *Twelfth Night* (1976) and *The Good Person of Setzuan* (1978) at Auckland's New Independent Theatre. 'John coaxed me into the company, shrieking approval when I did a tango turn with "Come Away, Death" and wrote some Brechtian sambas. It was a long way from that rather severe Wilde setting of 1968.' Playwright and director Mervyn Thompson also regularly worked at the New Independent; at the time, he was developing a new song–drama along the lines of his successful *O Temperance* (1972) and *Songs to Uncle Scrim* (1976). 'Mervyn wanted to investigate the injustices that the Pakeha land courts had dished out to the tangata whenua over the years. He'd seen the work I'd done with John, and asked if I'd be interested in writing the music.'

To begin with, Thompson worried that Dart was a *pasticheur* – 'he'd heard the punk pop songs I'd written for Brian McNeill's ill-fated play *New Zealand Heroes*' – but his doubts were quickly allayed. 'Mervyn fed me the lyrics song by song. It was an intense period of writing, but in three weeks we had a show.' Thompson had a fervour Dart had not experienced in the worlds of either musicology or schoolteaching. 'Nothing could distract him – not even his son playing billiards with my precious peanut butter glasses while we were both working at the piano.' *Songs to the Judges*[5] was premiered in Thompson's

Maidment Summer Theatre season in February 1980; the following year the company toured the production under the auspices of the New Zealand Students' Arts Council, with the shadow of the Springbok tour looming on the horizon [CD track 9].

The success of *Songs to the Judges* encouraged Dart to work again in the medium of song–drama, and in 1981 he collaborated with John Curry and Ross Fraser on *Give Us a Kiss . . . And We'll Tell You.*[6] Billed as 'New Zealand's first gay revue', the format posed a structural challenge. 'The succession of songs didn't carry the momentum of *Judges*. Rather than try to create a dramatic crescendo, we opted for a cabaret format in which the sentimental, political and satirical would sit next to each other in happy and, we hoped, effective contrast.' *Give Us a Kiss* toured the country in 1982, again under the auspices of the New Zealand Students' Arts Council. Like *Songs to the Judges*, *Give Us a Kiss* was performed in theatres, galleries, schools and training colleges; also like *Judges*, it generated its share of controversy. '*Truth* gleefully proclaimed that *Give Us a Kiss* had been banned from playing at the Waikato Art Museum.[7] In the end we did the shows in the New Place Theatre, over at the university.'

The early 1980s were a period of transition for Dart. His last three years of schoolteaching were part-time and he finally made the break at the end of 1982. 'In my last year of schoolteaching Ross invited me to be part of *Art New Zealand*, which was edging its way towards its twenty-first issue, and I worked as his assistant. Until then, I'd managed to juggle teaching and freelancing, but something had to give and I resigned from Edgewater at the end of the year.' When Fraser suffered a debilitating stroke in 1986, Dart was thrown in at the deep end. 'Issue 39 was my first big test as editor. Ross was a huge help, but it was a steep learning curve.'

The experience on *Art New Zealand* stood him in good stead.

> *Music in New Zealand* started with dreams and schemes and informal commissions. I talked all around the place, and when the first scripts came in I realised that I had better make it happen. From the beginning, it had a strong commitment to every facet of our country's music. I felt that it had to present that music in all its diversity, totally across the board. Looking back over old issues, one finds extraordinary bed-mates listed on the various 'Contents' pages. Issue 11, which presented a big symposium on Lilburn's Third Symphony, also featured Terry Vaughan's marvellous shaggy-dog tale about the Kiwi Concert Party and Schubert's 'Ave Maria' and, a few pages after that, Roy Colbert's

rather nifty profile of Dunedin songwriter Martin Phillipps, with some particularly choice photos.

Dart is responsible for the production of *Music in New Zealand* from text editing to typesetting, and contributes articles and reviews when time permits, but he passes credit for the magazine to the musicians and the contributors: 'I'm just an organiser – a marshal for all these talented people.' Although the production values of *Music in New Zealand* are not as high as those of *Art New Zealand* – it doesn't carry enough advertising to pay for glossy colour reproductions, and the magazine depends for its life on the support of Creative New Zealand and the Lilburn Trust – the format is the same, and images are just as important. 'Early on, I remember pleading with the *Auckland Star* to borrow a copy of a stunning production photo from David Farquhar's *A Unicorn for Christmas*, with Ngaio Marsh, script in hand, standing over a very demure Honor McKellar.' Dart has also made a point of commissioning photographic portraits. 'Geoffrey Smith did a series for us: Donald McIntyre doing his blokey thing on a rocky foreshore, and elegant portraits of Eve de Castro-Robinson and Michael Houstoun.' His own vast collection of musical ephemera also enriches the pages of the magazine. 'It continues to shock me how our musicians are not photographing events that could be of some historical importance. We're in awful danger of losing our history. It's slipping away and we're not always making the effort to rescue it.' From the beginning, each issue of *Music in New Zealand* has carried at least one substantial interview; as well as carrying profiles of established New Zealand musicians from Annea Lockwood to Ivan Zagni, Dart makes a point of introducing readers to new and younger composers. 'It's a question of communication. Words can provide valuable gateways into music which is potentially difficult, even for the willing listener.'

Words can also be destructive. In a television interview following the 1995 Rugby World Cup in South Africa – at which she had sung the cup theme song – one of New Zealand's more famous musical exports made an ill-considered and ill-informed remark about the state of New Zealand composition. 'She was asked whether she would be performing any New Zealand music on her visit to South Africa. She grimaced, and out came the comment, "No, I'm sorry. We haven't got a wealth of composers out there unfortunately." And then the afterthought – "We might have a little Maori song".'[8] Dart got together the collective outrage of thirty New Zealand composers and the responses flowed into *Music in New Zealand*. One of his favorites, a tart response from Edinburgh-based Lyell Cresswell, included a fragment of Edward Tregear's poem 'Te Whetu Plains' ('All still, all silent, 'tis a songless land'), set especially for the diva.

Dart also keeps a personal dossier on the indignities that New Zealand music has suffered at the hands of other critics.

> In the past one couldn't avoid the temptation of comparing a particularly wooden tenor to the Kaingaroa Forest, or wondering whether a cello broke its own string in protest at a woeful performer, but I get more incensed now by bigger issues: lack of collegial support at concerts – by both composers and fellow musicians – and arrant negativity on the part of reviewers who don't realise how an ill-considered few sentences can deprive a second concert of valuable audiences. I simply can't imagine why a critic would want to live in this country and ignore its culture. How could one local reviewer write up two concerts by the Auckland Philharmonia, enthuse about Mahler and Bruckner, and totally ignore a twenty-minute work by a New Zealand composer which was on one of the programmes?

A worse sin for Dart than simple illiteracy – 'one of them doesn't even know the difference between pathos and bathos' – is the attitude he detects in some critics of complacent arrogance, especially in relation to contemporary music.

> The *Listener* recently asked a Taranaki journalist to cover a week of New Zealand music played on Concert FM, and he launched his column with the words, 'I don't know much about music. I don't even know what I like. Not till I've heard it two or three times, anyway.' He then proceeded to offer glib little pronouncements on the composers whose music turned up on various programmes. They just couldn't get away with it writing about New Zealand literature or the visual arts. There'd be howls of protest.

Music in New Zealand exists as a corrective to such knee-jerk sound-bites which so often pass for criticism in daily or weekly publications.

Dart's contempt for 'cruel and stupid' writing about music is simply another manifestation of his passionate defence of the people who make and perform music in New Zealand. 'I can't comprehend the self-pride of critics who go to a concert, hear a new work for the first time, and then write about it ten minutes later.' When asked to review a new guitar concerto by Dunedin composer Anthony Ritchie, Dart studied the score, went to the concert, and listened to a recording of the performance half a dozen times before he felt ready to write about the work. 'The effort that goes into a major work needs to be respected. This is the music that grows out of who we are, what we are and where we are. It needs someone to speak up for it.'

Dart has special praise for musicians who are prepared to undertake the often thankless task of commissioning and performing new New Zealand works. 'The contemporary ensemble 175 East has been giving cutting-edge concerts of new music since 1996 – but they still struggle for audiences and reviews.' Bouquets also go to the Auckland Philharmonia. 'It's always insisted on being part of what's happening here. You'll find New Zealand music in all the main series programmes, in the Kiwi Kapers school shows, and in all the Philharmonia Ensemble's chamber music programmes. The Philharmonia has the country's longest-running composer's residency, and it's been organising composers' reading workshops for years.'

Although he is evangelical about local music in all its guises, Dart is also not afraid to go out on a limb in defence of what he regards as artistic integrity. 'We've made a national monument out of that E*N*ZSO horror. It's appalling to see a fragile little Tim Finn song clubbed to death by the combined forces of the NZSO, the National Youth Choir and Kiri. I like the cross-over, but it's the motive that concerns me: it's nothing to do with art – it's to do with making money.' He is equally dismissive of 'clumsy bicultural events' like 'Taaua', the short-lived musical partnership forged in 2000 between Tainui and the NZSO. 'In his 1946 address to the first Cambridge Music School, Douglas Lilburn predicted a future for New Zealand music – but he predicts with such graceful caution, and he is so sensitive when it comes to how we might catch some Polynesian ethos within our music, that one wishes that more people today had this sensitivity.' Dart detects glimpses of this ethos in works such as Gillian Whitehead's *Taurangi* for flute and piano, in the wailing bird-calls of Lilburn's electro-acoustic works, in the passing flash of Polynesian voices in Crowded House's 'Four Seasons in One Day', and in Mahinarangi Tocker's 'Heart Winds'. 'Mahina talks about being part Jewish, part Scottish and part Maori. That cultural mix is very New Zealand to me. In this part of the world we must be open – forever open – to the new sounds and experiences that are around us.'

Dart's own eclecticism also marks his university teaching style. Since 1998, when he was appointed to the staff of the music department at the University of Waikato, he has taught everything from New Zealand music to the history of the musical. One of his pleasures has been seeing students in his course on Rock Music warm to the 'hard-core' country music he includes in the syllabus;

but then country music is one of Dart's passions, a taste he shares with his partner, Don. Dart has also had an on-campus presence as a performer: in September 2000, he accompanied soprano Patricia Wright in a song and lieder recital. Only a few months later, he could be heard in rather a different venue, playing rather different repertoire. In February 2001, Dart and trombonist Paul Booth were invited to perform a 5 am gig at the party following Auckland's Hero Parade. Dart arranged two works for the occasion: 'a sort of Weberian duo concertante on Village People themes' and a longer medley for solo piano.

> I wanted to create a cocktail of music by gay composers. It began with a splash of Handel hornpipe, sighed with a Schubert impromptu, took a dip in Saint-Saens's aquarium, and eventually travelled – via a Poulenc *Mouvement Perpétuel* and a few phrases of Lilburn's *Sings Harry* – to the blues that Aaron Copland wrote for the pianist William Kapell. It was almost spooky the way that the pieces segued so obligingly into one another.

The themes of Dart's personal medley, as it segues from pianist to composer to teacher to broadcaster to journalist and back to teacher again, are often heard simultaneously. But, no matter what the key, Dart believes the song is essentially the same.

> All musicians are travelling towards the same destination, which is communication with the listener. They just approach that goal from different perspectives. Perhaps it's my obsession with communication that has driven me to explore as many ways I could find of touching people with music. I'm a populist, I suppose, and what I've done has been to try and spread things. I think that's been worthwhile. I *hope* it has.

1 The Radio Corporation of New Zealand established TANZA ('To Assist New Zealand Artists') – the country's first local record company – in 1948. TANZA's first release, Ruru Karaitiana's 'Blue Smoke', was released in 1949 and sold over 20,000 copies. 'Opo the Crazy Dolphin' was the hit of 1955. Production had ceased by 1956.

2 William Dart, 'Film Censorship in New Zealand', *Landfall*, Vol. 24, No.1 (Mar. 1970), pp.67-73.

3 Ross Fraser (1935-96) founded *Art New Zealand* with Peter Webb in 1976. His poetry includes *Poems from the Greek Anthology* (1988) and *Metaphysics for Fun* (1991), and several posthumous volumes. Poems and essays were also published in *Landfall*, *Arena* and *The Poetry Yearbook*.

4 William Dart, 'Hubert Parry and Cyril Scott: Two post-Victorian song writers. With an introductory essay on the musical problems of Great Britain in the 19th century', PhD dissertation (University of Auckland, 1975).

5 William Dart, *Songs to the Judges* (Wellington: Playmarket, 1983; Kiwi-Pacific LP, SLD-69, 1982).

6 William Dart, *Song Book* (Wellington: Waiteata Music Press, 1995). A collection of fourteen songs selected by the composer from *Songs to the Judges*, *Give Us a Kiss* and *Away with the Fairies* (1983).

7 Bill Blades, 'Town Fathers Give Gay Fun the Kiss-Off', *NZ Truth*, 20 Apr. 1982, p.3.

8 'Kiri-Speak: Dame Kiri Te Kanawa on New Zealand Music', *Music in New Zealand* (Spring 1995), pp.8-13.

Hirini Melbourne : He Tangata Puoro

In the past, music had its own profound function in every aspect of life. I can't say how another tribe should use the instruments today, but as far as I'm concerned there's only one rule – the survival of the art-form. As long as the instruments are looked after and treasured, they should be heard.

The strands in the life of Hirini Melbourne (born 1949; Tuhoe, Ngati Kahungunu) as a musician and as a teacher are inextricably interconnected. Of those many strands – he is known as a writer for children, a translator, an editor and an historian, and is associate professor of Maori at the University of Waikato – Melbourne's name is perhaps most often associated with his activities as a composer of songs for young people, and with the traditional instruments he has helped rediscover and revive. 'Music wasn't incidental for Maori. It had its own magic, its own origins, its own esoteric purposes – not just to help conceive a baby and help a child to grow, but to ease the pain of labour and of tattooing, and to usher people from this world. There wasn't anything music didn't touch. But along the way we seem to have lost the reason to sing.'

Hirini Melbourne was born in the strongly Tuhoe community of Ruatoki in the northern Urewera. Not long after his birth, his mother took him to the hospital in Whakatane for a check-up, where a nurse suggested she should call him Sidney. 'My mother had never heard of Sydney, Australia, so the joke was a bit lost on her.' Melbourne kept the name until he started recording his own songs in the late 1970s, when the shy musician adopted the transliteration Hirini as a pseudonym. Since then, Hirini Melbourne's short, lyrical songs about birds and trees and the sounds of the city have introduced successive generations of youngsters to the sound of te reo. The popularity of those songs has helped the pseudonym to stick.

Melbourne attended the local high school at Ruatoki until form five. He failed School Certificate at his first attempt – 'surprise, surprise' – and from his second year in the fifth form he attended Te Aute College in Hawke's Bay. Until then, he had taken for granted his marae and its music, his family's immersion in te reo, and the sounds of the bush. 'I didn't realise how important that was until I left the area. It was then I realised that the rest of the country was not like Ruatoki.' Melbourne soon found he had to speak English 'in order to survive on a daily basis' at boarding school. 'I built up a relationship with another student who was also Tuhoe, from Waikaremoana. I'd gone to Te Aute thinking I would be able to use Maori, but he told me, "Hey, they don't speak Maori here." The only thing Maori about it was its name.' However, Hirini took pleasure in the school's music activities. 'We did a lot of community singing, and we knew if we didn't make the old ladies at the front cry, we hadn't done a very good job. That was when I realised the power of the voice.' Had it not been for that singing, Melbourne's expulsion from Te Aute during his seventh-form year would have given him little cause for regret. 'I used to be really good until I was made to take on roles and responsibilities. One night we thought, "What the hell!" and invested our money in alcohol. We got found out, and that was the end of that. But I remember thinking how much I'd miss the singing. It had a huge effect on me.'

Expulsion did not impede his academic progress: a scholarship to teachers' college in Auckland and a BA in history and Maori brought him back to the Bay of Plenty to teach Maori and social studies at Whakatane High School. 'I really wanted to go to a small school, but ended up going to about the fourth-biggest high school in New Zealand. It was a bit chaotic, but I was able to do ambitious things, largely because I was so naïve.' In 1974, Melbourne's first year at Whakatane, the school mounted a production of *The Pirates of Penzance*. The relevance of Gilbert and Sullivan to young Maori begged a question, and the following year Melbourne found himself devising a multimedia production based on the narrative of Rangi and Papa. 'The local radio station 1XX was just starting up, and all these ambitious young recording technicians wanted to become part of the production, so we did a whole lot of multi-tracking – it was a very Pink Floyd-ish sound. Everything was cued off the tape.' The gods were played by strapping lads from the first fifteen who had returned to school to go on a rugby tour of the South Island.

> As long as they didn't have to say lines and their faces were hidden by masks, they'd sing and they'd act – and do all sorts of things to prolong the battle scenes. It was

> amazing. In the end the coach had to come and beg me to tell them to go on the tour. That was the beginning of music for me – of starting to use music to say something.

Ironically, it was partly Melbourne's identification with Maori youth which prompted him to leave the classroom. 'As often happens with Maori teachers, you end up being a kind of social welfare officer, enforcing rules you had no part in shaping.' The incident of the kowhai tree – the only native tree growing in the school grounds – typified his predicament. The tree represented security and familiarity for the group of Maori boys who gathered under it to eat their lunch. The school found this threatening in some way, and passed a rule preventing students from sitting under the trees – 'they said it was so the trees wouldn't get damaged' – and from then on everyone had to spend their lunch-hour in the open. Melbourne increasingly found that the problems of young Maori in the school were becoming his responsibility. 'I ended up with all the "bad" students. I loved that, but I didn't want to end up carrying all this other baggage for the school, on top of what I was doing in the classroom and as warden of the school boarding house.'

In 1975, a position came up editing Maori texts for the School Publications section of the Department of Education. Hirini and his wife Jan moved to Wellington with their baby daughter, Mahina. 'One of the things that made my job difficult as a teacher had been the lack of resources in Maori – especially materials that were appropriate to the level and interests of the students I was teaching.' At the time, very few authors were writing in Maori; those who did used rather stilted and formal language. 'And they mostly came from rural backgrounds. They tended to romanticise rural life, and saw urban life in negative terms. I knew that at least seventy percent of the people learning Maori had urban experiences. That was a whole new challenge, and the job gave me an opportunity to do something about it.' During his four years in Wellington, Melbourne took over *Te Wharekura* and *Te Tautoko* – journals for secondary students fluent in Maori – and initiated the series *He Purapura* – full-colour storybooks in Maori for emergent readers.

However, the move to Wellington meant the loss of regular contact with whanau. 'I really wanted my kids to grow up with their grandparents, but I knew that in Wellington they wouldn't. So if they didn't get the language from me they wouldn't get it from anywhere else.' Mahina loved Pakeha nursery rhymes and lullabies. 'I didn't know them, so I taught her the songs I learned as a child so that she would learn to like the sound of the Maori language.' Melbourne complemented those ancestral oriori with his own songs. Their melodies were often folk-inspired, but formally and thematically they owed most to traditional pao – epigrammatic, two-line couplets on topical subjects. 'I tried to reflect on the urban environment for what it was. We lived in Hobson Street, and swore that the train went through our lounge. That was a dominant sound, so I started doing songs based on train rhythms. I opened my window out onto the Wellington street and took it from there.'

Melbourne used what he describes as 'a simple process of observation' to devise the melodies and texts for his waiata, balancing songs about the sounds of the city with the sounds he had started to miss in Wellington – the sounds of the bush. 'I wrote about birds and insects and trees, and cranes and trains and lifts and escalators, and tried to capture a child's ear for new sounds.' He had learned that if Mahina loved the sound of a word she would repeat it.

> I worked with really complicated words, and with combinations of sounds. People said they were too difficult for children. At the time, you had to work within a basic graded vocabulary for the school journals, but I didn't have to apply that to my songs, so I went the opposite way. I invented words, and revived words, and used old words to capture the movements and sounds of the bush.

Although he had never previously learned how to play the guitar, he taught himself to finger-pick in order to evoke those sounds. 'I wanted the guitar to help communicate what I was singing about. Birds were easy. So was the weta, because I knew what a weta sounded like: it makes a rasping sound when it scrapes its hind legs, so I just had to scratch the string.' But the weta also thumps. 'I was sleeping under a tree one day, and all this wood dust started falling on my face. I looked up to see a weta cleaning out the debris from its nest inside the tree – the pitapitaweta. He was thumping the tree to shake off the dust. That's how I came across the rhythm for that song.' Depicting the sound of a jumping grasshopper proved a little harder, as did creating the effect of water dripping in a cave for 'Titiwai', Melbourne's song about a glow-worm. 'In the end, that sound came from listening to water dripping off a pile of dishes in the kitchen sink.'[1]

These songs were not at first intended to find an audience beyond the family. However, while on a visit to a marae in Hawera, Melbourne came across an elderly woman singing traditional songs about birds. Her songs were being recorded by Hami Mitchell, a trainee reporter from Radio New Zealand's Maori section. 'She started singing a song about a skylark, and it caught my ear – "Pipiteri, pipiteri, pipiteriteri" – so I sat down beside her.'

Melbourne told her about his song 'Te Rere a Tirairaka' – the flight of the fantail – and she asked him to sing it. 'We started swapping songs. She'd sing a song about pipiwharauroa, and I'd do one of mine, and of course by this time I'd quite forgotten Hami was recording them.' Mitchell returned to Wellington to edit the tape. It happened to be during the build-up to Maori Language Week in 1977, and children's radio producer David Somerset walked past the studio and heard the songs. 'At the time, he was introducing the birdcalls prior to the news and wanted to do a small section on each bird – a bit of a story about the bird, and a song about it – so he arranged for me to record them. There was an amazing response during that week, and it took off from there.'

In Maori terms, Hirini Melbourne is a tangata puoro – a man of music. As such, he does not undertake composition lightly.

> The Maori did not compose just for the sake of it, but for a specific reason. If you walked along whistling it was said you had a ghostly companion – a spirit travelling along beside you. If you were on the ocean and you began whistling, you'd be asked if you were trying to whistle up the wind, because the wind is the whistle's friend and that's not a good thing to happen at sea. That sort of music making was not wise. You needed to have a reason for singing.

Melbourne has analysed the origins of the reasons for singing and of their loss, and of the corollary fragmentation of traditional musical forms and instrumental knowledge. 'There are a number of traditions which talk about the origins of music. I particularly like the Kai Tahu one. It begins, "Te waiata tangimai te atua ko te timutanga o te ao" – "the gods sang and the world came into being." Our music started when the gods created the universe – when sound made things happen.' Musical sound, therefore, was the extension of thought into the physical world, and a potent force for weaving together the flux of the spiritual and the material. Ngati Porou used the purerehua to summon rain; in the south the same instrument is known as the hamumu ira garara, and was used to lure lizards out of their holes. A porotiti whirled over the chest of a sleeping child would relieve the congestion of a cold or flu; the same instrument could also help alleviate the pain of rheumatism and arthritis. 'You could play a koauau to make a baby and to stop a baby being made. Entertainment was music's least important function. In all its forms, music was tied up with the deities who governed everything they did in everyday life.'

However, this music was fragile by its very nature. Traditional forms were often highly tapu and therefore surrounded by restrictions. They were kept in the hands of a few old people, and taught very formally to the youngest generation – much like carving and other specialised forms of knowledge. The disease and epidemics which followed the encounter with Pakeha took their greatest toll on the old and the young, devastating the oral preservation and transmission of musical knowledge. The situation was compounded by the fact that instrument manufacture and technique were highly specialised art-forms, and therefore already fragmented: not only were making and playing different skills, but performers tended to specialise in one instrument. 'The knowledge was never widespread, so you just had to take a few people out from one particular generation, and you'd lost the whole tradition.' Pakeha instruments, on the other hand, were not in the least tapu. 'They took to them with great glee and great expertise. In fact, Pakeha musical instruments – especially metal jew's harps – were often stipulated as part of land transactions.'

Although Melbourne maintains that the tradition was becoming fragmented well before the arrival of missionaries, Christianisation inevitably took its own toll on the rituals, the language and the ceremonies with which the music was associated. 'And of course the new God brought new sounds, too. A new voice liberated the Maori voice – open-throat singing. Suddenly the valleys were echoing with hallelujahs. They took to the voice of the new God with great glee.' Traditionally, singing had been characterised by a closed-throat technique, which still has its place in moteatea and manawawera. 'Closed-throat singing requires a certain amount of control. The ability to maintain composure was paramount no matter what the occasion.' The song form which evolved from the two cultures meeting – the waiata a ringa or action song – had no formal restrictions. 'It became a very popular means by which Maori people expressed themselves.'

Melbourne dates his commitment to the revival of traditional instrumental knowledge to a family trip to the Auckland War Memorial Museum, where he caught his first glimpse of a putorino – an aerophone about a foot long, widest in the middle and tapering at each end – lying in a glass case. 'It made me very curious, not only because I couldn't hear its voice, but because it was identified with my own tribal area. I wanted to find out more about it. Why was it in the museum? Who gave it to them? That was really the beginning of my journey to find out who we were, and what we were, musically.'

In the early 1980s, Te Puna Waihanga – an organisation spearheaded by artists Para Matchitt, Cliff Whiting, Ara Wilson and Hone Tuwhare – had been formed to support and promote the work of Maori artists and writers. The group planned a hui on koauau for 1981, to be held in Te Araroa. 'I knew one or two other people who were interested, so we shot up there. Joe Malcolm – Koauau Joe – was there as a kaumatua. I'd known him in Wellington, but he was the only player I knew then.' Malcolm too was in pursuit of lost knowledge about traditional instruments; others at the hui had also set off down the same road. 'I met Richard Nunns there, who was already a very competent player, and another Pakeha guy called Brian Flintoff, who was a maker. But I didn't do very well at that workshop. I was a smoker in those days, and couldn't produce a sound from the thing.' Nunns and Flintoff had known each other previously – 'they'd already got their heads together to copy some koauau they'd seen in museums' – but it was Nunns who grabbed Melbourne's attention. 'It was the metaphor he used. He said that traditional Maori knowledge was a mat. The different art-forms make up the warp and weft, but the strand holding the musical tradition together had been severed. I went up to him afterwards and said, "Let's fix it, then."' The job required a combined effort, and the sharing of knowledge and skills. Nunns and Flintoff had liked Melbourne's songs about birds, and proposed that he write a song for each kind of instrument. 'I told them I'd need to know about the instruments, and learn how to play them. That's really how we started. I gave up smoking and concentrated on the one thought in my mind – learning how to play the instruments so I could hear their voices.'

Together and separately, Melbourne and Nunns travelled to marae, talking to the old people about their most distant memories, and returning to them with their developments. 'We found that hearing an instrument, or seeing it, was very important for people. I'd been going around the Waikato, asking old people if they knew about the koauau. Nobody knew anything until I showed them one. It turned out they had a totally different name for it – they called it the whio.' Wherever they went, they found talking about instruments unlocked far distant memories. 'We were talking to people in their nineties, and they were remembering not their parents, but their grandparents. The traditions died out very early, so these were memories going back before the nineteenth century.' Some instruments were reconstructed from oral accounts: the ororuarangi – a flute made from the long neck of a gourd or a long bone such as an albatross's, with two finger holes placed side by side at the centre – had not been noted in the literature or found in museums. It was remembered as having a voice that leapt large intervals, not unlike yodelling or leaping into falsetto. 'We came across all sorts of interesting things. We even found an old man who had been taught how to play the putorino in the traditional manner. What we know about playing the putorino comes directly from him. All the other instruments are found in other indigenous cultures, but the putorino seems to be unique to Aotearoa.'

Melbourne did not hear the voice of the putorino – the instrument he'd seen languishing in a glass case in Auckland – until 1982. He has since made it his special study. 'Even when I heard the putorino played for the first time, I knew I had heard it before, as I was growing up. It was the sound of the voices of the old men and women. It was the sound of the water and of the wind. It was not a new sound.' The instrument dismissed by ethnomusicologist Mervyn McLean as an acoustic failure[2] is in fact two instruments in one, its 'male' and 'female' voices suggested by Johannes C. Andersen's 1934 description of the putorino as an 'alto bugle-flute'.[3] Thirty to sixty centimetres long, the putorino tapers to a mouthpiece at one end and to a tiny aperture at the other; a figure-of-eight tone hole marks the instrument's widest mid-point. In shape, it resembles the pupa stage of the native bag moth or case moth, also called the putorino. 'The case moth has an interesting life-cycle: egg, caterpillar, chrysalis, but only the male emerges with wings.' The story goes that the female case moth – Hinerauka-tauri, the goddess of flute music – remains in the cocoon, and sings. The male hears her voice. They mate, and the male immediately dies. 'Unfortunately, the kokako also heard her voice, and ate her. That's how we hear the voice of Raukatauri: through the kokako. The stories give us an idea of what sort of sounds we're looking for, and of playing techniques.' [CD track 10]

Putorino also means 'bringing together three voices'. Melbourne produces three quite distinct sounds from the instrument: the trumpet-like male cry, the softer flute-like female sound, and the low thrumming sound of the kokako. The instrument also 'brings together three voices' in that it can be played for the sound of the instrument alone, the player can also add his voice to that of the instrument by speaking or singing through it, and every now and again a third 'spirit' voice appears – occasionally, when two putorino are being played together, the frequencies of the instruments overlap, resulting in a third pitch. 'It feels as though there's somebody behind you, singing. Usually a female voice. It doesn't happen often, and when it does it's quite spooky.'

Melbourne recently discovered that the putorino is triple in yet another way. 'We'd heard talk about the secret of the putorino – that it had three parts. They're made in two parts from wood that splits along a straight grain, and then bound together. We couldn't work it out. We presumed the two halves of the instrument plus the binding made three parts, but it didn't seem like a very good secret.' When Flintoff and Melbourne heard of a damaged instru-ment at Te Papa, they persuaded the museum not to repair it until they had

had a chance to examine it. 'We just needed to encourage that last thread of binding to fray.' Inside, they found the secret. 'From the outside, it looks like it's just been hollowed out and joined, but when you open it up you see there's a straight bore at the top end where you blow, which opens out into an open chamber under the finger aperture, and then narrows right down to the end. So the inside is in three distinct parts.' This terminal conical bore means that back pressure builds up inside the instrument, enabling the player to sustain notes. 'We'd been using straight bores, and of course you just run out of breath.' Melbourne and Nunns have since established that all traditional flutes – koauau, nguru and porutu – had tapered bores.

The audiocassette and booklet *Toiapiapi* (1991),[4] the first commercial recording of the taonga puoro (treasured musical instruments) and the songs Melbourne had written for them, was the result of ten years' research by Melbourne and Nunns, and makers Brian Flintoff and Clem Melish. Many of the waiata on *Toiapiapi* – the name mimics the sound of birdsong – speak of, and for, the wairua of the birds. In turn, the wairua of the birds sing through the singer and the instruments.

> Song is a way of conveying greeting from one realm to the other. Whakapapa is not just about identifying yourself as a beneficiary of a particular tribal authority. It's also about relating yourself to other beings sharing the same space. Birds and insects are seen as brothers and sisters through the same progenitor. Those are very important concepts to understand. They're not hierarchical links. They're lateral ones.

Other waiata were specially composed to convey the name and the use of a particular instrument. The simple text of the waiata aroha composed for the nguru, for example, makes plain Melbourne's position on the playing technique of this controversial instrument:[5]

Ko te ngu o taku ihu
mohou e te tau.
Ko te tuki a taku manawa
mohou e te tau.

The sigh from my nose
is for you, my love.
The beat of my heart
is for you, my love.

Although an expensive coffee-table format had been suggested for *Toiapiapi* and its accompanying booklet, its final modest form stemmed from an injunction from the old people who had given their permission for the instruments to be used. 'They told us that the instruments and their secrets had been given to us freely, and that they wanted any resource material to be accessible to the people who were the rightful inheritors of the tradition.' Melbourne's guitar features in many of the songs. 'Instead of making a leap into the past, we decided to take a middle road. It was really done to entice people – young people in particular. We wanted to show that the old instruments needn't be restricted to just ritual performance. They can also take their place in a modern setting.' The first edition sold out in a matter of weeks, and *Toiapiapi* was re-released in 1993 and 1995. 'It still gets a great response from teachers and kids. The kids say, "Oh, sir, don't play that music. It's too spooky." That's the type of feedback I really like. It tells me the sound does something for them, and they respond to it, but the only way they can verbalise it is to say it's spooky.'

Melbourne believes the response the children are struggling to articulate finds a parallel in the Maori concepts of ihi, wehi and whana. 'Those three words sum up Maori responses to the environment, to listening to music, and to performance.' Ihi is similar to awe: a psychological, emotional response with its own physical manifestations – goose pimples or raised hair on the back of the neck. Wehi is a response to the presence of powerful psychic forces. 'I took some mates up to the Waipoua forest, told them to close their eyes and stood them in front of Tane Mahuta, the great kauri. When they opened their eyes the air just got sucked out of them, and they fell to the ground on their knees. They knew they were in the presence of the God of the Forest.' Whana is for the ephemeral.

> It's what people mean when they say, 'You should have been there.' It's for the moment of the performance. I think the kids were going through those experiences. But now they have no way of acknowledging that except by clapping, and somehow that whole thing is broken, because when you perform it's not you performing. The spirits of the ancestors have entered you. You've become them during the performance.

The taonga puoro themselves also have a wairua or life force, which to a large extent dictates the shape of the relationship between player and taonga. 'Everything has its own life force – animate and inanimate objects as well. You provide the breath that gives a voice to the taonga, but the music is a combination of the two.' The carving on the instruments makes this collaboration quite explicit: the face of the object itself is the most common form of decoration. 'You can tell by looking at the instrument how it's meant to be played. If it's got a single nostril, that's the end you play. If it's got two nostrils at the other end, that's where the combined sound emerges – your breath plus the wairua of the instrument.' The function of each instrument is determined by the category to which it belongs, and by the deity who rules its material. 'They're in the material, and in the process of making. They're still there in the process of music-making, so when you perform you're not only playing to people. You're also playing to the deity, to the thing surrounding that particular instrument and its particular voice.'

For *Te Ku Te Whe*,[6] their next collaboration, Melbourne and Nunns decided the taonga puoro didn't need the support of the modern guitar: the only sounds on the recording are those of bone, stone, wood, shell and the human voice. 'The Tuhoe whakapapa that accounts for the origins of the spiritual and physical world includes the origin of sound: te ku me te whe. Te ku are the softer sounds associated with the forest and the birds, and te whe are the sharp sounds which include the metallic sounds. As I'm a bush person, that's where I start from.' 'Purerehua' is composed around the sound of the bullroarer. 'Tangi Koauau' demonstrates the sound of koauau made of five different materials, and 'Poiawhiowhio' features instruments which imitate bird calls, including the karanga weka. 'We wouldn't have known about this instrument without Brian. It's a good example of the process of recovery of knowledge about these taonga.' On a visit to the Hall of Mankind at the British Museum, Flintoff found an unusual small stone flute identified simply as 'weka call'. The instrument no longer existed in New Zealand and appeared to be one of a kind. He made a replica and brought it back; the original remains in the British Museum.

The idea for *Te Ku Te Whe* came from Keith Hill, one of the co-founders of Rattle Records. In 1993, Rattle had produced their first CD: *Different Tracks* was a compilation of new New Zealand music, and included a short version of the tangi 'Raureka'.[7] 'They were amazed by the interest it generated. For a lot of people it was their first contact with traditional instruments. Keith asked us if we'd like to do our own CD, and we said, "Yeah! We'll do it!"'

The pair were given a week of studio time.

> Richard and I walked in and had a talk. We felt we'd come a long way on our journey to repair the mat of sound, so we decided to use the idea of the whariki or mat that is traditionally laid out at birth and death. We'd roll out the birth mat – the birth of sound – with instruments which were used to make important announcements: the long pukaea trumpet and the conch-shell trumpet or putatara.

> Then we'd simply weave the sounds together until we got from one end of the mat to the other, and end it whenever we wanted to, with takapau tuwhara – the rolling-up of the mat at the end of life. Once we got over all the technical problems, we just laid out all the instruments and moved from one to the other, from one idea to the other. We did it in a day and a half.

Nunns and Melbourne assembled a repertoire of their own compositions for *Te Ku Te Whe*. 'We didn't use existing or traditional waiata because they're taonga, and they're tribally owned. The tribe they belong to are their guardians, and we'd have had to obtain their permission to use them. It's a tricky area.' Travelling around talking to people about the instruments, Melbourne observed marked differences in attitudes to the preservation of traditional knowledge. 'Only a few men know about the tradition, and they give out that information sparingly, but women are the opposite. They know a lot more, but they are also more willing to share what they know. Men seem to have the notion that somehow their mana, their life force, is tied up with that knowledge and if they give it away they're left like an empty vessel.'

Those differences manifest themselves not only along gender lines. A hui about the future of nga moteatea, convened by Melbourne and held at the University of Waikato in 1998, split over the issue of the guardianship of traditional song forms. 'Before we got together, everybody was clear that moteatea was a dying art-form, and that something pretty amazing needed to be done to arrest its demise. The purpose of the hui was to see how we could revive the tradition and develop it.' Extensive audio and video recordings were to be made so the hui itself could later be used as a resource. Although all participating groups had agreed before the meeting to share their taonga, a group from Ngati Porou decided they could not allow their sessions to be recorded. 'I asked this group why they'd changed their attitude, and they said they were in the middle of a Waitangi Tribunal hearing about intellectual property rights and flora and fauna. They felt their property rights extended to moteatea.' No session on copyright had been planned, and the issue became a burning one.

> One speaker put it beautifully. He said, 'Exchanging gifts has always been part of our culture. We call it tukutaonga. If you give a cherished gift in the right way, you know it will be looked after, and passed through the generations.' He said he'd come to the hui with his kete, from which he would give gifts, and in return he'd take away gifts that had been given by others.

This kaupapa appealed to many people, but the problem remained. By the end of the hui, a substantial archive had been amassed, and Melbourne told participants of his plans for an audio and video resource kit. 'Before I could do that, though, I told them there were copyright issues we needed to address, and I asked them for permission to go ahead with it. Of course everyone said yes.' Then the group from the East Coast – by that time reduced to two hard-liners – asked Melbourne for the conference package. 'I just smiled and I shook my head. I think it resolved itself quite nicely. Ngati Porou have since joined a group trying to raise the level of debate over the issue.'

Other groups came to the hui with a less conservative attitude. 'Tuhoe talked about a song called "Taku Rakau" they had released for use in schools, to assist the process of reviving the language. They felt that by restricting access you're also helping the demise of the tradition.' The host people, Tainui, had their own story. After the wars in the Waikato, the government confiscated the lands of the Tainui hapu Ngati Apakura. They became refugees in their own land and migrated to the Taupo area, where most succumbed to disease.[8] The lament 'E pa to hau', written after the death of Te Wano, who had been leading Ngati Apakura out of Tainui, is now sung throughout Aotearoa. 'The host people said it gave them a sense of pride that their memories were being preserved by others. It's as good a way as any to confront the loss of land, the loss of language and the loss of culture: by sharing our stories and our burdens we can overcome our sense of loss, and maintain our dignity and our unity as a people.'

1 Melbourne's waiata about the bush and its creatures are collected on *Te Wao Nui a Tane* (Wellington: Huia, 1999). This book and CD won the non-fiction section of the New Zealand Post Children's Book Awards in 2000. Waiata on urban themes, conservation, education and unemployment are collected on *Hinepukohurangi* (Wellington: Radio New Zealand Replay Radio Audiocassette, n.d.), *Te Matauranga* (Hamilton: Kia Ata Mai Educational Trust Audiocassette, n.d.) and *Toiapiapi* (Wellington: Shearwater Associates Audiocassette, 1991.)

2 'It is apparent that the puutoorino was a compromise instrument, perhaps explaining its early obsolescence. It was evidently not very effective in any of its applications.' Mervyn McLean, *Maori Music* (Auckland: Auckland University Press, 1996), p.184.

3 Johannes C. Andersen, *Maori Music with its Polynesian Background* (New Plymouth: Avery, 1934), p.273.

4 Hirini Melbourne, *Toiapiapi: He huinga o nga kura puoro a te Maori* [Toiapiapi: a celebration of the traditional instruments of the Maori] (Wellington, Shearwater Associates: 1991).

5 The playing method of the nguru or nose flute has been the centre of considerable controversy. Notwithstanding Richard Nunns's success at producing a focused and musical sound from the instrument using a nose-blowing technique, ethnomusicologist Mervyn McLean maintains it is unlikely that such a method was much used (see *Maori Music*, pp.189-94). Melbourne's attitude is even-handed: '[The nguru] can indeed be played with the mouth koauau-style. However it can also be played with the nose, producing a sobbing, weeping voice. In this it has a similar quality to the sounds of a person in distress. So where does the truth lie? Whatever, it can be played with both the mouth and the nose.' (Hirini Melbourne, *Toiapiapi* booklet: pp.32-3).

6 Hirini Melbourne and Richard Nunns, *Te Ku Te Whe* (Rattle CD, RAT D004, 1994).

7 *Different Tracks* (Rattle CD, RAT D003, 1993).

8 Sir Apirana Ngata, *Nga Moteatea, Vol. 1* (Auckland: Polynesian Society, 1959), pp.236-7.

Wilma Smith : Family Matters

Having children has put into perspective all of the wonderful things I might have done professionally. The family is more important to me than anything else.

Violinist Wilma Smith (born 1956) has been the concertmaster of the New Zealand Symphony Orchestra since 1993. Although she had already been playing professionally for fifteen years, her appointment raised a few eyebrows. Quite apart from the fact that she was a woman in a position usually occupied by men, a good deal of her prior ensemble experience had been gained not in symphony orchestras but in string quartets, initially as the founding first violinist of the Boston-based Lydian String Quartet and later as the foundation player of the New Zealand String Quartet. 'I think the people who were surprised at my appointment didn't realise that playing in string quartets is actually a fantastic preparation for being a concertmaster. In a quartet you're playing as a soloist all the time. Your ears have to be developed to an extraordinary extent. It's the best musical education on earth.'

Smith was born in Suva. Although she was not yet five when her family emigrated to New Zealand, Wilma has vivid memories of Fiji, especially of extended visits to her mother's parents' home in Levuka on the island of Ovalau. A combination of factors led to Margery and William Smith's decision to move to New Zealand. William Smith, a marine engineer, suffered from a kidney disorder and, during a holiday visit to New Zealand, doctors told him the tropical climate was not helping his condition. New Zealand also promised professional and educational opportunities, and by 1961 the family had settled in Mt Eden.

Wilma started private piano lessons at the age of eight, and within a year she had begun group violin lessons at Maungawhau Primary School, where the energetic and enthusiastic music teacher insisted everyone should learn an instrument. 'He gave us all ear tests, and if you could hold a tune he suggested one of the harder instruments, and even if you couldn't he gave you a recorder to play.' Wilma was offered a violin and, although she had never heard of the instrument or even seen one before, she began lessons with nine other children under the watchful eye of teacher Helen Hopkins. 'We must've just got a TV, because one of the things she taught us was the theme from *Bonanza*.'

Her first private teacher was Violet Lewis, who was largely self-taught – and a tennis fan.

> She'd liken the follow-through of a great tennis swing to the follow-through of a bow stroke. Her teaching of the fundamentals of sound production was so solid that I only needed to make minor adjustments later.

Lewis was already fairly elderly when Wilma started learning from her, and when she retired she gave Wilma her violin. 'I was still playing it in the States.'

By the time Wilma left school she was studying violin with Heather Smith, herself a former student of Lewis, and intended to continue with her. Piano lessons with Rosemary Mathers, then studying at the University of Auckland with piano lecturer Janetta McStay, edged Wilma towards piano study at university.

> I'd been in the top stream at Epsom Girls' Grammar and lots of my friends were aspiring to be doctors and lawyers, but I wasn't motivated enough to push myself that hard. I did just enough to get by. Music won out for me because it was what I could do best, with least effort. It was only later that I realised it was going to be very hard work. But to begin with, I did it because it was the most natural and easiest thing to do.

Smith had been at university for more than a year, studying piano with both McStay and Bryan Sayer, before she decided to change to violin. 'I hadn't yet learned to apply myself, and of course Janetta knew it. The piano finally got on top of me. When I told Janetta I was going to switch, she said, "Bryan *will* be relieved."' Smith completed her violin studies with David Nalden. 'David was very methodical and meticulous, and taught with a definite system. He was especially particular about technical foundations: he took all his students back to open strings.'

Ironically, however, Nalden's regime meant that Smith nearly missed out on an experience that would help determine her future. When applications were called for the New Zealand National Youth Orchestra (NYO) of 1974, she was still working on open strings, and therefore unable to audition. Although that was disappointment enough in itself, the Youth Orchestra planned an extensive international tour for 1975, and membership of the touring orchestra would be drawn from the pool of 1974 players. 'I hadn't been playing in the orchestra in 1974, so I wasn't really eligible to go on the tour. In the end I snuck into the 1975 orchestra because I played the piano as well as the violin: one of the works needed a pianist and they didn't want to take an extra person just for that.'

The NYO was only the second orchestra to visit China after the Cultural Revolution – the Philadelphia Orchestra had been there just before them – and the players received the warmest of welcomes. 'We were treated like royalty wherever we went.' The political atmosphere, however, was still highly repressive. 'We were told what we could and couldn't play. Beethoven was out, for example, because the authorities felt he wrote "absolute" music, and of course music that didn't have any meaning outside itself was decadent intellectuals' music. Music was supposed to further the cause of the revolution.' Conductor Ashley Heenan's programme for China included *The White-haired Girl*, 'written by a committee of Chinese composers', Kodály's *Dances of Galanta* and John Ritchie's *Concertino for Clarinet and Strings*, played by the young Christchurch clarinettist Keith Spragg.

On the same trip, the NYO attended the International Festival of Youth Orchestras in Aberdeen, which culminated in a combined orchestra concert in London. 'The combined orchestra played Richard Strauss's *Death and Transfiguration* in the Albert Hall, under Claudio Abbado. It was an absolute revelation – a very special concert for everyone, I think. At the end of the performance Abbado had tears pouring down his face.' The tour marked a turning-point in Smith's life. 'Before that, music had been something I'd fallen into, and did, and it was fun, but I'd never really considered it as a career. After that I never seriously considered anything else.'

With professional music now firmly in her sights, Smith moved to Wellington in 1976 to study with Peter Schaffer, newly appointed as concertmaster of the NZSO. Although she joined the NZSO the following year as a rank and file member, she was not yet ready to settle down: 'I knew I was going to study more overseas, so my job with the NZSO was temporary.' Her decision about where to study was not as straightforward as it might have been for someone in her position even ten years previously. 'We were fairly big on Royal Schools and Trinity College exams in this country, so there was still that colonial pull to the motherland, and people a bit ahead of me were still heading in that direction. But by the time I came along the tide was turning. People were branching out a bit more.' She even considered studying in the Soviet Union. 'I went to the extent of starting to learn Russian, so I must have been pretty serious about it.'

Peter Schaffer presented studying in the United States as a viable alternative to the London colleges, and Smith applied to music schools in the USA. She was offered a place at the New England Conservatory in Boston, but Schaffer instead encouraged her to study with his own former teacher Roman Totenberg, then teaching at the Longy School in Boston. 'While I realised that Roman Totenberg was – and is – a terrific teacher, I found the school itself didn't really suit my needs. It's changed now, but in those days it was very small – a kind of community college.'

Smith arrived in Boston on a Friday afternoon. After a brief visit to the Longy School she spent the weekend considering her options, and the following Monday presented herself at the New England Conservatory. 'I told them I'd already turned down a place at the conservatory, but that I'd had a change of heart.' As it turned out, the New England Conservatory was short of violin students. 'They pulled my file out from the bottom drawer, and there I was.' Almost by chance she found herself in the class of violin guru Dorothy DeLay. 'Everybody seemed to be putting DeLay down at the top of their list of teacher preferences, so I thought she must be all right and did the same. Looking back, I was appallingly ignorant, because she was probably the most famous violin teacher in the States at the time, and I didn't know anything about her.' Twice a month DeLay commuted to Boston from her teaching base at the Juilliard School in New York to give masterclasses; in the alternate weeks, her students had lessons with her assistant Hyo Kang. 'It was a terrific system for me: you had to actually get up and perform in front of your fellow students every two weeks, and the private lessons were with someone who was an excellent teacher in his own right. It was the best of both worlds.'

Another major musical influence in Boston was violinist and teacher Louis Krasner, with whom Smith studied chamber music at the New England Conservatory.

> He taught me to listen, which was probably the most important thing I learned in my time in Boston. You don't learn to listen in one easy lesson – it's not that simple

> at all. It was gleaned over the course of many chamber music coachings with him, and also in some individual sessions. His comments led me to start listening much more closely. I started to hear things I wouldn't have noticed before. I learned that ear training is the most important thing for a musician: you must learn to listen, and listen every split second.

Not long after her arrival in the US, a stroke of good fortune opened a path to professional work in Boston. During her first summer, she attended a two-week summer school in Sarasota, Florida, where Joseph Silverstein, the concertmaster of the Boston Symphony Orchestra, was tutoring violin. He had brought with him his young son, an aspiring horn player. Smith's chamber group had prepared Brahms's trio for violin, horn and piano, and Silverstein took his son along to hear the work. In effect, the performance was an informal audition: 'Next season I was surprised and thrilled to be asked to do some casual work with the BSO, which spilled over into lots of other interesting freelancing in Boston.' Smith went straight from Sarasota to the summer music school at Aspen, Colorado, where Dorothy DeLay was in residence. 'She encouraged all her students to go. That year, I played in a chamber orchestra with Itzhak Perlman – a former student of DeLay – who was playing and directing some Mozart violin concerti.'

Smith made the most of the musical opportunities Boston offered. Although her studies at the New England Conservatory became increasingly fragmented, other activities more than compensated for the disruption. Freelancing with the BSO brought first-hand experience of some of the world's great soloists and conductors. 'Simon Rattle was still quite young then, but he had such conviction and focused energy and intensity.' At the time, the BSO would hold open rehearsals immediately before concerts, for which tickets could be purchased at a reduced price. Audiences would come expecting a concert performance. 'Rattle still had quite a bit of rehearsing to do, so he stopped and started, and went over things. At the end of the rehearsal, he was actually booed. There was hardly any applause and we all wandered off the stage. I admired his fortitude: he was absolutely uncompromising about his musical priorities.' Kurt Masur also impressed the young violinist. 'It was fascinating to see what makes a great conductor – to see the charisma and authority, both personal and musical, which lets them hold sway over ninety-odd hard-core professionals. Kurt Masur had that sort of stature. Then of course there were the soloists who visited – people like Perlman, Yo Yo Ma, and Jessye Norman.' Boston was also a lively centre for period instrument performance of baroque and classical music. Smith freelanced with Banchetto Musicale and performed at the 'Mostly Mozart' festival in New York in a period instrument orchestra conducted by Christopher Hogwood.

At the end of 1980, Smith's second year in Boston, another musical opportunity presented itself. Robert Koff, a former member of the Juilliard Quartet, was teaching violin at Brandeis University on the outskirts of Boston. Koff wanted to establish a string quartet in residence at Brandeis, to teach and perform on campus. 'At that stage it was very part-time, so they couldn't hope to attract a well-established quartet. They were rather thinking they might put one together.' Smith had been playing with a violist at the New England Conservatory, and she knew another violinist, who knew a cellist. 'We threw ourselves together, and spent two days preparing an audition. Robert Koff must have thought we had potential, and offered us the position.' Despite the low pay, they decided to take the job. 'We were all at similar stages in our careers – everybody had just finished their studies and had no definite plans. It was an option that we felt didn't have too much risk involved: if it didn't work out after a year or so we could just abandon the idea.' After two years of expert coaching and guidance from Koff, the Lydian Quartet felt ready to test themselves on the international string quartet competition circuit.

> Our first competition was in Evian in France, then we did one in Banff in Canada, one in Portsmouth in England, and then the Naumburg Award in New York. We were placed in all of them, which was very nice, but we didn't win one until the Naumburg in 1984. That was a really good credential to bandy about, especially in the States, where everybody had heard of it.

Success in competitions gave the quartet an advantage in securing equally competitive concert bookings, especially after the Naumburg Award, which led to performances at the Los Angeles Olympic Arts Festival, the Library of Congress in Washington DC and the Alice Tully Hall at New York's Lincoln Center. 'But the best thing about the competition circuit was meeting lots of other quartets who were working around the world doing the same sort of thing. It's a very weird and wonderful lifestyle, and it takes another quartet player to understand what you go through.'

Apart from its musical distinction, the Lydian Quartet was notable for the fact that its members were all women. When the quartet was founded this was a rarity. 'The Primavera Quartet in New York had received lots of publicity as the first all-women string quartet in the United States, but I think we were the second all-female group that started to make a name for itself. We didn't use the fact particularly, but we didn't fight it, either.' Smith believes an all-women ensemble does have a 'special dynamic':

> A quartet is a complicated relationship, because it's a relationship between various pairs in the group. And there are lots of permutations of those pairs. So if you can imagine that your relationship with another woman is different from your relationship with a man – for whatever reasons – it's that, times quite a few. Any quartet is complicated, because they're one-on-one relationships, several times over. And then there's the collective voice, too. It's very interesting psychologically.

String quartet playing eventually brought Smith back to New Zealand. The Music Federation of New Zealand (now Chamber Music New Zealand) had decided to establish a national string quartet, to be funded by the federation, the Arts Council and the Stout Trust. The quartet would spend part of the year working intensively as a quartet, and part of the year in rank and file positions in the NZSO. 'The federation was scouting around looking for likely candidates. Because I was involved with the Lydian Quartet, and had kept in touch with Elisabeth Airey, the general manager of the federation, she had me in mind as a candidate for the first violin position.' Airey approached Smith in Boston and asked if she would be interested in putting together the New Zealand quartet. 'It wasn't an easy decision for me, but it seemed that, if I was going to come home at all, this was at the right time and for the right job. About two years after making that decision I actually was back, so it took quite a while to get it all going.'

As first violin, Smith was responsible for assembling the rest of the quartet, notwithstanding the logistics of living in Boston. 'I came home for a few weeks at the beginning of 1987, having arranged for all sorts of other New Zealanders – living both in New Zealand and elsewhere – to gather at my parents' house in Auckland. I devised a complicated scheme whereby everybody got to play with everybody else in various quartet formations.' Smith's roster resulted in three-quarters of a quartet: the New Zealand violinist Gillian Ansell had been studying in Germany and at the Royal College of Music in London; Smith and cellist Josephine Young had known each other in Wellington, and later in New England. The three women travelled to Boston and London to audition violists, finally appointing Italian Sandro Costantino. The New Zealand String Quartet gave its first concerts in May 1988. Initially its members played part-time in the NZSO, but by 1990 it had become a full-time quartet. From the beginning it also had a close relationship with Victoria University of Wellington. 'They provided us with rehearsal space, and we did some teaching there. That became more and more full on as the quartet's involvement with the orchestra decreased.' In 1991 the quartet was appointed quartet-in-residence, teaching the performance string students and coaching chamber music. Smith counts as highlights of her years with the New Zealand String Quartet a Musica Viva tour of Australia, and recording Anthony Watson's three String Quartets.[1] 'Douglas Lilburn was the driving force behind that recording project. The Lilburn Trust made it financially possible.'

In 1992 the concertmaster's position in the NZSO became vacant. Pregnant with her daughter Jessye, Smith applied for the job. By the time of her audition, she was the only 'live' applicant left: all the other candidates were to be heard on tape. 'Auditions are held behind a screen to make sure they're anonymous, but I'm sure everybody knew it was me, and I certainly knew who was out there. It was a bit ludicrous, really, but I quite liked not having to look at them. It's hard enough to audition for your peers and people you grew up with without having to see them too.' Knowing the trial period which followed the audition would be drawn out by the birth of the baby, due in March 1993, Smith resigned from the quartet. 'It would have been unfair to keep them hanging around for another year while I found out, so I left the quartet at the end of 1992, not knowing whether I had the concertmaster's job or not.' Two and a half months after Jessye's birth, Smith began a three-month trial, and was appointed concertmaster in September 1993.

Although she came to the position with a wealth of chamber music experience, Smith found crucial differences between playing in a string quartet and leading a symphony orchestra.

> The biggest difference is that the orchestra has a conductor, whose job it is to shape the music. Everyone in the orchestra, including me, has to help the conductor's interpretation of the music come alive. Of course there are strong individual musical personalities in every orchestra and good conductors allow the musicians to flourish, but basically we're being given directions, and being told what to do. In a quartet that doesn't happen. You've got four people who have an equal say in how a piece is going to go, and therefore there's a great deal of negotiation and discussion. In the end you've got to come to a unified approach, otherwise it's not going to make sense to yourselves or to your audience. But to get to that point is a long haul, because you've got four very strong musical personalities who may not agree on everything.

As concertmaster, Smith's role is not purely musical. Apart from the extra hours spent adding bowing to her section's parts, she also attends meetings of the players' committee with the orchestral management. 'It's important to have information flowing both ways. The players need information about how the orchestra is being run, and the management team needs to have information about how the orchestra feels about things.'

Although Smith is passionate about music she does very little playing purely for her own amusement, without the incentive of a concert.

> We used to do it a lot as students – chamber music reading parties and things. But after twelve years of playing in two professional quartets, and having the satisfaction of playing something reasonably well, and in tune, and together, with all the work that represents, I can't imagine group sight-reading for the sake of it would be all that enjoyable any more. In fact, when I'm not doing something I need to do – practising, or working in the orchestra or whatever – I really like not having the violin with me. After concerts I like putting it on the truck and getting on the plane just with my handbag.

This apparent detachment belies the fact that Smith's violin is clearly more than a tool of trade. It is a Guadagnini made in 1761, which belonged to Eric Lawson, a former deputy leader of the NZSO. 'He very, very generously sold it to me for a fraction of its market value when I was still living in Boston. He didn't know at that point that I was going to be moving back to New Zealand.' When she did return, she was pleased to be able to bring the violin 'home' too, so Lawson could see it and play it regularly. 'During his last few years I'd visit him when I was in Auckland for concerts, and we'd play duets together. He had another violin which he continued to play until his death in late 1999.'

Despite her heavy schedule with the NZSO, Smith still finds time for chamber music: Felix the Quartet consists of Smith, plus other NZSO players Vesa-Matti Leppänen (violin), Andrew Thomson (viola) and Rowan Prior (cello). 'We did our first concerts in 2001 in Christchurch, Wellington, Waikanae and the Wairarapa. We've also begun touring for Chamber Music New Zealand.' Smith has also enjoyed a profound musical relationship with pianist Michael Houstoun, with whom she first collaborated in Washington DC in 1980. 'Playing with Michael has been an inspiration for me. I feel like I've done some of my best playing with him: he lifts me out of myself, because of his own consummate musicianship.' Smith has taken special pleasure in working with Houstoun on the Beethoven sonatas. 'I've enjoyed playing those just about more than anything.' [CD Track 11]

Smith also finds herself gravitating towards the orchestral repertoire of the classical period. 'I'm getting narrower in my choices now. I used to listen to lots of different music – rock and jazz as well as "classical" music – but now if I put something on it tends to be classical: a really good recording of the Beethoven symphonies, or a Mozart piano concerto.' In practice, however, Smith finds she rarely listens to music. 'Because it's such a big part of my life anyway it doesn't occur to me to go home and put the stereo on. More often it will occur to one of my daughters, or we'll listen to their Suzuki violin CDs while we're all busy in the kitchen.'

Smith's family is the mainspring of her life, and the measure by which she judges all her other achievements. She and her partner Peter Watt have three daughters: Jessye (named for Jessye Norman), Rosie and Sophie. Wilma and Peter first met 'a long time ago': Peter had been principal trombone on the 1975 NYO tour, and the two crossed paths again after Wilma's return to New Zealand. Now a computer consultant, Peter keeps normal office hours, and looks after the girls when Wilma is working at night. 'Our loyal nanny, Faye Hall, and my mother take over when we're both at work. Peter also has two children in Melbourne who have been regular visitors to Wellington for the last eleven years.'

Rosie, Wilma and Peter's second daughter, was born in January 1995. Her arrival was unusually spectacular.

> I have rather short labours. We only live five minutes from Wellington hospital but we still managed to be too late. We went through the barrier arm at the main gates of the hospital at 8.01 am, so we have a souvenir of her exact time of birth, because we had to take a little card with the time on it. About thirty seconds later, with Peter still speeding through the carpark and me in the back seat, there she was on my lap. I'd been in labour for about an hour and a half in total, but looking back on it, it was a very exciting way to have a baby.

Sophie's arrival in 1998 was even quicker. 'It was a forty-minute labour, but this time we made it to the hospital with about five minutes to spare.' Lenny, Wilma and Peter's first child, had also arrived quickly. 'Lenny was early – 34 weeks – but he weighed nearly six pounds, so at first he seemed quite healthy. But he had been infected by strep B. We only had him for twenty hours. You learn so much about grieving and about losing anything from an experience like that.' Lenny remains a member of the family. 'We visit his grave quite regularly, and the girls usually include him when counting the number of children in the family.'

The conditions of Smith's working life – the orchestra spends on average six weeks a year away from home – have largely suited her need for a balance between professional and maternal commitments. 'I've always felt that I wouldn't do well as a full-time mother. I like the variety of having a job as well: I was quite happy to go back to work about three months after the birth of each child.' Although she enjoys the fullness and the variety of her life, at times she feels a degree of frustration. 'I want to do my job to the best of my ability, and I also want to feel that I'm not seeing my kids just in a frazzled state. My short-term goal is to achieve that balance – and it's a very short-term goal, because kids are not small for very long. To do it I need to make more time.' She has become very efficient at working at the violin in her own time: 'practising well and purposefully is a necessity if it's to be fruitful in a very short time'. If attaining a relaxed blend of motherhood and professional life is Smith's short-term goal, her longer-term ambition is to consolidate both her personal and professional achievements. 'I want to be fully involved in whatever I'm doing, whether it's working on a piece in more depth, or sharing the girls' growing up in a full and calm way.'

Smith, now in her mid-forties, feels she has reached a 'mid-point' from which to evaluate her past and contemplate her future.

> I don't want to arrive at eighty and think, 'My God, what happened?' I want to arrive at old age with a calm understanding and acceptance of what I've done. I'm not saying I intend to get complacent in the second half of my life, but I do want to focus more. I'd like to have more time for my relationship, for instance. It's very easy to go for weeks – months, even – without any real time with your partner. You're in the same house and you're doing what has to be done, but not having time to hang out together. Peter's got a very responsible and consuming job too, so it's easy for our relationship to become the last priority, behind both our jobs and the children. My long-term goal is to focus on achieving the things I want to achieve in the rest of my life in a very calm, satisfying way.

1 *Anthony Watson: The String Quartets*, New Zealand String Quartet (Continuum CD, CCD 1065, 1994).

Peter Scholes : Connecting Threads

Towards the end of my studies I was spending almost as much time on the recorder as I was on the clarinet, but as the orchestra got busier the recorder became less important. Then more conducting work started coming in, and bigger commissions. It's been a shedding process, really: you extend your tentacles in all sorts of directions, but in the end some things have to go. There just aren't enough hours in the week.

During the 1980s, Peter Scholes (born 1957) was known throughout the country for his playing of the classical and romantic repertoire for solo clarinet, and for his advocacy of contemporary repertoire for the instrument. His own compositions placed him at the cutting edge of the contemporary music scene, while national tours with rock musician Ivan Zagni found him equally at home in improvisation-based idioms. As principal clarinet of the Auckland Philharmonia, he was familiar as an orchestral soloist; as the University of Auckland's 1988 Composer-in-Residence, he could be found exploring the acoustic properties of lengths of PVC piping fitted with clarinet mouthpieces. By the early 90s, however, something had to give. Since his resignation from the Auckland Philharmonia in 1993, he has continued to expand his career as a soloist, a composer and a conductor. 'If you study the successful people you know, you'll find they're never static. They're always aiming for somewhere else. Looking from the outside they may appear to be at the top of the heap, but ask and they'll tell you they're actually looking ahead for the next challenge.'

The youngest of five children, Peter Scholes grew up in Rotorua. Eric and Ena Scholes had emigrated from England in 1948 with their three older children, settling first in Titirangi, where Peter and his older brother Michael were born. However, the life of a dairy-owner did not suit the artistic and independent Eric. 'He'd been an aircraft engineer in England, and worked at De Havilland's during the war, but he always wanted to do his own thing.' The family moved to Rotorua. After a brief stint as moteliers, Eric and Ena Scholes bought the souvenir shop just outside the gates of Whakarewarewa. The souvenirs gave way to paintings and the Scholes Gallery quickly earned an impressive reputation as a dealer gallery in the lively arts and crafts scene of the 1960s. The business reflected the family's interest. 'My oldest brother, Jeff, was painting at that stage – he didn't become known as a potter until later – and my sister Rosemary married the art historian Peter Tomory. The house was full of artistic types. I remember an exhibition of Colin McCahon – one of his "Waterfall" series. Toss Woollaston and Gretchen Albrecht exhibited there as well.' The hallway between the gallery and the rest of the house was devoted to the work of the family's youngest artist. 'It was *my* gallery.' One night, while the rest of the family was preoccupied with an exhibition opening, the small boy sat behind the door into the hallway making his own paintings. 'I wrote "Two shillings" on the bottom of them and poked them under the door into the exhibition space. I think my cheek caused more of a stir than my talent.'

Scholes's musical talent proved rather more exceptional. As a third-former at Auckland Grammar School, he sat the standard musical aptitude test and the results indicated that he should learn an instrument. He was assigned a clarinet and a teacher: the highly regarded and much-loved clarinettist George Hopkins, then working as an itinerant teacher in Auckland secondary schools, gave Peter his first lessons. 'We had a recording of the Mozart clarinet quintet at home. At my first lesson my teacher picked up the clarinet and suddenly someone was making that same gorgeous sound, in the flesh. It took literally ten seconds, and I was hooked.' Sadly, Hopkins died little more than a year later, but those ten seconds had already determined the direction of Scholes's future.

Although the atmosphere of Auckland Grammar tended to induce a certain self-consciousness in musical students – 'I carried my clarinet case around in a duffle bag so it looked like it had rugby boots in it' – boarding school proved an ideal environment for establishing a practice routine. Impressed by his dedication, the school music master Ray Wilson gave Scholes a key to the music room. 'There was nothing to do from half past three until six, so I'd go in there every afternoon and do two hours' undisturbed practice.'

At the end of his seventh-form year, Scholes found he had been offered places at both the University of Auckland's School of Music and Auckland Medical School. 'I don't even remember deliberating about it. I wanted to see where music would take me.'

At university, Scholes came under the influence of another remarkable clarinet teacher. Lessons with Ken Wilson were tightly structured around the acquisition of fundamental musical skills. 'Learning technique and repertoire is as basic as learning your times tables. There's only one way to do it: you have to work.' Scholes rose to the challenge of Wilson's demanding régime. 'He was a wonderful player and a wonderful musician, but his standards were absolutely uncompromising. If you worked through what he set you, it would take four or five hours, every day. Then he'd listen, and if it wasn't right he'd tell you. He went straight for the jugular. My usual post-lesson feeling was a mixture of trauma and elation.' But lessons were not all hard work. Scholes was then a member of the early music ensemble Digorie, in which he played the recorder, the chalumeau – the seventeenth-century predecessor of the clarinet – and the crumhorn. 'I remember one mad session with Ken, sight-reading through some early music. I was playing a crumhorn and he was playing a virginal that my father had made.' Wilson would invite all his students out to his tiny cottage at Greenhithe for evenings of clarinet ensemble playing. 'We'd play everything from arrangements of Vivaldi violin concerti and Haydn string quartets to Ken's own *Variations on a Theme of Paganini* for clarinet quartet. It was a terrific way to develop intonation and musicianship skills.' Wilson also secured Scholes his first professional work. 'Ken was doing a lot of session work for Radio New Zealand, and he'd get me along playing second clarinet. It was great experience.'

The young clarinettist also made the most of orchestral playing opportunities offered by the National Youth Orchestra, the Auckland Youth Orchestra and the Cambridge Music School. 'We covered a huge amount of repertoire at Cambridge. It was fantastic: real hands-on orchestral experience, with conductors like John Hopkins and Georg Tintner, and top tutors from all round the country. It was really important continuity between each university year.' At the same time, Scholes began extending his clarinet technique to encompass the remote reaches of the contemporary solo repertoire. 'I was drawn to the most horrendously difficult pieces, like Stockhausen's *Amour* for solo clarinet. It took a phenomenal amount of practice.' He would take these works to Wilson for comment. 'Ken would help with the tricky bits, but in those days people were trying to make some pretty weird noises on the clarinet, and I'm not sure how much he approved of all that.' Scholes is now tempted to concede Wilson's point. 'While it's quite nice to be able to use extended techniques in live performance, electronic technology has pretty much taken over that job now. But electronics can't emulate lyricism and beauty – for that you need live instrumental music, and a soul.'

In 1979, when Scholes was three years into his four-year music degree, a position came up in the Symphonia of Auckland. He knew if he didn't grab that chance, it might be years before he had another. But no sooner was he settled in the second clarinet's chair than he found himself without a job: the Symphonia collapsed in July 1980, in acrimonious circumstances. 'When it went bust, we were all technically unemployed. It was all a bit traumatic, and a whole bunch of people disappeared. Many of the players wouldn't have a bar of anything other than a fully contracted salaried position, and there just wasn't the money around to guarantee that kind of security.' A core of musicians from the old Symphonia decided to form a new, player-run orchestra, and the Auckland Regional Orchestra gave its first concerts in November 1980 under conductor Georg Tintner. Players oversaw programming and the appointment of administrative, managerial and musical staff. 'The Auckland Philharmonia is basically still run like that. It's a very unusual structure, internationally.'

However, the new orchestra could pay its musicians only for each performance, and its schedule filled only six months of the year. Developing other musical interests was a financial and personal imperative for Scholes. 'Even though I was just a spring chicken, virtually straight out of university, Janetta McStay invited me to join the Auckland Chamber Music Players.' McStay had in mind a new, flexible touring ensemble which would play traditional repertoire and commission new New Zealand works. The core of the group consisted of Scholes and pianists McStay and Christine Cuming, plus violinist Mary O'Brien, cellist David Jenkins and soprano Wendy Dixon. In the four years of its existence, the Auckland Chamber Music Players premiered works by John Elmsly, Ross Harris, William Southgate and Gillian Whitehead. Scholes also toured for the Music Federation with pianist David Guerin, and the Auckland Wind Quintet. 'It was a wonderful period. I was totally immersed in the world of the clarinet.'

By now principal clarinettist of the Auckland Regional Orchestra, Scholes returned to the university's School of Music as the clarinet tutor. 'I coached chamber music as well, which was really the beginning of conducting for me.'

The Karlheinz Company planned a performance of Lou Harrison's violin concerto, with David Nalden as soloist. 'They needed a conductor, and I said I'd do it. That's what first gave me the bug.' Workshops with John Hopkins and Juan Matteucci laid a technical foundation in conducting. 'You have to learn stick technique – where the stick's pointing, the evenness and clarity of the beat. Beyond that, though, conducting is a process of simplification – of finding the most direct way of communicating the essence of the music to the players, and from there to the audience.'

The long unpaid months of the orchestra's summer recess were relieved by the Labour Department's Project Employment Programme, which offered six months' subsidised employment for performing artists. Scholes and three colleagues from the orchestra found themselves thrown together with four temporarily unemployed rock musicians. Under the directorship of English rock guitarist and composer Ivan Zagni, Avant Garage was born. 'It was my first contact with rock musicians, and it was quite an eye-opener.' The group was committed to creating everything they performed – a necessity, given their eclectic instrumentation: Scholes's *Garage Sale*, written for the group in 1983, is scored for flute, clarinet, cello, tuba, two electric guitars, bass guitar, percussion and voice. 'The classical musicians made written works, and some of them were quite heavily scored and intricate. The rock musicians didn't read music, but that didn't stop them having an equal contribution to those pieces.' The classical musicians too found themselves working in unfamiliar territory. 'I'd done some improvising in medieval and renaissance music, but the whole creative process of the rock musicians was based on improvisation. Working without a score was an entirely different way of thinking.' At the end of the six months, Scholes and Zagni formed the duo Music on the Wall – 'manic clarinet/saxophone meets disturbed guitar'[1] – which, under the auspices of the Music Federation, toured extensively from 1983 to 1985 [CD track 12].

Although he had already composed works for Digorie and had written incidental music for three radio plays for Radio New Zealand, Scholes's crowd-pleasing compositions for Avant Garage and his works for Music on the Wall added a new dimension to his reputation as a performer and composer. 'Ivan made me realise that getting up there and playing your own music was a tangible possibility – and that there was an audience who wanted to hear it.' Zagni's graphic score *Wireless* provided the seed for Scholes's first major composition for solo clarinet. Zagni's score didn't use conventional notation, offering instead a conceptual nucleus for Scholes's tightly structured three-movement work. 'A kind of scenario evolved as I was finishing *Wireless for Clarinet*.[2] The opening section explores the first endeavours to harness radio waves for the transmission of sound. By the second section, the new technology allows transmission of music, and the third part celebrates the new-found medium.'

Scholes completed the work in London, where he and his partner Katherine Harris were spending six months on study leave from the orchestra – Scholes to study clarinet with Thea King and Alan Hacker, and Harris to study violin. While in London, Scholes saw an advertisement for the 1987 Rotterdam International Gaudeamus Interpreters' Competition. He used the competition as the incentive to prepare a programme of contemporary works for solo clarinet, making the most of intensive lessons with Alan Hacker, himself a renowned interpreter of contemporary scores. 'The Gaudeamus competition was unusual in that you could play whatever you wanted, and it was open to groups of up to nine players, all competing against each other.' Scholes's programme – including New Zealander Chris Blake's *Towards Peace* (1978) for solo clarinet – took him to the final round of the competition, ahead of seventy entries from twenty countries. His recital for the final round, broadcast live on Dutch radio, featured the first public performance of *Wireless for Clarinet*. He was placed third overall; *Wireless for Clarinet* earned him special commendation from adjudicator and virtuoso bass clarinet player Harry Sparnaay.

The next few years saw Scholes juggling orchestral playing, concerto and chamber music appearances, teaching, composing, conducting and fatherhood: Peter and Katherine's first son, Eric, was born in 1990. By 1993, Scholes had been with Auckland Philharmonia and its various predecessors for thirteen years. 'Leaving wasn't a hard decision in the end. There were too many other things I wanted to do.'

Scholes's resignation from the orchestra coincided with the release of the soundtrack for Stewart Main and Peter Wells's film *Desperate Remedies*.[3] His seventy-five-minute score, played by the Auckland Philharmonia and conducted by the composer, took the overture to Verdi's *Force of Destiny* as its anchor. 'Stewart and Peter had already decided the Verdi encapsulated the spirit of the film. My job was to write original music, but blend it into that style.' In fact, the score consists of three distinct components: direct quotations from Verdi, Berlioz and Johann Strauss, music written using Verdi's themes, and a substantial original element. 'Film is a director's medium, so sometimes things I liked were lost, but you can't feel precious about that, or compromised. I think I was very lucky because the directors were so sympathetic. Very little was changed or cut.'

Radio New Zealand's selection of Scholes's *Islands II* for clarinet and electronic processing as the New Zealand entry in the 1993 UNESCO International Rostrum of Composers further enhanced his credentials as a composer. Premiered by Scholes at the Wellington International Festival of the Arts in 1992, *Islands II* is the second in a series of three compositions loosely connected by a single geographical idea. *Islands II* uses a Yamaha SPX900 effects processor (in turn controlled by a Macintosh computer) to modify the sound of the clarinet in real time. 'The sequencing software which runs during the performance generates controller curves on the screen. They look like landforms on the horizon. But the *Islands* sequence also relates very much to my own life: island holidays, especially on Great Barrier, were an important part of how I grew up.'

At the time, Scholes was apprehensive that the piece's particular computer requirements would make the work difficult, but not impossible, for other performers. Gretchen Dunsmore, a former student of Scholes's from the University of Auckland, was completing graduate study in London and asked if she could include *Islands II* in her final recital. Warning her of the work's technological difficulties, Scholes sent her the software and the score. 'She took the software into the college's technology department, and they told her it couldn't be done. That made me absolutely livid. Of course it could be done.' Scholes packed the gear into a suitcase and took it to London. 'We rehearsed it, and she played it, and it was fine.' Ironically, Dunsmore's London recital would be one of *Islands II*'s last live performances: the equipment needed for the work was stolen in a burglary of Peter and Katherine's Ponsonby home in 1994. 'It could only be done on that gear. It's obsolete now, and irreplaceable. I could adapt it for other equipment, but re-creating it would take more work than it took to write in the first place, and in five years' time that would be obsolete as well.' The preoccupied couple allowed the burglars to walk in. Their second son, Eliot, had been born in January 1994 with life-threatening congenital heart defects. 'Eliot had just had surgery. It's hard to describe the state you go into. It's your worst nightmare, really – you hand over this tiny bundle and you might not see him again. We just went out and left the back door open.' Eliot continues to make progress. 'There is still a lot of unfixable stuff, but he's an absolute soldier. He's a very brave little boy.'

The year of his resignation from the Auckland Philharmonia, Scholes met English composer and arranger, and front-man for the English post-Punk band Killing Joke, Jaz Coleman. 'We were using Jaz's Parnell studio to record the soundtrack of *Desperate Remedies* and one day he brought in the score of his First Symphony. I really fell for it, and recording it with the NZSO in 1993 was the first of many projects Jaz and I did together.'[4] The producer on that occasion was London-based Chris Kimsey, whose next project was a symphonic 'cross-over' CD of the music of the Rolling Stones, *Symphonic Stones*.[5] Kimsey had booked the London Symphony Orchestra and George Martin's Air Studios, and invited Scholes to conduct the three-day recording session.

The first two days went smoothly. '"Jumping Jack Flash" had been scheduled for the last day, but by lunchtime the arrangement still had not arrived. The whole orchestra was sitting there waiting, with the clock ticking over – over a hundred musicians each being paid a hundred pounds a session.' The music finally arrived an hour and a half into the three-hour session. 'I had to learn the score while the parts were being handed out, but we got it down with time to spare. It wasn't a particularly straightforward arrangement, either – lots of time signature and tempo changes – but their phenomenal ensemble skills made for a great recording.' Half the arrangements used singers. 'Mick Jagger, Marianne Faithfull and Michael Hutchence put their tracks down later: they watched a video of the orchestra and listened through headphones. I didn't need to be there.'

The album met with a lukewarm critical reception. 'It was the first project we'd done, and we had three different arrangers working on it, so stylistically it wasn't terribly cohesive. I don't think mixing vocal and symphonic tracks worked particularly well, either.' Scholes feels that later cross-over projects – purely orchestral, with Jaz Coleman as sole arranger – have been stylistically more coherent, and therefore more successful. 'They're carried by the quality of the music and the power of Jaz's arrangements.' *Us and Them*,[6] Coleman and Scholes's reworking of the music of Pink Floyd, ran for seventy-eight weeks in *Billboard* magazine's cross-over charts; US sales topped 350,000. Scholes has subsequently conducted cross-over CDs of Led Zeppelin and The Who, and most recently the music of The Doors, arranged by Coleman as a violin concerto and recorded by the Prague Symphony Orchestra.[7] Once again, the orchestral track was recorded without the soloist. 'Nigel Kennedy was unavailable for the orchestral sessions, so he overdubbed his solo part later. Jaz likes to apply rock'n'roll production techniques to the orchestra – everyone is individually miked – which means you can have complete control in the production stage.' Scholes missed not only meeting Nigel Kennedy, but also the birth of his third son, Harrison, who arrived while he was in Prague. 'We hadn't been expecting him for another month, but Katherine insisted I not come home. We needed the money, and anyway I'd made a professional commitment, so I stayed in Prague. But I do regret not being there for Harry's birth.'

Scholes has also been involved in local cross-over projects. Eddie Rayner, the original keyboard player and arranger for Split Enz, approached Scholes and the NZSO with the idea of recasting some of the band's hit songs for symphony orchestra in a project which became known as E*N*ZSO. 'When Eddie came to me with the idea for the E*N*ZSO collaboration there wasn't a single dot on the page. We talked about it, and I passed on all I knew from the previous projects, and left it to him.' Unable to read or write music, Rayner made the arrangements with music notation software, composing the full orchestral score on a MIDI-controlled synthesiser keyboard. Scholes maintains that, as Rayner had originally used a bank of synthesisers in Split Enz to approximate the sound of a symphony orchestra, E*N*ZSO represented the realisation of his very first intentions. Other original band members participated in the project. Tim and Neil Finn and Noel Crombie contributed to *ENZSO* (1996).[8] *ENZSO*^{2} (1998) drew the vocal talents of popular culture icons Dave Dobbyn, Sam Hunt, Jon Stevens, Boh Runga, Margaret Urlich and Dame Kiri Te Kanawa.[9] Again, the critical response to the CDs and spin-off orchestral tours was mixed, but Scholes defends the project with the same enthusiasm he displays for all his musical ventures.

> Some rock critics say it shouldn't be done – they say the band did it right, and they've got the CD to prove it. But that's a very conservative and limiting attitude, because there's no final form of a rock song. Notation doesn't come into it, and every time the band plays it they do it differently. So if this is how Eddie Rayner wants the music to sound, where's the problem? Classical critics don't want to hear orchestras playing this kind of music either, but, if orchestras are to survive, they've got to reach out. It's no good pandering to just three percent of the population. They've got to pander to ninety-seven percent of the population.

Reaching out to audiences of the future forms another strand of Scholes's diverse musical life. Until resident conductors took over the Auckland Philharmonia's non-subscription engagements in 1999, Scholes conducted the orchestra's annual school holiday music programme, beginning with his own

Terry and the Violin Case (1989), a collaboration between Scholes, writer Stephen Ballantyne and Murray Lynch's Tantrum theatre company. One of the work's most ingenious musical sequences involves the hapless lovers Ted and Melissa, parked in Ted's tow-truck on Bastion Point. Around them the orchestra evokes the sounds of nature at night: 'my biggest challenge was getting the horn to sound like a morepork.' The orchestra takes an equally active role in *The Clown's Birthday* (2000) for two actors, narrator and orchestra, written for children by Scholes and Margaret Mahy. 'Margaret Mahy came up with the idea of casting the orchestra as a forest. When you look at the orchestra it's obvious, really.' Other projects for the Auckland Philharmonia's annual school music programme have included *Drums Across the Pacific* in which Scholes combined a Cook Islands drumming ensemble with a symphony orchestra, and *Tale of the Birdcatcher* (2000), commissioned by Class Act Opera and Creative New Zealand to a libretto by Catharina van Bohemen.

Scholes has also devised a work for schoolchildren in collaboration with Witi Ihimaera. The writer had long admired the composer's work, and introduced himself in the foyer of the Aotea Centre. 'He told me about his idea for a piece for orchestra and narrator, retelling legends from around the world.' The four stories making up the *Symphonic Legends* (1996) come from New Zealand, Asia, Greece and Ireland. Ihimaera's criteria were that the narratives should be affirmative and offer positive role models for young women. Scholes used *Peter and the Wolf* as the model for the music, which weaves in and out between the narratives.

Scholes has also collaborated with dancers, working closely with choreographer Ashley Killar to produce a score for the Royal New Zealand Ballet's 1995 production of *A Midsummer Night's Dream*. Fascinated by the collisions between the play's two worlds, Scholes assembled an incongruous ensemble of string quartet, saxophone quartet, percussion and piano, producing music that 'bewitched and bedazzled with a myriad of sounds ghostly and gleeful, tremulous and tender'.[10]

The soundtrack for Niki Caro's début feature film, *Memory and Desire* (1999),[11] confirmed Scholes's status as a writer for film. A haunting marimba solo establishes the mood of his poignant score, and the spare texture of flutes, harp and sustained strings does much to strengthen the film's atmosphere of calm tragedy. 'I began with the idea of the marimba: instead of starting with an orchestra, with all its colours already in place, I sometimes like to start with a particular sound, and build up the orchestra around it.'

He was involved with the project from the rough-cut stage, which brought its own frustrations.

> Sometimes you write a piece of music that goes from point A to point B in the film. Then they change it all around, and that music has to be thrown out and you have to start again. You pull your hair out sometimes, but it's great sitting back and watching the movie, and seeing the part you played in the bigger project. Although you're just a cog in the wheel, a movie is often nothing much at all without the soundtrack.

While Scholes's film, theatre and recording activities have often had him acting as 'musician for hire', he has remained in demand as a soloist, performing clarinet concerti with the Auckland Chamber Orchestra, the Auckland Philharmonia, the New Zealand Symphony Orchestra, the Southern Sinfonia and the Wellington Sinfonia. He also appears regularly with the New Zealand String Quartet, with whom he has performed the Brahms, Mozart and Weber clarinet quintets. And in 1994 the quartet and Scholes premiered Neville Hall's *A Splinter of Silence in the Belly of Time*, written during Hall's tenure as composer-in-residence with Chamber Music New Zealand.

Scholes has also played a key role in the founding and development of the Auckland Chamber Orchestra (ACO), established in 1999 to fill a particular niche in Auckland's professional musical scene. The ACO's predecessor, the Auckland Sinfonietta, had been founded in 1990 by pianist Tamas Vesmas, with the intention of giving freelance professional musicians the opportunity to play works from the chamber orchestral repertoire. The Sinfonietta was starting to attract critical attention when growing friction with the Auckland Philharmonia began to hamper its activities. Frustrated by programming, personnel and financial difficulties, Vesmas resigned as director in 1994, and when Scholes was appointed musical director the following year he found an orchestra with no Creative New Zealand support, struggling to attract private sponsorship. Firmly believing that a city the size of Auckland should be able to support a part-time professional chamber ensemble, he sought the advice of arts patrons Linda and Frank Olsson. The Auckland Sinfonietta was wound up and the Auckland Chamber Orchestra established in its stead. 'The players were the same, but this time we set it up as a trust.' Enough funds were raised to mount a short concert series, and by the end of its second annual series the orchestra was well on its way to overcoming the ensemble problems which plague part-time orchestras. 'Music is the main job for most of the players, but they need to play together more. And to be able to plan concerts, we need consistent funding. It's the same old problem.'

Scholes's programming is in keeping with the scale of the ensemble. In December 2001 the ACO presented a single concert performance of Mozart's two-act opera seria *La Clemenza di Tito*, directed by Raymond Hawthorne and performed in the Auckland Town Hall's Concert Chamber.[12] 'There are so many wonderful operas we'll never see here because they're not big blockbusters. I see a real need to present this fabulous smaller-scale repertoire in a small venue.' Scholes also plans to programme Mozart piano concerti, more opera, and New Zealand music.

Even though the orchestra's projects are comparatively modest, fundraising remains a constant struggle, especially when public funding bodies are hamstrung by lack of resources.

> I've sat on the Creative New Zealand music funding panel, and the processes are fine. The problem is the gap between the amount of money they've got to give out, and the amount of money the arts require to really flower in this country. As a panel member, it's frustrating. You think you've been appointed to make decisions about the lifeblood of the artistic health of this country, but it's nothing like that. It's like walking into a nuclear bomb zone with a suitcase full of medicine.

Scholes's musical versatility, however, means that his own professional life is not unduly hampered by the vagaries of public sponsorship.

> I want to make the Auckland Chamber Orchestra work because I'm an Aucklander, and I want to contribute to the Auckland community in that way. But I've also got irons in the fire with writing and conducting and playing. I love the diversity, and working with many different types of artist. It's wonderful to be able to supply something that's really needed. I love being part of a team, and I love being useful.

1 Anthony Nevison, 'Ivan Zagni and Peter Scholes', *Rip it Up*, July 1984.
2 Peter Scholes, *Wireless for Clarinet* (Wellington: Waiteata Music Press, 1990).
3 *Desperate Remedies* soundtrack (EMI CD, 4713012, 1993).
4 Jaz Coleman, *Symphony No. 1, 'Idavoll'* (RCA Victor CD, 09026-627171-2, 1996).

5 *Symphonic Stones* (RCA Victor CD, 09026-625262, 1994).
6 *Us and Them: the Symphonic Music of Pink Floyd* (Point Music CD, 446-623-2, 1995).
7 *Kashmir: Symphonic Led Zeppelin* (Point Music CD, 454-145-2, 1997); *Riders on the Storm: The Doors Concerto* (Decca CD, 467-550-2, 2000).
8 *ENZSO* (Sony/Epic CD, 483870.9, 1996).
9 *ENZSO*[2] (Sony/Columbia CD, 492852.2, 1998).
10 Eve de Castro-Robinson, 'The Royal New Zealand Ballet's *A Midsummer Night's Dream*', *Music in New Zealand* (Autumn 1996), p.53.
11 *Memory and Desire: Music from the Film* (Polygram CD, 98002, 1998).
12 Tara Werner, '*La Clemenza di Tito*', *NZ Herald*, 11 Dec. 2001.

Helen Medlyn : Serious Fun

I've never been able to put acting before singing, or the other way around. They're inextricably mixed – although I entertain through music, I always come from the lyric of a song. That's the connection between acting and singing: the words have to sing as much as the notes.

Mezzo-soprano Helen Medlyn (born 1958) describes herself as a singing actress. Her talent is rare among musical and theatrical professionals in that she is equally at home – and earning equal critical acclaim – singing Mahler, Noel Coward or Stephen Sondheim, and acting in 'straight' or musical theatre. But no matter what her medium, her goal is always the same: to seduce and transport her audience. 'It's not falling off a log for me. It's hard work, and the involvement is absolute. I do it for myself as well as for the people I perform for: I have a huge need to be loved. When people laugh and clap and throw flowers it makes it all worthwhile.'

Helen Medlyn was born in Falmouth, Cornwall, where her father's family had a small chain of butchery shops. 'My father and his two brothers were all trying to make a living out of the business, and my parents really struggled. Dad hawked meat out of the back of a van to pay the bills.' Encouraged by a friend from the Falmouth Operatic Society who had already emigrated to New Zealand, Helen's mother, Irene, started saving for her family's fare; Helen was three and her sister Margaret five when they sailed on the *Rangitata*. 'The ship was leaking as we came through the Panama Canal. I got measles and ate grapes in the sick bay.' Helen also remembers shipboard fancy-dress competitions, which the sisters kept winning. 'Mum was a wizard at making costumes out of seemingly nothing. I was Puss in Boots and Margaret was Bo Peep.'

The family settled first in Ohawe Beach, just out of Hawera, and about a year later moved to Auckland – first to Ranui, and then to Parrs Cross Road in Henderson Valley. 'It was pretty rural out in West Auckland in those days. There were orchards all around us, and the roads were unsealed when we arrived. We had a chemical loo for five years, and had a loo party when we finally got sewerage. Everyone had to bring a loo roll.' Irene threw herself into local amateur dramatics, and didn't have to encourage her extrovert younger daughter to join in. 'I couldn't *wait* to get on the stage. I was one of those, "Pick me! Pick me!" kids.' Helen's first theatrical coup was as a tiny pirate in her mother's production of *The Pirates of Penzance*. 'One of her pirates had to pull out, and I said, "I'll do it!" I was eight, and about four foot nothing, and I had to fight a man who was about six foot four. The big joke was me poking his tummy.'

The little diva was not always in the limelight. When she was about six, Oratia Primary School made the mistake of casting her as only one of the three kings in the school nativity play. 'I wanted to be Mary. *Mary* was the star of the show. Why wasn't I Mary?' However, Auckland Children's Light Opera gave her plenty of opportunity to shine. 'I was the only alto in the chorus – I had such a huge booming voice they didn't need anyone else. It wasn't that I wanted to show off: I just sang loudly because I loved it.' Medlyn's first character role was the Mayor of Munchkinland in *The Wizard of Oz*, followed by the Hobgoblin in *The Snow Queen*. 'The ultimate was playing one of the ugly sisters in *Cinderella* when I was about ten.' Even at that young age Medlyn's talent for ad-lib comedy was obvious. 'People fell about all over the place. I loved it.'

Although himself very musical, Helen's father, John, did not perform music theatre until 1976, when he joined the chorus of St Thomas's Light Opera Club's performance of *Annie Get Your Gun*, starring Helen and directed by Irene. 'I think he got lonely at home by himself so he decided to come with us. After that there was no stopping him.' The family also made music at home. 'We did a lot of singing around the piano. We could even manage the Verdi *Requiem*: Dad sang bass, Mum tenor, Margaret did the mezzo and me the soprano.'

With Margaret on an academic path to her own career in music, Helen decided to go her own way. 'I went to seventh form, but I got bored and didn't finish the year. I wanted to be out in the world. Margaret was studying music at university by then, but I just didn't have a hankering for that kind of life, ever. I didn't see the point.' Helen's first job was as an invoice clerk at

Universal Homes. Front-of-house positions in American Express and then Travelodge suited her better, but she found herself most at home in the world of advertising, first as a receptionist at MacHarman's and eventually as producer at Saatchi & Saatchi. 'Advertising is as close as you can get to theatre, without being in theatre. There's a great deal of creativity going on, under great pressure. There's an enormous sense of fun, too. We worked hard and played hard.'

Medlyn became known at MacHarman's not only for her speaking voice – still often used as a voice-over in commercials – but also for her singing. 'I used to sing around the agency a lot, and my colleague Jane Berney asked why I didn't do more with it. She was convinced I could make money out of it, but I'd never thought that way about singing – it was easy and fun and I loved it.' Berney saw an advertisement for a singer at the Diamond Restaurant, and pointed it out to Medlyn. 'I said I'd apply, but of course I never did. In the end she rang up pretending to be me and got me an audition. I swanned in there and sang for them, and got the gig.' With resident pianist Murray Duncan, Medlyn expanded her repertoire of jazz standards and strengthened her harmony singing. Together they worked the Auckland dine-and-dance scene of the late '70s – 'the Palomino out in Henderson, Fisherman's Wharf, El Matador – the whole sheboof'.

Medlyn was still working in advertising by day, but her confidence in herself as a professional performer was growing to the point where she felt able to audition for the 1981 New Zealand tour of *Evita*. 'They said my singing was fine, but were more interested in whether I could dance or not. When I was about eighteen I'd done a year's beginners' classes at Bernice McGough's dancing academy – me and all these five-year-olds – but somehow I must have convinced the audition panel.' Medlyn remembers the production as much for the after-show jazz improvisation sessions, which nearly cost her her voice, as for her chorus singing and dancing role. 'We were sitting around having drinks after the show, and I started singing, as you do.' Jam sessions with jazz bassist Andy Brown and *Evita*'s musical director jazz pianist Dave Fraser turned into regular post-show gigs. 'Of course jazz and drink go together, and I was a bit of a smoker in those days – Camel cigarettes. Just about as strong as you could get. I'd just sit at a table and smoke and drink and sing – after bellowing "Evita, Evita" for hours on end.'

By the end of the four-month tour, Medlyn could speak only in a hoarse croak. 'When I got home I went to see a throat specialist. He told me I had blisters on my vocal cords, and if they burst they'd scar and turn into nodules.

I wasn't allowed to talk for a *week*.' When the inflammation had gone down she had to re-learn how to use her speaking voice. 'I went to a speech therapist for six months, just going "Ah, ah, ee, ee." It was awful.' That was only the beginning. Medlyn then had to learn how to sing again. 'My sister had just finished studying at university, so I went to see her teacher Anthea Moller. All she would teach me was opera, and I did *not* want to be an opera singer. That was Margaret's bag.' Moller overcame Medlyn's resistance to the point where she was able to sing again. 'She introduced me to repertoire I still sing – Mahler's "Liebst du um Schönheit" and "Mon coeur s'ouvre à ta voix" from *Samson et Dalila* – and as a way of helping me regain my confidence she entered me in the Pukekohe competitions. I came last. But at least she got me up on stage again.'

After the *Evita* tour, Medlyn returned to temporary office work, and by the time the Mercury Theatre advertised its 1982 production of *Jesus Christ Superstar* she felt well enough to audition. 'I introduced myself to the production team, and told them I was going to sing "I don't know how to love him", which I did – exactly like Yvonne Elliman.' The panel – director Simon Phillips, choreographer Cath Cardiff and musical director Penny Dodd – patiently sat through her imitation. 'Then they asked me to sing it again, the way *I* would sing it, and straight away it was something totally different. I'd always imitated other people because I never thought my own interpretations were good enough.' Cardiff then asked her to dance. 'I'd come from the office and I was wearing a tight pencil skirt, so I took my skirt off and did the dance audition in my petticoat. They said thank you and good-bye, and I thought I'd heard the last of it.' The next day she was offered the role of Mary Magdalene. 'During rehearsals for that production Simon Phillips took me to mental and emotional places I'd never been before. I cried a lot: it was as though he undid some kind of psychological zip, and all my innards fell out on the floor. Mary Magdalene was a huge catharsis – and I did it bloody well, actually.'

Early the following year Medlyn played a season of Tom Lehrer's *Tomfoolery* at Palmerston North's Centrepoint Theatre, again directed by Phillips.

> It was a five-hander, with Carmel McGlone on the piano. We were billeted in the jockeys' quarters at the Awapuni racecourse. It was summer and the shearing gangs were coming through, so there was us – five little theatrical types simpering around the place – and these huge men sharpening their shears. There were literal and figurative sparks flying everywhere. We had a great time.

On her return to Auckland, Medlyn found the musical theatre scene in a temporary lull. She went back to advertising, working first in a minor production role and then as a production assistant to Mackay King's Roy Meares, with whom she worked until she left advertising in 1989. 'By that time Saatchi's had taken over Mackay King, and I was in charge of a few things myself – all small-time, and mostly in radio. I had a real interest in sound, and the voice.'

Meares gave Medlyn time off to perform. 'Jonathan Hardy cast me as Nickie in *Sweet Charity* in 1984, but then he proceeded to break me into little pieces. He told me I couldn't sing, and couldn't act, and couldn't dance. I think I would be able to handle it now, but at the time I couldn't, and went under. I didn't sing for three years.' Medlyn made an ambivalent return to singing in 1988, performing the Bernstein *Mass* with Viva Voce and the Auckland Choral Society, under the baton of John Matheson. 'I didn't think I was singing very well, so when John told me he thought I was going to be a great opera singer I shrugged it off. But I think he gave me a bit of confidence to go on.'

With the collapse of the National Opera Company in 1983, the Mercury Theatre had found itself with an extra Arts Council allocation earmarked for opera, and Medlyn sang in the chorus of several of the Mercury's productions, including *Madama Butterfly* (1983).

> The Butterfly was a wonderful soprano called Sharon Spinetti, who'd come over from the States. I was one of her geisha girls, so I got to stand quite close to her. I was completely fascinated by the enormous sound coming out of this tiny body. I'd seen and loved both Elisabeth Hellawell in *Tosca* and Malvina Major in *La Bohème* when I was about fifteen, but I hadn't been that *close*. I was gob-smacked.

Medlyn's growing curiosity about opera coincided with her growing disillusionment with advertising. 'One Friday morning I woke up and thought, "I don't want to do this any more." I was earning huge money, but it just wasn't enough: I wasn't being praised enough for good work, and that's always been important to me.' The following Monday Raymond Hawthorne rang to offer her the part of Martha in the 1989 production of Gounod's *Faust*. 'Everything seemed to fall into place.' The small role helped allay Medlyn's lingering anxieties about opera. 'I had a little bit to sing here and there – no arias – and it was in English, so it felt like a show. I didn't have any trepidation about it whatsoever.' Thereafter, Medlyn became a Mercury regular, taking chorus parts in operas and larger roles in musicals, including Fruma Sarah in *Fiddler on the Roof* (1989) and Nettie in *Carousel* (1990).

By 1990, Medlyn was ready to rise to the challenge of Raymond Hawthorne's uncompromising directorial approach. Cast in the *buffa* role of Berta in the Mercury's production of Rossini's *The Barber of Seville*, she found she couldn't get a handle on the character at all. 'I had gone back to my superficial acting, and Raymond hated it. I remember his face in my face, shouting with frustration: "I *know* there's talent in there. Why can't I see it? Stop pissing about and *show* me!"' After Hawthorne had finished, Medlyn stomped off to the bathroom to cry. The production's Figaro, baritone Robert Honeysucker, followed her. 'I thought he was going to tell me that Raymond was a bastard, but he said, in effect, that Raymond was right. I was appalled, and told him in no uncertain terms to get out of my toilet.' However, where Jonathan Hardy's approach had left Medlyn deflated, Hawthorne's spurred her on. 'I went home and watched the old black and white version of *Rebecca* with Judith Anderson as Mrs Danvers, and *A Room with a View* with Maggie Smith. All of a sudden I was overwhelmed by a vision of Berta as a sexually repressed spinster.' The next day she slicked back her hair and took her composite character to the rehearsal.

> Raymond didn't say anything. He just took what I had to give, and at the end of the day he turned to me in his inimitable way and said, 'Good girl.' I knew I'd nailed it. I was able to be funny by being real, and that's what he wanted. With Raymond there's never any excuse for being superficial. He's not interested in acting. He wants being.

Hawthorne added his own touches to the character. 'He said, "Let's make her a sherry-drinking madwoman." It was set in the 30s, so every time the cocktail trolley went past I'd take a quick snifter.'

Medlyn's next Mercury success was the acting role of Joy Gresham in the 1991 production of William Nicholson's *Shadowlands*. 'It was the very first *big* straight play I'd done. Paul Minifie took a big gamble in casting me – all the actresses in the world wanted to play Joy Gresham.' When Medlyn and actor Ross Duncan read through the script together she knew the part was meant for her. 'Sometimes you look at something, and you go, "Whatever happens, this is for me." It just sang off the page at me.'

However, it was Medlyn's role in *The Barber of Seville* that proved to be the professional watershed. This was the first time she had sung an operatic aria by herself, in Italian, and it made her think more seriously about singing lessons. 'I rang up my Mum and asked her who I should go to. She had tried to take me to singing lessons before, and I'd hated it. I would *not* be told what to do.' This time Irene Medlyn suggested the singing teacher Janice Webb, with whom she had worked in amateur theatre. Medlyn was initially a reluctant pupil – 'I thought I knew it all already, so I pouted a lot and gazed at the ceiling' – but Webb won her over. 'She'd always say nice things about the nice notes and never say anything about the bad ones. Just constant encouragement and support. She teaches the old Italian way of singing and believes in letting the voice out, and letting the soul sing.'

When the Mercury Theatre closed in 1992, Janice Webb threw down a gauntlet. She knew Medlyn was out of work and in need of a musical goal. 'Janice told me if I gave her four months of my life she'd prove that I could be an opera singer. She gave me two lessons a week for four months, and just drilled me.' Webb also knew how vital it was to steer her reluctant student towards the right repertoire. 'She realised that I came from the lyric, and if a lyric didn't grab me on an absolutely visceral level I just wouldn't be fagged singing it.' Webb chose a programme of Brahms, Donizetti and Wagner for the *New Zealand Herald* aria competition of 1992, and Medlyn swept the pool: the lieder prize, the Dan Ford Scholarship for music theatre, and the aria competition itself. 'The prize money wasn't huge, but the wins proved Janice's point – that I could do it if I worked, and that opera didn't have to be boring.'

Medlyn scored her second professional triumph of the year when former Mercury Theatre musical director Brett Morris invited her to replace an indisposed singer in the Auckland Philharmonia's 'Light Side' series, which he was to conduct. 'Brett took a risk with me, just as Simon Phillips had with *Superstar* and Paul Minifie had with *Shadowlands*. The Philharmonia didn't know me then, so they took a risk as well.' The risk paid off. Since that 1992 engagement, hardly a year has passed without Medlyn starring in one of the Auckland Philharmonia's lighter concerts, a 'Last Night of the Proms' or a summer matinée in the grounds of Auckland's Government House. 'I love it, and there's a huge groundswell of appreciation for what I do. I walk among the crowd and be silly and sing to them face to face and all the men pretend to faint. It's fun, and it's funny.' She has also strutted her stuff with the Southern Sinfonia, the Christchurch Symphony Orchestra and the Canberra Symphony Orchestra, and in 2000 toured a programme of popular music with the NZSO.

Medlyn continues to balance her love of opera with the music of the lighter stage. 'I think if you start classical training too early you can never get rid of it. I came to opera late – I was thirty-three before I started singing "serious" stuff –

which means I can make the switch easily. Opera has to be absolutely strict and formal, but with jazz you've got much more musical leeway.' On occasion, however, she has been made to feel uncomfortable about her unconventional musical background. From dozens of international applicants, Helen and Margaret Medlyn were selected to join nine other singers for a series of masterclasses with German mezzo-soprano Brigitte Fassbaender, held at Brereton Hall in Cheshire in 1993.

> Brigitte Fassbaender is a goddess, basically, but in retrospect I wasn't ready for it. Although the sound of my instrument was better than some of the other girls who were there, I just didn't know how to use it: my technique wasn't as embedded as it is now. Brigitte would say, 'Do this, do that,' and half the time I didn't know what the hell she was talking about. She didn't get cross, but I could tell she was exasperated with me, and through stress and frustration I lost my voice.

Knowing Medlyn's background, Fassbaender then asked her to sing some jazz. This only made matters worse. 'As far as I was concerned I was there to learn how to sing opera, not to sing jazz. I know she was only trying to be helpful, but it was as though she considered I couldn't cut it as a classical singer, so she'd let me do what I was good at. I found it terribly upsetting.' However, the experience was not entirely negative. 'She was impressed with my acting skills, which I was chuffed about, and her own singing was a real eye-opener. It's a *huge* voice, and it's like steel. I remember standing about three feet away from her, and feeling like my head was being split open by a laser-beam of sound. It's a fabulous sound for an opera house, but up close it was really hard to take.'

A masterclass with Donald McIntyre later in the same year proved somewhat less distressing. 'I sang Erda's aria from *Das Rheingold*, and he sang Wotan's bits in the middle. It made me go weak at the knees. But I'd learned the aria from a record, and the singer had gone, "Weiche, Wotan!" at the top of her voice, so I did too.' McIntyre explained that the earth-goddess is pleading with Wotan not to take the ring.

> The earth has already been plundered, and Erda is warning Wotan that the ring will give him the power to destroy it entirely, so her voice must contain vulnerability. Sir Donald appealed to the actress in me, and a light went on. It came into my voice and I only got out one line before the sadness of it all overwhelmed

> me. I cried and cried. I don't think I was ready for him vocally, either, but from an acting point of view it was immensely interesting. He saw my limitations and taught within them. I adored him.

By 1994 the hard work and tears had begun to pay off. Her brief appearance as Kate Pinkerton in Auckland Opera's *Madam Butterfly* (1994) – a restaging of an original Ken Russell production – stole the show.[1] Medlyn imagined the usurping American wife as a kind of human iceberg. 'She walks into Butterfly's house with an arctic atmosphere surrounding her. She's going to take someone else's child, and she sits on a fridge flicking through a magazine.' Moffatt Oxenbould, the artistic director of Opera Australia, was in the first-night audience, and Medlyn's agent had arranged an audition the next day. 'I sang the "Habanera" from *Carmen*, but I'd been to the opening-night party of *Butterfly* the night before, and I was absolutely shattered, so it wasn't all that good. But I suppose it can't have been all that bad, either, because a couple of months later the Queensland Lyric Opera – acting on Moffatt's advice – rang to offer me the part of Maddalena in *Rigoletto*.'

Medlyn's Queensland performance attracted the further attention of Opera Australia, who invited her to sing the role of Maddalena in their 1995 production of *Rigoletto*. 'At the time, I think Margaret may have wondered why I made my début at the Sydney Opera House before her. We were singing similar repertoire at that stage, and she was much further on in her career.' But Medlyn believes her strength as an actor worked in her favour. 'I love playing fractured and complicated women. Maddalena's not on stage for long, but you have to show that beneath her sex-pot exterior she's torn between her duty to her brother Sparafucile and her love for the Duke, who she's trying to protect. Despite agreeing that someone else should die instead of the Duke, she's horrified by Gilda's murder. Death really is anathema to her.'

Medlyn's vocal acting skills also secured her the role of Prince Orlofsky in Opera Australia's 1997 *Fledermaus*. Medlyn was invited to step in at short notice for the Melbourne season, replacing mezzo-soprano Suzanne Johnston.

> I'd just done two big things in Sydney – a concert performance of *Die Walküre* with Edo de Waart and the Sydney Symphony Orchestra, and a *Messiah* with the SSO and Richard Hickox – and then it was straight into rehearsals for the Strauss. I had a couple of sessions with the rehearsal director in Sydney, flew to Melbourne, had a couple of walks-through with the cast and a technical rehearsal, and I was on.

Director Lindy Hulme gave Medlyn her head with the role of the androgynous Orlofsky.

> It's traditionally done by a mezzo playing a man, but we agreed that we didn't want it to be as clear as that. We felt the audience shouldn't know if the character was a man or a woman, because it's not sure, either. I wanted Orlofsky to be slightly icky, so I started doing icky things, like licking people, and stubbing cigarettes out in people's glasses. My idea was that you wouldn't want to be near this person, but you stayed with them because they had money.

Medlyn's Orlofsky was at once repulsive and comic. 'All this notwithstanding, I wanted the audience to be sympathetic. I wanted them to see it was all a big cover-up for a tortured character.'

Back in New Zealand in 1998, Medlyn delighted audiences and critics alike with her performance as Concepcion in Opera New Zealand's production of Ravel's one-act comic opera *The Spanish Hour*. The biggest role she had undertaken until then made the most of her sense of comic timing. The vampish Concepcion – 'a gloriously vulgar, brazen and desperately frustrated wife'[2] – manages to seduce three lovers in turn, all in the hour her husband is away winding the town's clocks. 'It was a frantic farce. I hid my lovers inside the clocks that were on either side of the stage, and rushed around trying to stop the lovers from seeing each other, or my husband.' One night she opened up a clock and the expected lover wasn't there. 'He'd missed his cue, and was up the back gassing to a dresser. After the initial shock, I swung into ad-lib mode, and just pretended I was calling for him. I don't think anyone in the audience was the wiser.'

Not long after completing *The Spanish Hour* season, Medlyn found herself on the brink of physical and emotional collapse. 'It was an amalgam of many things. I'd turned forty, and I honestly thought I'd be married, and have children – or have a career that was earning me a regular wage, or have a home to call my own.' A stressful interpersonal encounter tipped the balance into what would eventually be diagnosed as clinical depression. Her voice was the first thing to go. Medlyn had been booked to sing the Verdi *Requiem* with the NZSO. 'I went along to the first rehearsal and sang like a goddess. But the next day I woke up, and I was as sick as a dog. I went to my throat specialist, and all he could see was red. He said I could push myself now, and risk never singing again, or I could rest and have a voice for the Adelaide *Ring*.' Medlyn cancelled all her engagements for the next three months – including the Verdi

Requiem, and Opera New Zealand's production of Rossini's *La Cenerentola*. 'I was supposed to sing Tisbe, one of Cinderella's ugly sisters. I really wanted to do it: it was one of the very first roles I'd played as a child, and here was my chance, thirty years later, to play the role again. But it was ten performances and lots of dollars down the drain.' The financial pressure deepened the crisis. 'I didn't want to do anything. I didn't want to see anybody. I didn't want to be anywhere.' Medlyn's GP offered her the choice of drugs or psychotherapy. She opted for therapy. 'I've never cried so much in my life. I hadn't realised how much of a failure I felt because I didn't have that stable job, that stable relationship, or that stable home. But once I started to talk about it, I realised that other people have gone through the same, if not worse, and had found their way out of the darkness.'

After three months of therapy, the depression had abated to the point where Medlyn could contemplate working again. The much-anticipated State Opera of South Australia's 1998 production of *Der Ring des Nibelungen* was the result of inter-state rivalry, four years of planning and an $8 million budget: the state government of South Australia had initially earmarked the funds for a Formula One Grand Prix but the event went to Victoria instead, and South Australian premier Dean Brown diverted the money to a major cultural event which would, like the Grand Prix, attract visitors to the city. Adelaide's *Ring* – the first complete Australian cycle since 1913 – would restage Pierre Strosser's 1994 production for the Théâtre du Châtelet, Paris, under the musical direction of British conductor Jeffrey Tate. Australians and New Zealanders made up the bulk of the cast: Helen and Margaret Medlyn were offered roles as Valkyries and Rhinemaidens when they auditioned in 1994. 'Kate Ladner from Australia was No. 1 Rhinemaiden, Margaret was No. 2, and I was Flosshilde – the lowest-voiced of the three Rhinemaidens. And I was Schwertleite in *Die Walküre*.'

Although the critical response to Strosser's pared-down production was ambivalent,[3] Medlyn found her roles fulfilling both personally and musically. She was particularly impressed by Tate's attention to detail, and his sympathy for her intuitive approach to character. 'There's one tiny moment in *Götterdämmerung* where Flosshilde is trying to persuade Siegfried to part with the ring. At that moment, I'd thought of her character as evil and manipulative.' Tate, however, wanted the line delivered as a gentle reproach. 'He took me by the hand and looked me in the eye, and said that Flosshilde was quite serious when she says Siegfried should be nicer to women, and he needed me to sing it as sweetly as I could. Then when I nailed it he said, "Fabulous. Good girl." He made all of us feel special.' However, the production was less rewarding professionally. 'Career-wise it wasn't great: in small concerted roles you don't stand out, so nobody notices you particularly. But I just loved it. I'd do it all again tomorrow.'

Although she happily sings smaller roles, Medlyn also shines as a concert soloist. Her performance with the New Zealand Chamber Orchestra of Handel's cantata *Lucrezia* and Respighi's *Il Tramonto* in 1996 was a musical and dramatic triumph, and her incandescent *Das Lied von der Erde* in August 2000 elicited a rapturous response from *New Zealand Herald* critic Heath Lees: 'Medlyn excelled, now soaring above the musical firmament, now hushed and seemingly lifeless in the face of the void. Her contribution in "The Lonely One in Autumn" ignited an intensity of expression that gradually lit up the whole performance.'[4] [CD track 13]

A generous and professional ensemble performer, Medlyn saves her love of the limelight for her one-woman cabaret-style shows, devised in conjunction with pianist Penny Dodd. 'Somewhere along the line there comes a time when I just have to be the star of a show, and that's where the one-woman shows come in. Penny, in her inimitable way, lets me shine out the front.' Each show mixes torch songs and songs from the shows with poetry, lieder and prose recitations, and is loosely connected by a single thematic idea. *Hell on heels* (1998) is about the lengths to which women will go to secure fame, fortune and power; *to hell with love* (2000) looks at love 'through the eyes of a woman getting on for thirty-five or so'; and the women in *hellbent* (2001) are 'recklessly determined' in their pursuit of love or revenge, or freedom and justice.

Despite her glamorous stage persona, Medlyn describes herself as an old-fashioned girl.

> When people see me on stage they see the razzle-dazzle and the gorgeous frocks, and they think that I must be like that all the time – and that I go home to a fabulous house and someone who runs me a bath and brings me champagne. I wish! But the truth is, the other day I came home from a matinée and cooked dinner for me and my flatmate, and sat and watched telly. It's such a wonderfully ordinary life.

Medlyn is equally frank about her need for an audience.

> There's been a dearth of close personal relationships in my life, so I think my long-time love-affair is with the audience. I make myself very vulnerable when I'm on

the stage. As long as even a handful of people demonstrate their love for me openly and without holding back, I feel wanted and give more and more of myself. In the end it radiates through the whole audience. I don't think about it all the time, but I'm quite aware of how much I need to be loved in that way. It's a sort of obsession – and it's one which a lot of entertainers understand, I think. It's how some of us feed our souls a little.

1 William Dart, 'The Next Big Sing', *NZ Listener*, 30 May 1998, pp.38-9.
2 Rod Biss, 'Opera duet pleasant but a little on the light side', *Sunday Star-Times*, 5 April 1998.
3 David Gyger, '*Ring* comes to South Australia in a blaze of modified glory', *Opera-Opera*, December 1998.
4 Heath Lees, 'Performance', *NZ Herald*, 18 Aug. 2000.

Gareth Farr : Happy Camper

> When I'm writing I need to be by myself: you can't sit down, write, go and make some phone calls, then write some more, because it turns out crap. Composing is very solitary, and requires so much concentration that it makes you go a bit mental sometimes. That's why I need to perform as well. It's always been a balancing thing for me.

Gareth Farr (born 1968) has carved himself a uniquely colourful niche in New Zealand classical music. As well-known for his flamboyant drag persona Lilith Lacroix as he is as a percussionist and composer, Farr's multiple selves sustain and complement each other: the composer learned the fundamentals of orchestration counting rests at the back of the orchestra; Lilith is an outrageous flirt, Gareth maintains he is shy. But Farr's selves have at least one thing in common. 'Of course there's more to it than just wanting to be looked at and admired – and many classical musicians have a huge problem admitting that comes into it at all – but that's why I perform in the first place. I like people paying attention to me.'

Don and Jan Farr moved from Pukerua Bay to Auckland's Balmoral Road when Gareth was a few months old, and it was there that his bent for percussion first declared itself. 'I'd perch on the edge of the washing-machine and watch as the agitator went back and forth, back and forth. I loved the hypnotic rhythm.' When Gareth was two, the Farrs – plus baby Rebekah – moved to Birkdale, where Don's reel-to-reel tape recorder provided a more conventional source of musical fascination. 'I'd sing into it, and then push the reels around with my fingers, making it go a bit slower or faster. I was absolutely obsessed with it. When it broke it became my Meccano toy, then I just smashed it to bits with a hammer. I was that kind of child: quiet and a bit introspective, but destructive.' Jan's guitar came in for similar treatment. 'I adored it, but I had no idea what you were supposed to do with a guitar, so I used it like a resonating box. I was fascinated by the way that if you *belted* it the whole thing would vibrate. I'd sing Cher's "Gypsies, Tramps and Thieves" – which I really liked when I was about five – and bang it like a drum.'

Partly in an effort to divert her son's anarchic musical energy towards a less fragile instrument, Jan Farr decided it was time to have a piano at home. 'I'd make her play Mozart's "Rondo Alla Turca" over and over again, and then I'd pick it out with one finger. But I'd also bash out great handfuls of notes, and find little sequences I liked, and just play and play. I think my mother started getting me lessons out of desperation in the end, because I must have been driving everyone nuts.' To begin with, lessons were not a huge success. 'I'd play by ear – re-create stuff I'd heard – but I hated reading. I was a lazy little shit, basically. I'd never do any practice, and lessons would be torturous half-hours of desperately trying to follow the notes.' Although he persevered with lessons – if not with practice – through intermediate school, he and his teacher were saved further mutual torment when the family moved to the inner-city suburb of Grey Lynn. Don and Jan both worked in the city, Don for Actors' Equity and Jan as the editor of the Socialist Unity Party's weekly magazine. 'I couldn't have been happier, mostly because I didn't have to go to school in Birkdale any more. I hated Birkdale, and I *hated* school. I didn't like playing sports and I didn't hang out with the lads – I always had female friends when I was little – so I was picked on. The boys at school used to frighten the shit out of me.'

Things began to change once Farr started school at Auckland Metropolitan College in Mt Eden, where there was no uniform and few rules. Students determined their own syllabus, even to the point of deciding whether or not to sit exams. 'It was fantastic. It was a small school with very limited facilities and there were still bullies, but we called teachers by their first names, and they'd really look after you if they saw something was wrong. I blossomed from then on.' Musically, too, things started to look up. 'I started lessons with Lorraine Petousis – someone my mother had known years before – when I was about thirteen. She was fantastic, but I think I drove her to distraction: I still wouldn't practise. After I'd dragged out some Mozart sonata for the nineteenth time she finally sat me down and asked me what kind of music I liked.' Petousis gave him a transcription of Elton John's 'Song for Guy'. 'I loved it. I couldn't stop playing it. Then I did the theme from *Hill Street Blues*, and "Puppet on a

String".' When Farr eventually tired of those, Petousis produced a recording of *The Rite of Spring*:

> The string playing in 'The Dance of the Adolescents' was unlike anything I'd ever heard. It's very, very percussive – all those wild, violent down-bows – almost like someone hitting a bass drum. It had that real primal feel to it. Something to do with that music just instantly switched on the light. It wasn't that I didn't like classical music: I guess I was just missing the element of excitement.

Percussionist Don McGlashan brought a special brand of excitement to Metropolitan College. 'He only taught there for a year and a half, but he changed my life – even more than Stravinsky. With *The Rite of Spring* it was "Wow, I do like music after all". With Don it was "WOW! *That's* what music is".' McGlashan introduced his students to the rhythm games devised by the percussion ensemble From Scratch, of which he was a member. 'We'd never just sit in a music class with him. He'd bring along ideas that excited him. We'd stand in a circle and he'd say, "Here's this really cool clapping game we've been working on in From Scratch."' Farr would spend hours in his bedroom, clapping rhythmic patterns. 'Even walking down the street your footsteps make this fantastic natural metronome for practising cross-rhythms.' McGlashan also taught Farr basic percussion techniques. 'Realising I was a percussionist and not a pianist was an amazing thing.'

McGlashan was also responsible for the revelation that there was such a thing as composition. 'I'd always loved opening the piano and plucking inside because it made such a cool sound. That sort of experimentation is exactly what a composer does, but in a more controlled way.' McGlashan introduced Farr to the compositional concepts developed by From Scratch. 'They were fascinating – and completely mathematical, which really appealed to me. A 5/16 rhythm, a 6/16 rhythm and a 7/16 rhythm all going at the same time will go for a certain length of time, and then come back together. That was incredible for me at the age of sixteen.' At the same time, Farr continued with piano. 'Lorraine had to go away, so I asked Don if he knew a good piano teacher. He told me I should go to David Guerin. I'd never heard of him then, of course, and boy was he was *tough*. But by that point I'd been switched on to music to the degree that I was prepared to practise for six hours a day.'

Farr had been intending to study zoology and botany at the University of Auckland, until McGlashan told him that it was possible to study percussion there. 'I enquired at the School of Music, and they said I'd need UE music.' As

Metropolitan College didn't offer music as an academic subject for senior students, Farr left school at the end of the sixth form and spent 1985 taking some papers in German at university and studying University Entrance music by correspondence. 'I'd never done any real theory before: things like being given a question phrase, and having to write an answer for it. The teacher gave me lots of good feedback and I started to really enjoy it. I even wrote some pieces for piano. They are locked in a box and nobody will ever see them.' Towards the end of the year he auditioned for a place at the university. 'Don thought it wouldn't matter that I'd only been learning for a year. He thought I had enough potential and talent to get in, and that's exactly what happened. I certainly didn't get in on accomplishment. Wayne Laird told me later that my timpani playing was abominable, but they could tell I'd be easy to teach.'

At the end of 1986, his first year at university, Farr found he still had 'yearnings' to be a solo pianist and auditioned for university piano teachers Bryan Sayer and Tamas Vesmas. He narrowly missed out on a place, but continued to work hard with David Guerin. 'My friends at university were all entering the *Auckland Star* piano competition, so I decided I would as well. I learned the Mozart A major concerto, but even then I realised that the only part of the competition I could realistically pull off was the solo piece.' He prepared Douglas Lilburn's *Nine Short Pieces* for the 1987 competition. 'I chose them partly because I didn't think anyone else would be playing a contemporary piece and Edwin Carr was the adjudicator, but also because I loved them.' Farr was placed second. 'I think Ted appreciated me playing Lilburn, because Ravel is modern for most people. Works by modern New Zealand composers hardly got a look-in in those competitions.' The same year – his first year of studying composition at the university – Farr's *Water Songs*, a set of piano pieces for children, won first prize in the New Zealand Institute of Registered Music Teachers composition competition, and in 1988 his *Music from a High Altitude* for piano, percussion, cello and clarinet won first prize in the School of Music's annual competition. The work was subsequently performed in Hong Kong at the Asian Composers' League Young Composers Competition, where it won major acclaim. That year also saw Farr complete his performance diploma in percussion with the School of Music's highest marks.

In 1988 the Victoria University gamelan visited Auckland for a concert and some workshops. A curious Farr went along to hear what it was all about.

> We'd been told a bit about gamelan in lectures – about how it's a very interesting layering of textures, where the big instruments play very slowly, and the small

instruments play very fast – but when I heard it I was completely blown away. There were these huge gongs with enormous bass resonances that shook the whole room, and delicate smaller tinkling instruments, and quieter ones filling in the harmonies in the middle. It was quite the most incredible thing I'd ever heard.

Farr decided to move to Wellington on the spot. He joined the gamelan, freelanced on percussion with the New Zealand Symphony Orchestra and finished a bachelor's degree in composition and ethnomusicology under the guidance of composers Jack Body and Ross Harris, and gamelan expert Joko Sutrisno.

The characteristic rhythmic patterns and modalities of gamelan quickly found their way into Farr's own writing. 'When I first started playing in 1989 every single composition was influenced by gamelan – to the point of plagiarism. But I think the early works of any composer sound like their teacher. Early Beethoven sounds like Haydn, early Shostakovich sounds like Glazunov and early Farr sounds like gamelan.' Working through the influence took time. Farr charts an evolution from *Siteran* (1990) for Javanese gamelan and harp, through *Tabuh Pacific* (1995) for Balinese gamelan and symphony orchestra, to *From the Depths Sound the Great Sea Gongs* (1996) for symphony orchestra. 'By the time I wrote *Sea Gongs* I think I was about halfway through working out my relationship with gamelan. Now I'm quite consciously stopping myself from doing anything that's too overt. I needed to get away from the all-the-cultures-of-the-South-Pacific-in-one-piece thing. I didn't want to get typecast.'

With a Fulbright Scholarship, an Arts Council grant and an AGC Young Achievers Award tucked under his belt, Farr arrived at the Eastman School of Music in Rochester, New York, in time for the fall semester of 1991. 'I did a Master of Music in composition, but it also had a performance component: I had to submit a composition and do two percussion recitals, which suited me fine.' Farr's composition teachers David Liptak, Christopher Rouse and Samuel Adler – Rouse and Adler by coincidence both percussionists themselves – encouraged a rigorously analytical approach to his own writing.

Adler would put your score on the piano, and you'd have to play it, and justify every damned note in the piece. It was the first time I'd had to look at my own music, and treat it as a craft, not as a loose inspiration. It sounds like a stuffy old conservative thing to say, but my harmony and counterpoint class at Eastman was the first time I'd really forced myself to learn the rules. It's the best thing I've ever done. You've got to learn the basics. There's no way around it.

In 1993, at the age of twenty-five, Farr was appointed Chamber Music New Zealand's youngest-ever composer-in-residence. The appointment came with the expectation of three substantial works for chamber ensemble, and during his nine-month tenure Farr completed *Kebyar Moncar* for the Victoria University gamelan and *Owhiro* for the New Zealand String Quartet.[1] The idea for *Cadenza*,[2] written for the virtuoso contemporary chamber ensemble CandNZa, came from Jenny McLeod. 'Jenny suggested I write a piece as a birthday tribute to Pierre Boulez, but I wasn't particularly interested in glorifying Pierre at the time. I *hated* that serial stuff.' Farr's tongue-in-cheek programme note for *Cadenza*'s second movement, 'The Derivation of Musical Wisdom', shows exactly how he felt about the more arid reaches of high serialism. His note describes a nightmare scenario in which Pierre Boulez is hosting a television cooking show. As the composer drops long rows of notes into a pan with herbs, garlic and white wine he turns, looks straight at the camera and gives a knowing wink. 'Et voilà. He's just whipped up another load of rubbish.'

At the end of the residency, Farr returned to Rochester to start a doctorate. 'It was going to be a Doctor of Musical Arts, which was for composers who were performers as well. You did a recital, wrote some papers, and submitted a composition portfolio.' Farr completed most of the requirements for the degree: his doctoral dissertation was *Cheng Cheng* (1995) for two harps, percussion and Balinese gamelan angklung. Other works completed in Rochester, including *Kembang Suling* (1995) for flute and marimba,[3] *Tabuh Pacific* for gamelan and orchestra and *Le Temps est à la pluie* ('It looks like rain', 1995) for symphony orchestra,[4] were the result of commissions from New Zealand. Farr's last Rochester work, *Lilith's Dream of Ecstasy* (1995), commissioned by the NZSO for large symphony orchestra, evokes the chaotic, colourful – and very noisy – alter ego who flowered into a stage personality during Farr's second stay in upstate New York.

Lilith Lacroix did not burst upon the world fully formed. Farr's first memories of cross-dressing date from early childhood.

> We had a fantastic dress-up collection. My father was working at the Mercury Theatre, and he'd bring home cast-off costumes. I found most of them a bit boring, except for a blue fairy dress. It had a light blue bodice and a big tulle skirt with lots of sparklies on it. I just loved it. My friend Lisa would come around and she'd put on the prince's outfit, and we'd get married. My mother and grandmother would sit nearby having tea, calling me Garetina.

As an adolescent, Boy George and *The Rocky Horror Picture Show* sparked his imagination. 'I think *Rocky Horror* pushed many people over the edge into the drag world. I used to experiment with make-up, to see if I could do Frank-N-Furter, which was fun.'

Lilith wasn't named until 1992 when Farr was in Seville, playing at Expo with the NZSO. 'I was hanging out a bit with the only two openly gay men I knew in the orchestra, and one day they decided to go shopping. I didn't really want to go: it was hot, and I didn't have a hat, so I bought an enormous sunhat. It was at least eight metres wide. I was swanning around Seville looking like a grumpy Audrey Hepburn.' His two friends wanted a name to suit his mood. 'They decided Lilith was a good pouty name. I didn't like it at all – I thought it was that chick from *Cheers*.' But the name stuck. 'After we got back I had to go to a Halloween party in drag. I went in my flatmate's dress, no wig, a smudge of blue over each eye. It was really bad drag. Somebody asked me my name, and I said Lilith. That was it. Once you've used a name in drag once, there's no getting out of it.'

Farr had not discovered Rochester's vibrant drag while studying for his master's at Eastman. 'I'd heard there was a drag show in town, but I was working my butt off and never got there. Anyway, Rochester is a small town by American standards, so I thought it would be a lot of tragic old transvestites prancing about on stage.' When he finally visited Club Marcella in 1994, he discovered one of the best drag shows in the country.

> I just couldn't believe it: not only were all the performers flawlessly beautiful, but they were also astonishingly talented. They could all dance. They all had fantastic costumes. It was the best entertainment I'd seen in a very long time, and the crowd was going completely crazy. I thought, 'Ooo, that looks like fun. I wonder if I could do it?' I thought it would be really easy.

Egged on by his Eastman percussion tutor, Farr made his début as Lilith Lacroix. 'It was a nightmare. The lights were shining in my eyes, and I got completely thrown. I forgot the words, and I was so nervous that my mouth got dry and my lips stuck to my teeth. It was a complete disaster.' His costume didn't help. 'I was wearing a very small green velvet dress – size four – so I couldn't breathe, either. I got off stage and thought, "That was *terrible*. I'm going to have to do it again."' He did, and by the following year Lilith had become a regular member of Club Marcella's 'Life's a Drag' female impersonation show. 'We performed twice a week, like clockwork. The show had its regular patrons, so we'd rotate the numbers: you'd probably do the same one every three weeks or so.' Lilith also helped Gareth pay the rent.

> Boy, did they *tip*. On the other hand, the drag audience can be the most brutal crowd in the world. Even in stand-up comedy the very worst they do is not respond – at least they don't throw bottles! It's an incredible exercise in the bare-bones essence of performance. You don't have the abstraction of a classical piece – or even a musical instrument – in front of you, and you have to convince an entire roomful of people that you're performing your arse off.

Farr soon learned that Lilith was not just 'the chick from *Cheers*' but an altogether more interesting role model for an up-and-coming young drag queen. 'Ellen Koskoff, my ethnomusicology professor at Eastman, was a specialist in Jewish music and she'd done a lot of research on Hebrew mythology. It turned out that Lilith was Adam's first wife, but he kicked her out because she was too independent and dominant.' Enraged by her expulsion from Eden, Lilith turned herself into a night demon of exquisite beauty who enters the minds of men through their dreams, where she sows the seeds of lust and frustration. Although the biblical character is the symbol of sexual temptation, Lilith Lacroix is not remotely interested in male sexual attention.

> The gay men who came to the club related to queens as women because that was the only time they ever saw them. They may have absolutely idolised them, but obviously it wasn't going to be in a sexual way: visually, they're women. The occasional confused guy would sidle up to one of us, but we'd recognise the look on their face well in advance so we could just run away. That's the only romantic approach you'll ever get in a place like that.

The Rochester queens taught Gareth how to sew – he still makes most of his own costumes – and welcomed him into their fold, but not before one of them sent him to the most expensive wig shop in Rochester as a little welcoming present. 'That's how they do it. They help you a little bit, then put the knife in just to make sure you realise you're new.' He also learned about make-up. 'If I'm feeling slightly bitchy, the eyeliner goes out a little further and the eyebrows go up a little higher. I might not do the eyes as dark as normal if I'm feeling a bit softer or a bit playful. But, before you know it, there are lips, a bit of blusher, and I'm someone else.' The transformation is not just physical. 'I've never been able to quite figure out how it works, but from then on I'm more confident. No one believes me when I say this, but I'm fundamentally shy.'

Shyness did not stand in Lilith's way in Rochester's gay beauty pageants. Crowned Miss Sweetheart of 1995, first runner-up in Miss Gay Upstate New York 1995 and second runner-up in Miss Gay Rochester 1995, Farr had the pageant protocol down to a T. 'They're Miss USA style, and no less conservative. If your evening gown has straps your hair can touch your shoulders, but if your gown covers your shoulders, you must wear your hair up. You're disqualified if your evening gown is higher than the heel of your shoe, for God's sake.' Tiring of the scene's conservatism, Farr started to build percussion into his routine.

> The first time I played drums in Rochester it frightened the crap out of people. The audience expects a drag queen to come out and lip-synch Annie Lennox or something, and then go offstage. I'd come out and start this Gloria Estefan number, and in the middle of it I'd rip off the dress and underneath was a big set of drums. It took people a while to get the hang of it. Drag queens so often do very feminine postures, and when you stick a big drum between your legs and start belting it, it unsettles people a bit.

At the beginning of 1996 Farr made the decision to abandon his studies – and Club Marcella – and return to New Zealand. 'I could see the drag show pulling me along indefinitely, but I could also see it never going anywhere. Every week it's exactly the same. Same people, same crowd, same pop songs, same limits to what you can do. And then there was the drug issue. The drug scene and the drag scene were one and the same. It's everywhere.' He also realised his composition studies were edging him towards a career in which he had little interest. 'I realised that most of the people doing doctorates at Eastman were going to be teachers, and I didn't want to be a teacher, ever. I also realised that I was postponing a career in New Zealand to get the doctorate, which was crazy, because the point of getting the doctorate was getting a career.'

The immediate impetus for Farr's return came from choreographer Douglas Wright, who invited him to work on his new ballet. Farr's score for Wright's *Buried Venus* was one of four major commissions that made him the darling of the Wellington International Festival of 1996. Alexa Still and Farr performed the shakuhachi-inspired *Kembang Suling* (1995) for flute and marimba, and Michael Houstoun premiered Farr's toccata *Sepuluh Jari* (1996), which had been written for the pianist, at his request, in the style of a Bach toccata. *Lilith's Dream of Ecstasy*, played by the NZSO under young German conductor Marcus Stenz, dazzled the festival's opening-night audience. Farr now regards the work with some critical disdain.

> Looking back on pieces can be very painful, really. At the time, I thought *Lilith's Dream of Ecstasy* was exactly how I wanted it, but I can't listen to it now. It drives me up the wall. It's like an overture – a little presentation of all the themes that are going to come up in the opera, and the opera never happens. I learn an enormous amount every time I write a piece for orchestra, but by the time you hear the work for the first time – usually two days before the concert – it's too late to make major changes.

A string quartet might look at a new work a month before the performance, which gives the composer a chance to make revisions, but orchestral rehearsal schedules are much more stringent: a new, short work will inevitably receive less than two hours' rehearsal. 'If you revise anything after the first rehearsal, you only get one read-through of your revisions, so you have to be 100 percent sure about what you want to do on the first rehearsal. It's bloody terrifying.'

While generating musical ideas presents no problem to Farr, 'learning where to put them' is still a challenge. 'You've got the audience in your power for the length of the piece, and you take them on a journey. That journey has to have a very deliberate shape, because audiences have a terribly short attention span. If you've been in an audience when they've all lost their attention at the same time, you know – and when it's your piece, you *really* know.' It isn't just the sudden rustling of papers and shifting of feet. 'There's a whole drop in the mood, and they're gone. You quickly realise that you've got a certain amount of time at the beginning of a piece when you've got the audience's undivided attention, but there comes a point where you have to deliver whatever it is you've been promising in those first few minutes.'

Lilith Lacroix taught Farr a few tricks for holding an audience's attention.

> Performing drag I learned that it's a good idea to have a major climactic moment two-thirds of the way through a piece. If you come out wearing the new outfit you've just made from bananas or whatever, and you've got flashing lights on your headpiece, you don't even need to know the words of the song. The audience just goes, 'Whoa! That looks great!' You've got them in the palm of your hand for about thirty seconds, but then you've got to sock it to 'em – do some dance moves, sing a song that they all know, whatever.

Slowly the audience's energy subsides.

> Then there's the point exactly two-thirds of the way through a three and a half minute song when you will lose them if you don't do something else. All experienced drag queens – and composers for that matter – know that, and have a trick up their sleeve for that point. They might remove what looks like their only outfit and reveal a spunky little sequined number underneath, and the whole crowd goes, 'Wahoo!' With an orchestral piece it's exactly the same. There are moments when human beings do exactly the same thing every time. It's probably the only predictable thing about composition. [CD Track 14]

Farr is candid about what he regards as the structural flaws in his most popular work to date. *From the Depths Sound the Great Sea Gongs* was commissioned in two parts by the NZSO to commemorate the orchestra's fiftieth anniversary.[5] 'The Invocation of the Sea', the work's first part, was premiered in October 1996 – the anniversary of the orchestra's first rehearsals. The complete work was performed in March 1997, on the anniversary of the orchestra's first concerts.

> *Sea Gongs* Part II is another good example of something that irritates me to the point of not being able to listen to it. It starts off well – it's got these Ravelian orchestrations like little eddies whipping up the water – but there are sections that don't have any structure at all. It's like the middle of a huge Mahler symphony where nothing much happens – just tiny echoes of things. He can go on like that for fifteen minutes. You can't get away with that in a piece that's only twenty-three minutes long. If you were Mahler you probably could, but I'm not Mahler.

Farr is happier with the structure of *Ruaumoko* (1997), commissioned by the Wellington Sinfonia. 'It had an extra-musical structure before I even started work: it was about the four seasons, but in a South Pacific context.' Ruaumoko is the unborn god, who remained in Papatuanuku's womb. 'When he turns he causes earthquakes and when there's an earthquake the season changes. It's a great little structure: each movement has its own preconceived mood, and the percussion cadenzas between each movement are the earthquakes.' Because of the large-scale structural constraints, Farr found himself concentrating on substructures. 'I kept a very close eye on the amount of material I was using, and keeping themes recurring and developing throughout the piece. I'd make minor revisions before it's performed again – things that were awkward to play – but I wouldn't change much structurally. I was really quite happy with it.'

Farr attributes his magpie ear for colour and rhythm partly to growing up in central Auckland, and partly to being an orchestral percussionist. 'We had a Tongan church on the corner, and Cook Island cricket down at the park. The sound of Pacific music was just part of my musical environment.' He also found it easy to assimilate a feeling for orchestral colour:

> You spend a lot of time not doing anything in a percussion section. You go 'ting' on a triangle, and spend the next 250 bars counting – and concentrating really hard – so you don't miss your cue. I'd listen to the horn section and remember what they sound like when they're really low, or too high. The trick of orchestration is sitting at home in your studio and being able to summon up the sound of a piccolo, and know exactly what it sounds like in the range you're writing for it. As composers, percussionists have an unfair advantage: we just soak it all in. There's nothing else to do.

Scottish percussionist Evelyn Glennie has also turned the ability to soak up sound to her advantage. The profoundly deaf Glennie 'hears' sound not through her ears but through her entire body. She and Farr met on her first visit to New Zealand. 'I heard her play James MacMillan's *Veni, Veni, Emanuel* and was blown away. She came to the pub with all us percussionists after the concert. Someone gave her one of my postcards – the one with the castanet bra – and she thought it was hysterical. She said, "Och, it would be great if you wrote me a piece one day." I thought she was kidding.' Farr's agent Ross Hendy had arranged to meet Glennie the following day. 'He wanted to talk to her because he's also interested in publishing percussion music. I asked if I could gatecrash their meeting because I wanted to know if she was serious. She was *absolutely* serious.'

Glennie premiered Farr's *Hikoi,* a concerto for percussion and large orchestra, in September 2000 with the NZSO conducted by James Judd. The work's structure is narrative and episodic, and makes the most of Glennie's lithe physical presence.

> I wanted to create a work for her where the movements of the performer were a part of the composition. *Hikoi* is a journey. It tells the story of leaving the nest, cutting the ties of home and security and asserting independence in the world. It's a fairly typical experience in New Zealand culture – and certainly one that characterised the previous ten years of my own life.

The work begins with the soloist positioned in her familiar 'nest' within the percussion section at the back of the orchestra. After an extended sectional cadenza she leaves the group, taking her drums with her for her travels around the stage. 'There are many ports of call where she docks, puts down anchor, and interacts with the locals. Her travels lead her through forests of strange instruments and unfamiliar sounds to her ultimate destination – the multi-percussion set-up at the front of the stage – where she plays out her triumphant assertion of independence.' Only days after *Hikoi*'s New Zealand première, this 'celebration of excess and an affirmation of the richness of life'[6] was played at the Sydney 2000 Olympics Arts Festival.

Farr himself has largely given away orchestral and solo percussion – 'I've even lost my marimba calluses' – in favour of his 'one-woman show' Drumdrag, and the percussion ensemble Strike.[7] 'They're both very serious and carefully thought-out percussion performances, but there's a bloody great drag queen in one of them. She's the star of the show, with the supporting drummers behind.' Strike, on the other hand, is based on absolute equality.

> We play a piece of Murray Hickman's called *Cube*. It's set in an enormous scaffolding cube with the interior absolutely covered in percussion. The instruments are spread out, so it's incredibly hard to play: you have to leap from one corner to the other to get to them. But that's the point. It has to be even more synchronised than dance, because if one of us is a split-second late you'll hear it. We're like four little clones moving in absolute unison. There's no stars in that show, and I love it – because the spotlight's off *me*.

Scores for Hone Kouka's plays *Hide and Seek* (1992) and *Nga Tangata Toa* (1994), Witi Ihimaera's *Woman Far Walking* (2000) and Bruce Mason's *The End of the Golden Weather* (2000),[8] plus soundtracks for the television dramas *Duggan* (1999) and *Claire* (2001), also needed a composer who knew how to become part of the background. 'It didn't come naturally. Eighty percent of the music for television has to be absolute background, nineteen percent is mid-ground, and you get two chances of twenty seconds each to be in the foreground when there's nothing else happening.'

Farr is one of New Zealand's few composers currently able to make a living outside a teaching institution. 'That said, though, if I was just composing – and not doing a drag show here or a gig with Strike there – there'd be no way I'd be able to pay the rent.' However, since becoming a household name in the late 1990s, Farr has begun to re-evaluate the direction of his career.

> In my mid to late twenties I went through a phase of doing anything I could to advance my career. It got me a long way, but it got me nowhere at the same time. I

developed as a musician and as a careeraholic and other people got to know who I am, but it didn't get me very far in terms of who I am myself – and I got pretty close to getting so sick of it that I never wanted to do it again. I don't want to be doing things in such a mad panic that I don't even remember doing them. From now on, the fundamental issue is to make sure I enjoy everything I do.

1 Gareth Farr, *Owhiro* (Wellington: Waiteata Music Press, 1996); *Owhiro: Works for String Quartet* (The HRL Morrison Music Trust CD, MMT 2019, 2000).
2 Gareth Farr, *Cadenza* (Wellington: Promethean Editions); *Gareth Farr Chamber Music* (The HRL Morrison Music Trust CD, MMT 2020, 1997).
3 Gareth Farr, *Kembang Suling* (Wellington: Promethean Editions, 1997); *Gareth Farr Chamber Music* (The HRL Morrison Music Trust CD, MMT 2020, 1997).
4 Gareth Farr, *Tabuh Pacific* and *Le Temps est à la pluie*, *Gareth Farr Orchestral Music* (The HRL Morrison Music Trust CD, MMT 2021, 1997).
5 Gareth Farr, *From the Depths Sound the Great Sea Gongs* (Wellington: Promethean Editions, 1998); *Gareth Farr Orchestral Music* (The HRL Morrison Music Trust CD, MMT 2021, 1997).
6 Lindis Taylor, 'Farr voyage, Glennie at the Helm', *Evening Post*, 25 Sept. 2000.
7 *Strike: New Zealand Percussion Music* (The HRL Morrison Music Trust CD, MMT 2030, 2000).
8 Bruce Mason, *The End of the Golden Weather* (Wellington: Te Papa Press CD, 2000), retitled *Te Parenga* and released on *Gareth Farr: Warriors from Pluto* (The HRL Morrison Music Trust CD, MMT 2036, 2001).

CD CONTENTS

1. Dorothea Franchi, **Four Pioneer Portraits** (Waiteata Press), Song 2: 'The Bushfeller', Song 3: 'The Blacksmith's Wife' (words by Eileen Duggan). Dorothea Franchi (piano), Honor McKellar (mezzo-soprano). © 1960 Sound Archives/Nga Taonga Korero. Duration: 3.45

2. John Ritchie, **Concertino for Clarinet and Strings** (Novello), third movement: allegro. Alex Lindsay String Orchestra, Frank Gurr (clarinet). (Ex KIWI CD SLD-107) ℗ 1962 Kiwi Pacific Records Intl Ltd. Duration: 3.48

3. Edwin Carr, **Leo** from *The Twelve Signs* (Waiteata Press). Melbourne Symphony Orchestra, conductor Edwin Carr. (Ex KIWI CD SLD-101) ℗ 1972 Kiwi Pacific Records Intl Ltd. Duration: 2.38

4. Richard Wagner, **Wahn! Wahn! Überall Wahn!** from *Die Meistersinger von Nürnberg* (Act III, Scene 1). Sir Donald McIntyre with the New Zealand Symphony Orchestra, conductor: Heinz Wallberg. (Ex CD MANU 1317) ℗ 1991 Ode Record Company Ltd. Duration: 7.09

5. Jenny McLeod, **Tone Clock Piece No 1** (Waiteata Press). Margaret Nielsen (piano). Live recording. © 1993 Sound Archives/Nga Taonga Korero. Duration: 2.29

6. Gioacchino Rossini, **Una Voce Poco Fa** from *Il Barbiere di Siviglia*. Dame Malvina Major with the New Zealand Symphony Orchestra, conductor: Piero Gamba. (Ex KIWI CD TRL-075) ℗ 1990 Kiwi Pacific Records Intl Ltd. Duration: 5.47

7. Jack Body, **Turtle Time** (words by Russell Haley) (Waiteata Press). Michael Neill (speaker), Dorothea Franchi (harp), Heather Charlton (harpsichord), Rosemary Mathers (piano), William Dart (organ). (Ex KIWI LP SLD-30) ℗ 1972 Kiwi Pacific Records Intl Ltd. Duration: 6.28

8. Robert Schumann, **Papillons**, nos I, II, III, IV, XI and XII. Diedre Irons (piano). (Ex MMT 2041) ℗ 2002 The HRL Morrison Music Trust (www.trustcds.com). Duration: 7.03

9. William Dart and Mervyn Thompson, **On that Day** from *Songs to the Judges* (© Kiwi Music). Margaret Blay, Sharron da Silva, Arthur Ranford, Hemi Rapata, Mervyn Thompson, William Dart (piano). (Ex KIWI LP TRL-069) ℗ 1982 Kiwi Pacific Records Intl Ltd. Duration: 3.45

10. Hirini Melbourne, **Raukatauri**. Hirini Melbourne (voice, putorino matai, pakohe), Richard Nunns (putorino maire, iwi toroa, matai). (Ex RAT D004) ℗ 1994 Rattle Records. Duration: 5.05

11. Ludwig van Beethoven, **Sonata No 8 in G, Op 30 no 3**, second movement: tempo di minuetto. Wilma Smith (violin), Michael Houstoun (piano). © 1998 Concert FM. Duration: 8.53

12. Peter Scholes, **Postcard**. Peter Scholes (clarinet), Ivan Zagni (guitar). © 1986 Sound Archives/Nga Taonga Korero. Duration: 5.56

13. Gustav Mahler, **Der Einsame im Herbst** from *Das Lied von der Erde*. Helen Medlyn with the Auckland Philharmonia, conductor: Miguel Harth-Bedoya. Live recording. © 2000 Concert FM. Duration: 6.37

14. Gareth Farr, **Waipoua** (Promethean Editions). New Zealand Symphony Orchestra, Mary Scott (clarinet), conductor: Kenneth Young. (Ex MMT 2021) ℗ 1997 The HRL Morrison Music Trust (www.trustcds.com). Duration: 5.00

Total duration 75.05
Digital audio mastering: Wayne Laird